Industrial Internet of Things: An Introduction

Edited by

Sunil Kumar

*GLA University, greater noida
India*

Silky Goel

*School of Computer Sciences
UPES, India*

Gaytri Bakshi

*School of Computer Sciences
UPES, India*

Siddharth Gupta

*Graphic Era Deemed to be University
Dehradun and IIT Roorkee, India*

&

Sayed M. El-kenawy

*Department of Communications and Electronics
Delta Higher Institute of Engineering and Technology
Mansoura 35111, Egypt*

Industrial Internet of Things: An Introduction

Editors: Sunil Kumar, Silky Goel, Gaytri Bakshi, Siddharth Gupta and Sayed M. El-kenawy

ISBN (Online): 978-981-5238-18-1

ISBN (Print): 978-981-5238-19-8

ISBN (Paperback): 978-981-5238-20-4

need for a court order if at any point you breach any terms of this License Agreement. In no event will any delay or failure by Bentham Science Publishers in enforcing your compliance with this License Agreement constitute a waiver of any of its rights.

3. You acknowledge that you have read this License Agreement, and agree to be bound by its terms and conditions. To the extent that any other terms and conditions presented on any website of Bentham Science Publishers conflict with, or are inconsistent with, the terms and conditions set out in this License Agreement, you acknowledge that the terms and conditions set out in this License Agreement shall prevail.

Bentham Science Publishers Pte. Ltd.
80 Robinson Road #02-00
Singapore 068898
Singapore
Email: subscriptions@benthamscience.net

BENTHAM SCIENCE

CONTENTS

PREFACE

Machine learning approaches are highly considered in almost each application domain area. The continuous growth of computational approaches motivates the editors to work in this area. The editors worked and gather various book chapters based on the "Industrial Internet of Things: An Introduction" and selected a few chapters for this book.

The book content categorizes into various subdomains starting with an introduction to computational techniques, and the importance of computational techniques in Industrial IoT. Various challenges and issues related to computational techniques in Industrial IoT. The book also covers currently hot areas of IIoT that are mainly healthcare informatics, transportation system, *etc*. Case studies also related to designing and testing the IIoT frameworks were also highlighted. The book shared the implications of waste management for boosting the national economy. Some legal policies were also discussed before concluding the book.

The editors have good knowledge in the area of machine learning and deep learning techniques. The research interest of Mr. Sunil Kumar is deep learning in information analysis in the agricultural domain; Ms. Gaytri Bakshi is working in the area of deep learning approaches for Industrial information processing; Ms. Silky Goel has an interest in computer vision and deep learning techniques. Mr. Siddharth Gupta is keen interested in image processing with machine learning approaches. Mr. El-Sayed M. El-kenawy has been working in advanced ML techniques. This book is edited by these five editors with a good review process.

Sunil Kumar
GLA University, greater noida
India

Silky Goel
School of Computer Sciences
UPES, India

Gaytri Bakshi
School of Computer Sciences
UPES, India

Siddharth Gupta
Graphic Era Deemed to be University
Dehradun and IIT Roorkee, India

&

Sayed M. El-kenawy
Department of Communications and Electronics
Delta Higher Institute of Engineering and Technology
Mansoura 35111, Egypt

ACKNOWLEDGEMENTS

This book is based on the flourishing aspect of IoT technology in the industrialization of the upcoming economy of India. Machine learning techniques are playing a revolutionary role in these various arenas of industry. IoT with machine learning cultivates smart industrial systems and has brought the economy, intelligence and lifestyle to yet another level. I am very grateful to have a wonderful team for encouraging each other to constantly work together and put endeavours in the correct direction. With great pride we present the book "Industrial Internet of Things: An Introduction".

We would like to thank all the reviewers who peer reviewed all the chapters of this book. We would like to thank the editorial team of Bentham Science Publishers, for their immense support in the process of publication. Finally, we would like to thank all the authors who have contributed chapters to this book. This book would have been impossible without your efforts.

We hope that this book will enlighten a reader about both technologies, their amalgamation, their applications as well as their standardization rules into the industry sector. Moreover, it will open up doors for other researchers to come up with their own ideas. Once again, we would like to thank everyone who was a part of this effort.

Sunil Kumar
GLA University, greater noida
India

Silky Goel
School of Computer Sciences
UPES, India

Gaytri Bakshi
School of Computer Sciences
UPES, India

Siddharth Gupta
Graphic Era Deemed to be University
Dehradun and IIT Roorkee, India

&

Sayed M. El-kenawy
Department of Communications and Electronics
Delta Higher Institute of Engineering and Technology
Mansoura 35111, Egypt

DEDICATION

To all the ones who have zeal for IoT and machine learning for research and innovation.

List of Contributors

Amit Verma	School of Computer Science, UPES, Dehradun, Uttarakhand, India
Arjav Jain	University of Petroleum and Energy Studies, Dehradun, India
Arnav Kundalia	University of Petroleum and Energy Studies, Dehradun, India
Arjun Arora	Cybernetics Cluster, School of Computer Science, University of Petroleum and Energy Studies, Dehradun, India
Gaytri Bakshi	Department of Cybernetics, School of Computer Science, University of Petroleum And Energy Studies, Dehradun, India
Gagan Deep Singh	Cybernetics Cluster, School of Computer Science, University of Petroleum \& Energy Studies (UPES), Bidholi, Dehradun-248007, India
Hitesh Kumar Sharma	Cybernetics Cluster, School of Computer Science and Engineering, University of Petroleum and Energy studies, Dehradun, India
Inder Singh	School of Computer Science, UPES, Uttarakhand, India
Neha Mendirtta	Chandigarh University, Punjab, India
Rishabh Kumar	Larsen & Toubro, Infotech, Mumbai, India
Rahul Nijhawan	Thapar University, Patiala, India
Sunil Kumar	Chitkara University Institute of Engineering and Technology, Chitkara University, Punjab, India
Silky Goel	School of Computer Science, University of Petroleum and Energy Studies, Dehradun, India
Snigdha Markanday	School of Computer Science, University of Petroleum and Energy Studies, Dehradun, India
Swati Sharma	Cybernetics Cluster, School of Computer Science, University of Petroleum and Energy Studies, Dehradun, India
Shlok Mohanty	School of Computer Science and Engineering, University of Petroleum and Energy studies, Dehradun, India
Tuhina Thapliyal	School of Liberal Studies University of Petroleum and Energy Studies, Dehradun, India

Industrial IoT

CHAPTER 1

Algorithms and Activation Function-IoT

Gaytri Bakshi[1,*]

[1] *Department of Cybernetics, School of Computer Science, University of Petroleum And Energy Studies, Dehradun, India*

Abstract: In this new industrial era, IoT is an emerging technology. Industrialization has entered an entirely novel phase with the fusion or incorporation of deep neural network methods with machine learning (ML). Both sustainable living and economic prosperity have resulted from this. Predictive analysis has been both a boon to humanity and an improvement in the caliber of work produced. It has created an opportunity for people to improve society and assist the poor in numerous ways. IoT and ML integration enables humanity to create a single home on this planet.

Keywords: Algorithm, Activation function, IoT, ML.

INTRODUCTION

Engineering is an application that has taken into account the principles of maths and science to solve real-world problems. Humans have evolved technology with engineering to aspire to the next level of a smart and intelligent world. With the advent of technology, engineering has been given a new shape in terms of providing services as well as production. Engineering has dominated every industrial sector, such as civil, mechanical, automobile, chemical, electrical, electronics, computers, and instrumentation & communication. Technology in itself is an advanced version and the practical implementation of principles laid down by science. Scientific principles are embedded to create smart frameworks, which in turn develop smart systems. This has led to the fruition of the term Internet of Things, where the Internet as an architectural backbone connects everything within a system in terms of communication and actuation. IoT is an ecosystem that, enables humans to study and understand the physical environment in terms of digitization. The framework comprises sensors as the most atomic entity with a communicating protocol that connects the sensing node with the edge device and then later connects the entire system to the cloud. The received

* **Corresponding author Gaytri Bakshi:** Department of Cybernetics, School of Computer Science, University of Petroleum And Energy Studies, Dehradun, India; E-mail: gaytri@ddn.upes.ac.in

data is analyzed by applying algorithms of AI and ML to predict or perform actuation [1] (Fig. **1**).

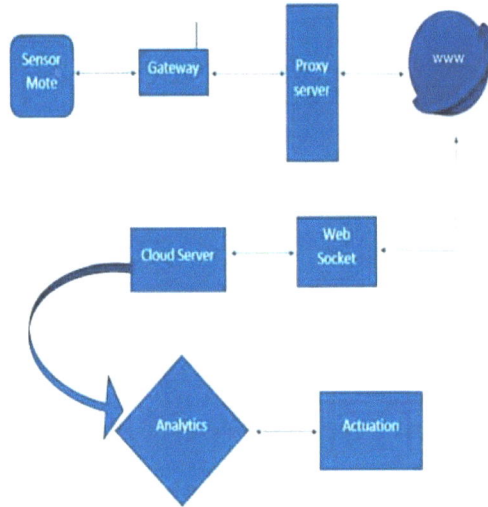

Fig. (1). IoT framework implementation [1].

IoT architecture is a layered architecture encompassing four layers, and its service-oriented architecture in each layer has multiple functionalities, as shown in Fig. (**2**).

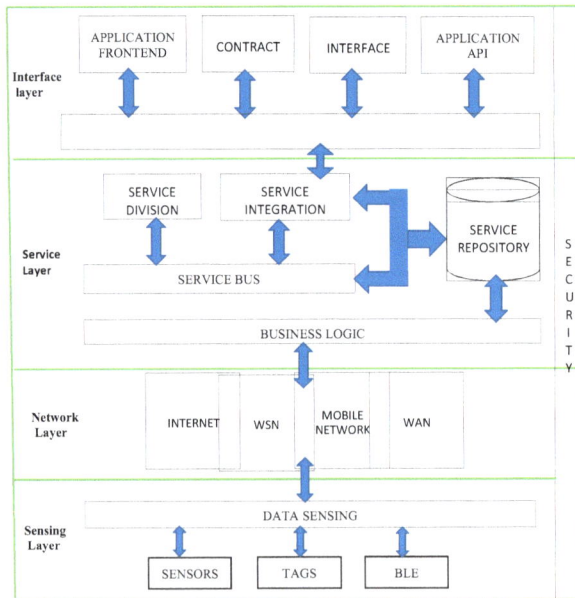

Fig. (2). Service-Oriented Architecture of IoT.

With the aim of reducing human intervention and maintaining sustainable development, IoT covers almost all the industrial sectors along with their services, as shown in Fig. (**3**).

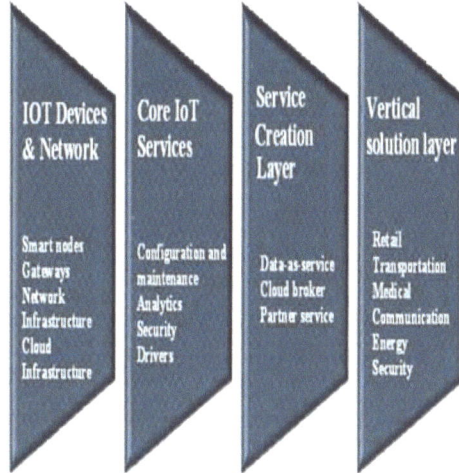

Fig. (3). IoT Service Layer.

INDUSTRIAL IOT VERSION

Almost all of the industrial sector has undergone a wider transformation with the advent and implementation of IoT. It has brought an immense revolution of modernization and intelligence to every industrial sector. In the degrading environment, the concept of sustainable development has also been inculcated. The industrial sector is now heading from version 4.0 to version 5.0 with the perceptions of smart, intelligent, and innovative solutions and services. The following sectors have different aspects of adopting IoT and embedding it with machine learning (ML) algorithms to quench public demands and develop a sustainable environment.

Building Infrastructure and Home Automation

This sector deals with creating smart setups, which include public sector buildings, urban development, and smart cities. Such cities deal with sustainable living with smart things that work independently and make life secure and easy [2]. This sector even works to develop secure devices that can continuously monitor the tensile strength of walls, bridges, and buildings [3 - 6]. The integration of ML with IoT investigates and predicts the construction outcomes with associated materials using strength models before the beginning of construction [7].

Security

This sector includes the physical security of humans as well as gadgets or hardware. In this sector, sensors are integrated with ML and DL algorithms to detect any human infiltration either in border regions or any private property. Many aspects of the identification of human movement and its classification in many complex conditions are the major areas of research in this sector [8, 9].

Natural Disaster Management

This sector requires smart equipment to detect humans and protect them in difficult situations of natural or man-made disasters [10, 11]

Manufacturing

This sector employs smart predictive systems that continuously monitors the wearing and tearing of manufacturing units in machines and alert to repair, replace, or maintain the part and prevent the system from any disaster or complete shutdown [12, 13].

Medical and Healthcare Systems

This sector has evolved from traditional health systems to smart systems where telemedicine, intelligent and smart health applications, and smart health monitoring systems have come into existence. With the incorporation of IoT, ML and deep learning (DL) models, predictive analysis of many diseases is done so as to take precautionary measures. Another aspect of this sector is to maintain health records with a smart system [14].

Environmental Monitoring

This sector deals with protecting and maintaining the environment. With the integration of both IOT and ML, the changing environment is continuously monitored and studied by many environmentalists [15, 16]. Protecting biodiversity and studying wildlife's habitat are also the aspects of this sector.

Energy Management

This is another sector where energy development harnessed from natural sources of sun, water waves, air, pressure, and metals is emphasized. Building a smart system is one of the attractive aspects of this sector [17]. This sector includes electricity distribution, maintenance, and surveillance [18]. A smart grid is one of the newest innovations in this sector, incorporating both IoT and ML.

Transportation

This sector includes many applications such as traffic routing and maintenance [19], smart parking, and travel tracking by air and trains. Another sector, named logistics, is fully dependent on smart transportation. Smart toll tax collection is one of the applications of this sector. The entire concept of smart transportation and smart roads can be implemented using telematics. Prevention of accidents in adverse climatic conditions is also one of the research areas of this sector.

Agriculture

This sector focuses on the smart way of cultivating crops. Many types of sustainable automatic agriculture methods have been adopted using IOT principles [20]. The study of agriculture covers topics such as plant care, crop and production management, soil care, disease care, weed care, water care, animal tracking, *etc*. By applying ML to sensor data and artificial intelligence system applications that offer more suggestions for decision-making, whole farm management can be further enhanced. Adopting ANN-based ML algorithms helps improve plant management systems [21].

ALGORITHMS USED IN THE IOT SSCTOR

Traditional Algorithms for IoT Applications

Support Vector Machine (SVM)

It is a supervised ML algorithm that is widely used for categorization and regression tasks. The benefits of SVM include:

- Effective in high-dimensional spaces.
- Robust to overfitting.
- Versatile and flexible.
- Effective in small sample sizes.
- Handles outliers well.
- Theoretical guarantees.
- Works well with both linear and non-linear data.

It is worth noting that SVMs may have some limitations as well, such as the need to choose appropriate kernel functions and tune hyperparameters. Additionally, SVMs can be statistically pricey for copious datasets, particularly when using non-linear kernels. However, overall, SVMs are a robust and conventional machine learning algorithm with several benefits in various domains. The decision function for a linearly separable issue with three samples along the border edges—referred to as "support vectors"—in h-dimensional spaces is seen in Fig. (**4**).

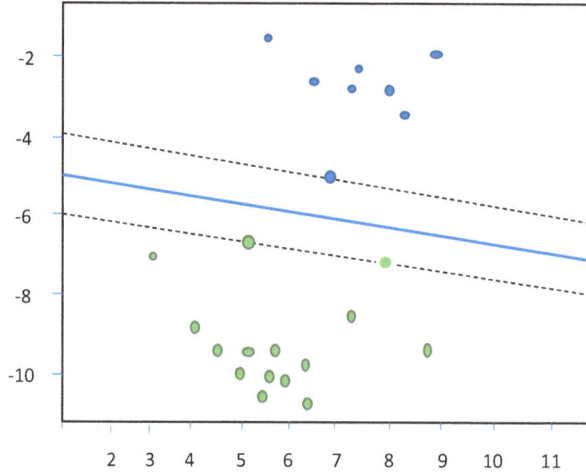

Fig. (4). Decision function for a linearly separable problem using SVM.

K-Nearest Neighbours (KNN)

It is a popular machine learning algorithm used for both categorization and regression tasks. Here are some benefits of KNN:

- Simple and intuitive.
- Non-parametric.
- No training phase.
- Flexibility in decision boundaries.
- Robust to noisy data.
- Adaptability to new data.
- Versatility in distance metrics.
- Interpretable results.

Despite its benefits, KNN also has some considerations. It can be numerically high-priced, specifically when applied to enormous datasets, as mathematically, the algorithm evaluates gaps between all training instances. Furthermore, determining the optimal rate of k and selecting the appropriate distance metric are vital concerns for achieving good performance with KNN. Overall, KNN is a flexible and intuitive algorithm that can be effective in various scenarios, particularly when the dataset is not large and the decision boundaries are complex or not well-defined.

Fig. (**5**) shows cases of two distinct categories, namely Category A and Category B, and with the upcoming new data point, the classification issue arises. To solve such issues, the K-NN algorithm is used.

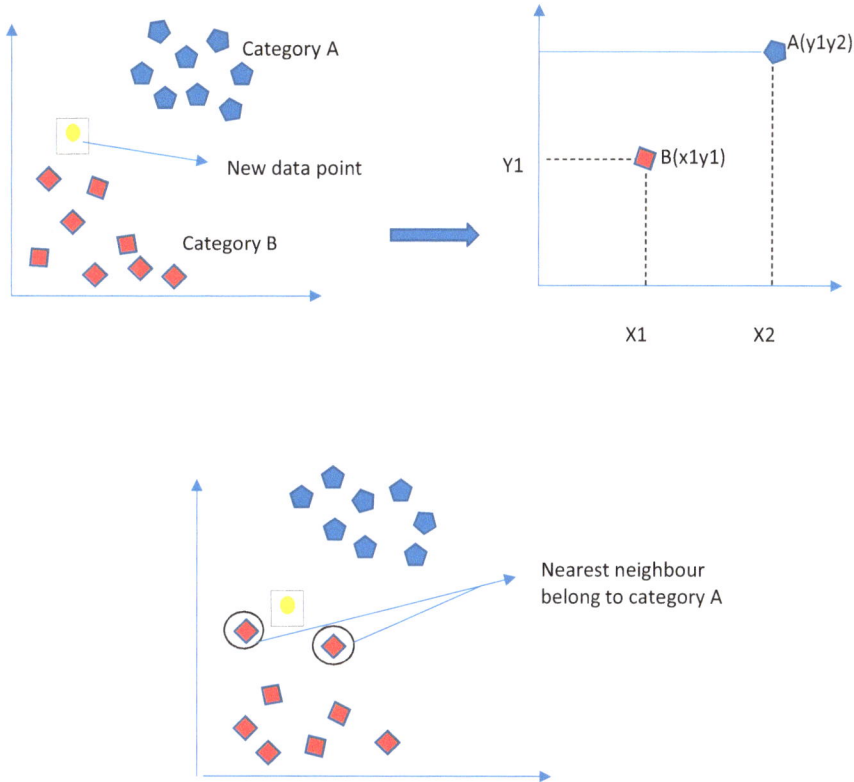

Fig. (5). K-NN working for class classification..

Linear Discriminant Analysis (LDA)

Linear discriminant analysis (LDA) is a dimensionality reduction technique and a classification algorithm. It is commonly used for feature extraction and pattern recognition tasks. Here are some key points and benefits of linear discriminant analysis:

- Feature extraction and dimensionality reduction.
- Supervised learning.
- Assumes Gaussian distributions.
- Effective with small sample sizes.
- Computationally efficient.
- Interpretable results.
- Can be combined with other classifiers.

While LDA offers several benefits, it is worth noting that LDA assumes that the data follows Gaussian distributions and that the covariance matrices are equal. These assumptions may not hold in all scenarios. Additionally, LDA is a linear technique and may not be suitable for datasets with complex non-linear relationships. LDA is a powerful technique for feature extraction, dimensionality reduction, and classification tasks, particularly when the class separability is well-defined and the assumptions of the algorithm are met. Fig. (**6**) depicts the different criteria for developing a new axis.

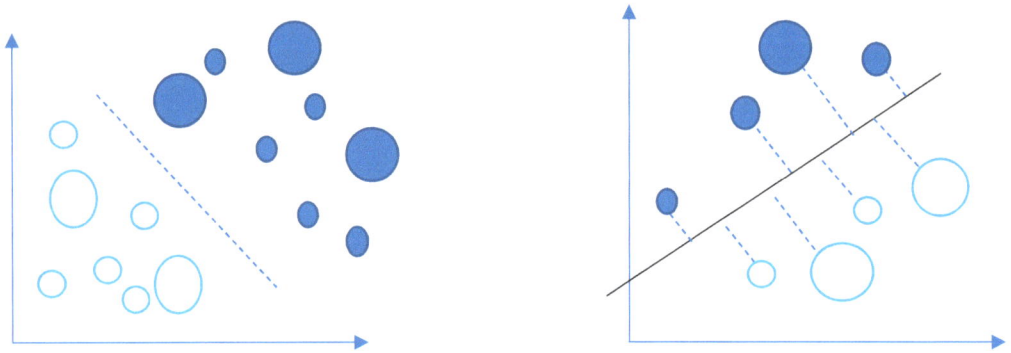

Fig. (6). Conversion of 2D plane into a 1D plane using LDA.

Naive Bayes (NB)

It is a machine learning algorithm based on the likeliness that is commonly used for categorization tasks. This algorithm formation is based on the principles of Bayes' theorem and supposes autonomy between features. Here are some key points and benefits of Naive Bayes:

- Simple and fast.
- Probabilistic framework.
- Independence assumption.
- Handles high-dimensional data.
- Works well with small training sets.
- Easy to interpret.
- Handles categorical and numerical features.
- Incremental learning.

While NB has several benefits, it is important to consider that the independence assumption may not always hold in real-world data. In such cases, other algorithms that can capture dependencies between features may be more appropriate. Additionally, NB can be sensitive to the presence of irrelevant features, as the independence assumption assumes that all features are equally informative.

NB is a simple and competent algorithm that is broadly operated for tasks dealing with categorization into a number of classes, especially in situations where the unconstrained hypothesis accommodates well or while working with high-dimensional data.

Random Forest

It is a collective learning methodology that amalgamates the predictions of compound decision trees to form an accurate prediction. It is widely used for both grouping and regression tasks. Here are some key points and benefits of random forest:

- Ensemble learning.
- Decision tree-based.
- Reduction of overfitting.
- Feature importance estimation.
- Robust to outliers and missing data.
- Handles high-dimensional data.
- Less prone to overfitting.
- Scalable and parallelizable.
- Versatile and flexible.

While RF has numerous pros, there is an urgency to state that it might not be the most reliable choice for all scenarios. For instance, if interpretability is a critical factor, the individual decision trees within the random forest are more interpretable than the ensemble itself. Additionally, RF may not perform well on datasets with high levels of noise or heavily imbalanced classes.

Overall, RF is a powerful and widely used composite learning methodology that addresses the limitations of individual decision trees, providing improved prediction exactness and robustness.

Advanced Algorithms for IoT Applications

Artificial Neural Networks (ANNs)

This term is inspired by the biological neuron and its network, which eventually forms the entire human brain. These networks feature the interconnection of neurons at numerous levels. These artificial neurons are termed as nodes. These networks of neurons are motivated using methodologies of genetic algorithms, providing the ability to a machine to grasp the features or information and give a decision analogous to the human brain. The artificial neuron is represented in Fig. (7).

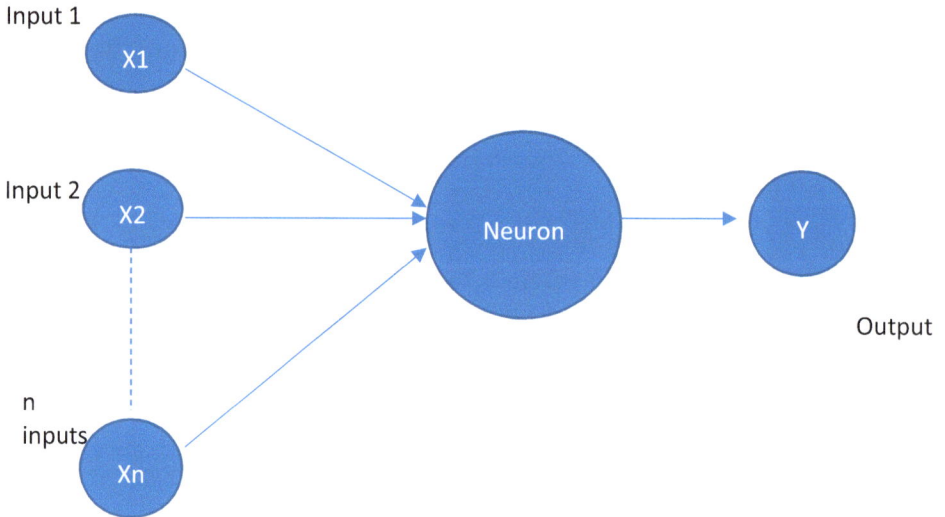

Fig. (7). Artificial Neuron.

DL

Artificial neural networks are the superset, while deep learning is its subset. These networks are illumed by the organization and maneuvering of the human brain. Deep learning is one of the vital constituents of subjects such as statistical and predictive computation and analysis. This helps with faster calculations and critical analysis of substantial volumes of data. With the commencement of deep learning in the era of analytics, predictions have been automated. Deep learning methodologies have outperformed conventional ML algorithms. It is a highly preferred network to be employed in areas such as recognition through images, recognition through speech, reproduction of enhanced images, and classification or categorization of objects. Feedforward neural networks, convolutional neural networks (CNNs), and recurrent neural networks(RNNs) are the three most popular DL architectures [22]. These models are known as deep neural networks because these models apply the concept of hidden layers, which are actually networks of neurons. A deep network can have around 150 hidden layers. The DL layer architecture is shown in Fig. (8).

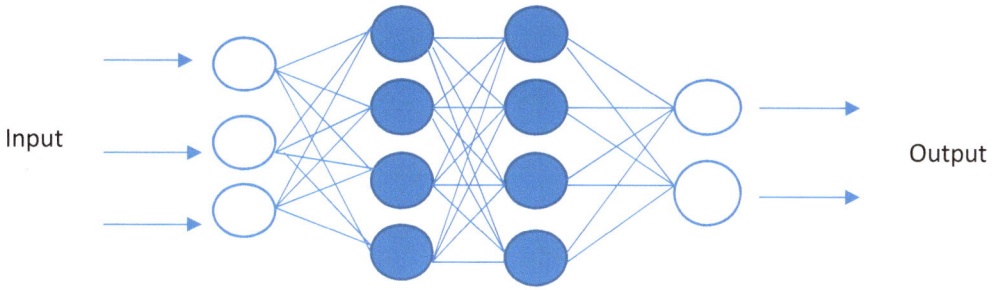

Fig. (8). Deep neural network architecture.

CNN

It stands for convolution neural network and is one of the DL approaches. Models based on this approach work on determining different objects by learning about weights and biases. These models are analogous to the neuron connectivity in the human brain. The entire working of this methodology is represented in Fig. (**9**).

Conv_1Convolution Max pooling Conv_2 Convolution Max pooling Fully Connected Relu Activation Fully Connected Neural Network.

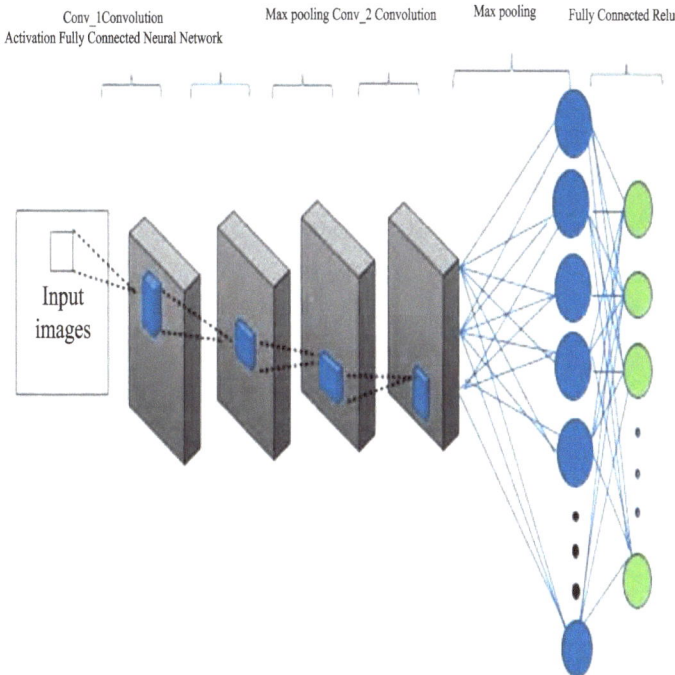

Fig. (9). Block diagram of the architecture of CNN.

CONCLUSION

IoT is an upcoming technology in this new era of the industrial world. With the integration of ML and deep neural network algorithms, industrialization has stepped into a new version of 5.0. This has led to economic growth as well as sustainable living. Predictive analysis has marked an upgraded standard of work performed as well as a helping hand for the human race. It has generated a scope where humans can uplift society and help the underprivileged in many aspects. Integrating IoT with ML helps the human race make this world one home.

REFERENCES

[1]   G. Bakshi, "IoT Architecture Vulnerabilities and Security Measures", In: *Security Incidents & Response Against Cyber Attacks. EAI/Springer Innovations in Communication and Computing.,* A. Bhardwaj, V. Sapra, Eds., Springer: Cham, 2021.
[http://dx.doi.org/10.1007/978-3-030-69174-5_10]

[2]   S. Somani, P. Solunke, S. Oke, P. Medhi, and P.P. Laturkar, "IoT based smart security and home automation", *2018 Fourth International Conference on Computing Communication Control and Automation (ICCUBEA),* pp. 1-4, 2018.
[http://dx.doi.org/10.1109/ICCUBEA.2018.8697610]

[3]   A. S. Xakimovich, "Analyzing the Results of Monitoring the Situations that May Occur in Emergency Situations of Bridges Through Various Optical Sensors", *Global Scientific Review,* vol. 8, pp. 80-88, 2022.

[4]   W.K. Kim, J. Kim, J. Park, J.W. Kim, and S. Park, "Verification of Tensile Force Estimation Method for Temporary Steel Rods of FCM Bridges Based on Area of Magnetic Hysteresis Curve Using Embedded Elasto-Magnetic Sensor", *Sensors (Basel),* vol. 22, no. 3, p. 1005, 2022.
[http://dx.doi.org/10.3390/s22031005] [PMID: 35161748]

[5]   W. Zhang, J. Gao, B. Shi, H. Cui, and H. Zhu, "Health monitoring of rehabilitated concrete bridges using distributed optical fiber sensing", *Comput. Aided Civ. Infrastruct. Eng.,* vol. 21, no. 6, pp. 411-424, 2006.
[http://dx.doi.org/10.1111/j.1467-8667.2006.00446.x]

[6]   J. Kim, J.W. Kim, C. Lee, and S. Park, "Development of embedded EM sensors for estimating tensile forces of PSC girder bridges", *Sensors (Basel),* vol. 17, no. 9, p. 1989, 2017.
[http://dx.doi.org/10.3390/s17091989] [PMID: 28867790]

[7]   J. Kim, and S. Park, "Field applicability of a machine learning–based tensile force estimation for pre-stressed concrete bridges using an embedded elasto-magnetic sensor", *Struct. Health Monit.,* vol. 19, no. 1, pp. 281-292, 2020.
[http://dx.doi.org/10.1177/1475921719842340]

[8]   G. Bakshi, and A. Aggarwal, "Non-Invasive Methods of Detecting Human Using Computer Vision by Incorporating Machine-Learning Techniques in Open Environment at Diverse Viewpoints", *10th International Conference on Reliability, Infocom Technologies and Optimization (Trends and Future Directions) (ICRITO),* pp. 1-5, 2022.
[http://dx.doi.org/10.1109/ICRITO56286.2022.9964601]

[9]   G. Bakshi, and A. Aggarwal, "Computational Approaches to Detect Human in Multifaceted Environmental Conditions Using Computer Vision and Machine Intelligence– A review", *2022 Third International Conference on Intelligent Computing Instrumentation and Control Technologies (ICICICT),* pp. 1547-1554, 2022.
[http://dx.doi.org/10.1109/ICICICT54557.2022.9917742]

[10]   P. Pandey, and R. Litoriya, "Elderly care through unusual behavior detection: a disaster management approach using IoT and intelligence", *IBM J. Res. Develop.,* vol. 64, no. 1/2, pp. 15-1, 2019.

[11]   M.D. Kamruzzaman, N.I. Sarkar, J. Gutierrez, and S.K. Ray, "A study of IoT-based post-disaster management", *International Conference On Information Networking (ICOIN),* pp. 406-410, 2017.
[http://dx.doi.org/10.1109/ICOIN.2017.7899468]

[12]   S. Nangia, S. Makkar, and R. Hassan, "IoT based predictive maintenance in manufacturing sector", *Proceedings of the International Conference on Innovative Computing & Communications (ICICC),* 2020.
[http://dx.doi.org/10.2139/ssrn.3563559]

[13]   R. Badarinath, and V.V. Prabhu, "Advances in internet of things (IoT) in manufacturing", *Advances in Production Management Systems. The Path to Intelligent, Collaborative and Sustainable Manufacturing: IFIP WG 5.7 International Conference, APMS 2017, Hamburg, Germany, September 3-7, 2017, Proceedings, Part I ,* Springer International Publishing., pp. 111-118, 2017.

[14]   G. Bakshi, A. Aggarwal, D. Sahu, R.R. Baranwal, G. Dhall, and M. Kapoor, "Age, Gender, and Gesture Classification Using Open-Source Computer Vision. In Emerging Technologies in Data Mining and Information Security", *Proceedings of IEMIS,* vol. 2, pp. 63-73, 2022. [Singapore: Springer Nature Singapore.].

[15]   GRARI, "Using IoT and ML for Forest Fire Detection, Monitoring, and Prediction: a Literature Review", *J. Theor. Appl. Inf. Technol.,* vol. 100, no. 19, 2022.

[16]   K.N. Shivaprakash, N. Swami, S. Mysorekar, R. Arora, A. Gangadharan, K. Vohra, M. Jadeyegowda, and J.M. Kiesecker, "Potential for Artificial Intelligence (AI) and Machine Learning (ML) applications in biodiversity conservation, managing forests, and related services in India", *Sustainability (Basel),* vol. 14, no. 12, p. 7154, 2022.
[http://dx.doi.org/10.3390/su14127154]

[17]   P. Bedi, S. B. Goyal, A. S. Rajawat, R. N. Shaw, and A. Ghosh, "Application of AI/IoT for Smart Renewable Energy Management in Smart Cities", *AI and IoT for Smart City Application,* pp. 115-138, 2022.

[18]   E. Sarmas, E. Spiliotis, V. Marinakis, G. Tzanes, J.K. Kaldellis, and H. Doukas, "ML-based energy management of water pumping systems for the application of peak shaving in small-scale islands", *Sustain Cities Soc.,* vol. 82, p. 103873, 2022.
[http://dx.doi.org/10.1016/j.scs.2022.103873]

[19]   G. Bakshi, R. Kumar, and U. Rajnikanth, "A Smart Approach to Detect Helmet in Surveillance by Amalgamation of IoT and Machine Learning Principles to Seize a Traffic Offender", *Proceedings of the International Conference on Paradigms of Computing, Communication and Data Sciences: PCCDS 2020,* pp. 701-715, 2021.

[20]   N. Gondchawar, and R.S. Kawitkar, "IoT based smart agriculture", *Int. J. Adv. Res. Comput. Commun. Eng.,* vol. 5, no. 6, pp. 838-842, 2016.

[21]   R.R. Gandhi, J.A.I. Chellam, T.N. Prabhu, C. Kathirvel, M. Sivaramkrishnan, and M.S. Ramkumar, "Machine Learning Approaches for Smart Agriculture", *6th International Conference on Computing Methodologies and Communication (ICCMC),* pp. 1054-1058, 2022.

[22]   S. Thennavan, D. Gokul, and A. Jayapalan, "Deep Learning Based Fake Stamp Detection", *2023 International Conference on Computer Communication and Informatics (ICCCI),* pp. 1-4, 2023.

CHAPTER 2

Deep Learning-Based Prediction Model for Industrial IoT: An Assured Growth

Tuhina Thapliyal[1,*]

[1] *School of Liberal Studies University of Petroleum and Energy Studies, Dehradun, India*

Abstract: Industry 5.0 is a revolutionary change for the traditional industrial domain with an amalgamation of interactive computational techniques. However, the Industrial Internet of Things (IIoT) is referred to as communication between various battery-enabled physical devices. The present IIoT sector faces issues like complex decision-making, enhancement of productivity capabilities, management of the cost of assets, uninterrupted connectivity, and security. Traditional computational techniques were partially successful in finding an appropriate solution for existing issues in IIoT. In this study, the author highlighted a deep learning-based prediction model that further assists the industry while making major decisions. This approach is currently used for various problems in agriculture, healthcare, coal and petroleum, entertainment and sports, surveillance, and retail and marketing industries.

Keywords: Artificial intelligence, Healthcare, Industrial IoT, IIoT, Machine learning, Smart industry, Smart agriculture, Smart education, Supply chain management.

INTRODUCTION

The term "Industrial Revolution" implies adopting smart ways and features that can change the workflow of traditional industries. The Industrial Revolution, which began in the late 18th century (1760-1840) with the invention of machinery such as steam engines, marked a significant milestone in human achievement. The introduction of the first weaving loom in 1784 led to the emergence of various small industries catering to both individual clients and large organizations [1]. This digital transformation, encompassing IIoT stakeholders and the application of Industry 4.0 and 5.0, has captured the attention of industry owners, spurring increased investment in the IIoT market. The market size grew to approximately $124 billion in 2021 and is poised for further growth this year [2, 3]. Such an increase in IIoT infrastructure set up by the industries further requires an intelli-

---

[*] **Corresponding author Tuhina Thapliyal:** School of Liberal Studies University of Petroleum and Energy Studies, Dehradun, India; E-mail: tthapliyal@ddn.upes.ac.in

Sunil Kumar, Silky Goel, Gaytri Bakshi, Siddharth Gupta & Sayed M. El-kenawy (Eds.)

gent data analysis system so that the streams of data generated by the IIoT devices can be processed and analyzed to derive the information that is important for the industry's growth.

As Fig. (**1**) depicts, deep learning (DL) is a division of machine learning (ML) and artificial intelligence (AI) [4]. Both machine learning (ML) and deep learning (DL) are derived from artificial neural networks (ANN), which are key technologies that form the basis of the Fourth Industrial Revolution (Industry 4.0) [5].

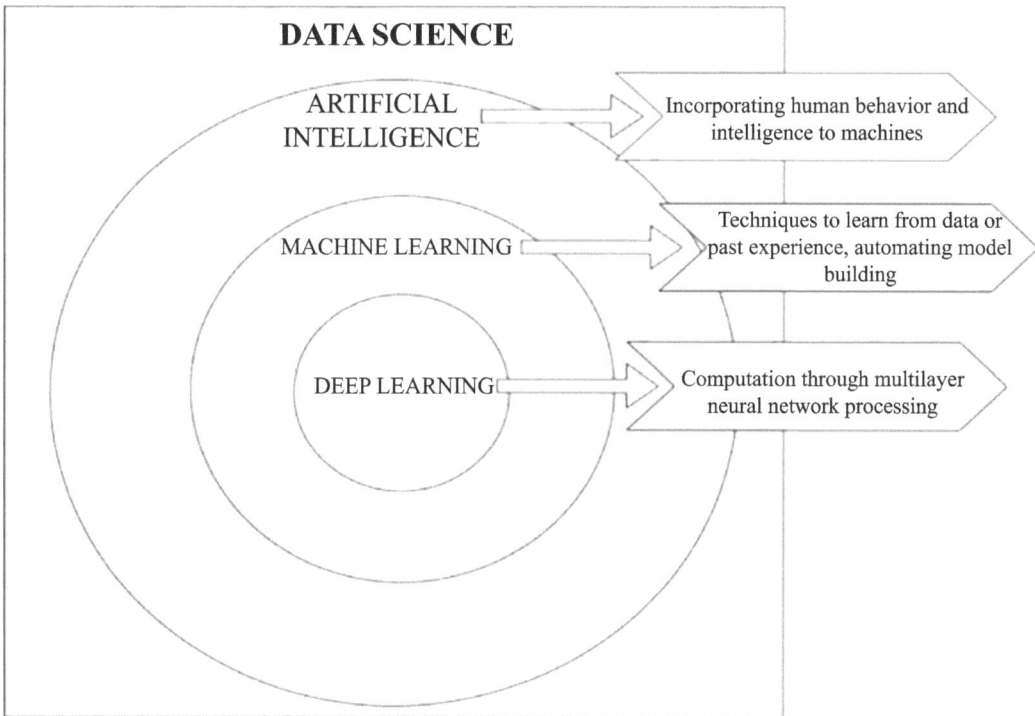

DATA SCIENCE

ARTIFICIAL INTELLIGENCE — Incorporating human behavior and intelligence to machines

MACHINE LEARNING — Techniques to learn from data or past experience, automating model building

DEEP LEARNING — Computation through multilayer neural network processing

Fig. (1). Layers of computational techniques.

DEEP LEARNING: DEFINITION

DL can be defined as a technique that allows a machine to perform what is natural in humans. DL operates on the premise that similar to human babies, it gradually learns from its surroundings and the resources provided to it. This process continues, and the knowledge base develops as babies grow.

This unique property that humans have is the key to DL algorithms. The success rate in problem-solving through deep learning is very high. The concept of driverless cars making them so accurate is decision making, following board signs, and stopping to let pedestrians pass; all these have become possible because of DL. In some instances where a machine must deal with classifying objects in images, DL has simply left the humans behind, which is commendable [6].

Another definition of Dl is "DL is an AI that imitates the way humans gain certain knowledge." DL has high importance in data science, and it includes figures, data, numbers, and predictive modeling as it eases data processing and makes it quicker.

François Chollet, a French software engineer and creator of the Keras deep-learning library, released in 2015, defines AI as an effort to automate intellectual tasks normally performed by humans. A simple definition of AI by Merriam-Webster (an American book publishing company) is "A branch of computer science dealing with the simulation of intelligent behavior in computers" [7].

DL is studied as it has a proficient collection of techniques. The emulsification of DL methods in industries can optimize smart manufacturing processes by incorporating information processing into its multilayer architecture. This facilitates the smart optimization of industry resources. The deep learning properties, for instance, pattern identification, self-learning capabilities, decision making, and above all, automatic feature learning, make it worthwhile as an implementation of a separate algorithm is not required [8].

Deep learning has extraordinary self-learning properties that allow it to learn from data. DL is in a boom these days. DL has a whole set of learning algorithms; it is not just an algorithm. It can be applied to various complex problems and prediction models.

WORKING MODEL OF DEEP LEARNING

Deep learning works on feature extraction of the raw data by implementing multiple hidden layers to derive all the required properties of input data. DL works by transforming the input into DL. It is considered more effective than machine learning in terms of high performance in data extraction, and with the support of highly advanced high-end hardware, its potential has significantly improved [9].

As shown in Fig. (2), the layers in the DL model are the smallest unit of constructive elements, which are associated with a weighted input value that is converted using some functions; further, these values are presented to other layers as an output. Layers altogether construct the whole deep learning model. DL approach can be imagined as a function of artificial intelligence that mimics the human brain to process data.

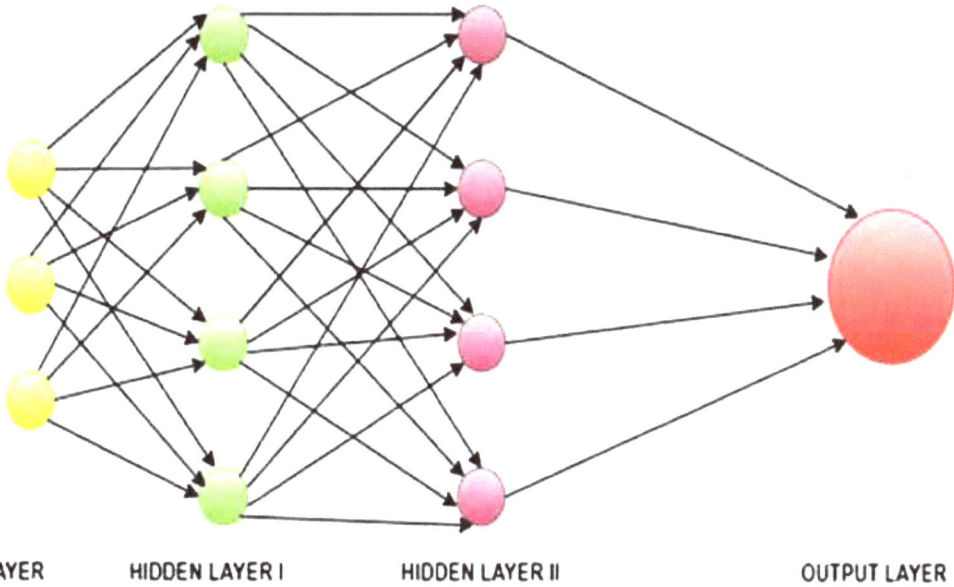

INPUT LAYER   HIDDEN LAYER I   HIDDEN LAYER II   OUTPUT LAYER

Fig. (2). Working model of deep learning techniques.

DL is a hierarchical structure with a collection of stages, and in each stage, some layers of information processing are present. These layers contain input and output layers. Fig. (**3**) shows a basic architecture of how the whole process of deep learning approaches is applied to the data supplied by the industries. First, the data from the various divisions of a firm or industry is collected like the input layer represented in deep learning. Then, using some data pre-processing tools, the information is extracted from the data, which is represented as the hidden layers. This information is then supplied as an input for a DL model. The output of the process is the result that is analyzed.

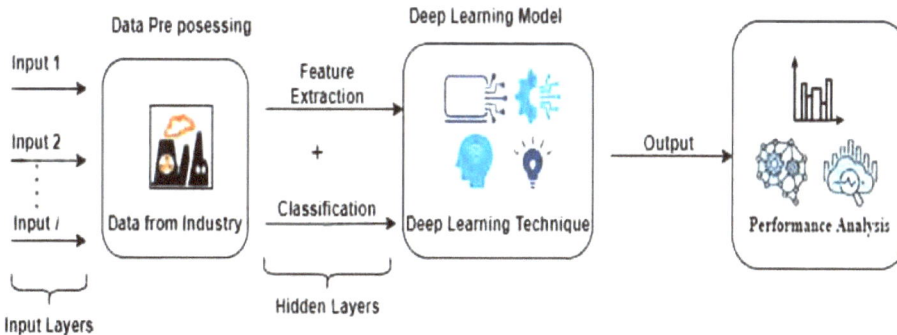

Fig. (3). Basic deep learning architecture.

The term 'deep' refers to the number of hidden layers in a DL model; it generally has more than 2 or 3 hidden layers. Most DL models have 10 to 100 or more layers, unlike traditional neural networks. Earlier, the feature extraction process was supervised, which means the programmer must be very specific with the details it is looking for in the data; the accuracy of the result was totally dependent on the level of details provided. The DL, on the other hand, is unsupervised, which means it creates its own feature set for extraction, which makes it faster and more accurate. Here, the computer learns through its previous experience. By collecting concepts and relationships between these concepts, knowledge is created, so there is no requirement for human inputs to the machine.

DEEP LEARNING IN INDUSTRY

Over the years, industries have undergone several revolutions. For example, during the First Industrial Revolution in the 18th century, water power began to be used. Spinning wheels were replaced by mechanized spinning wheels, electrical energy devices were introduced, and assembly lines were installed for manufacturing products. Additionally, computers were first introduced in the textile industry [1]. The Industrial Revolution 2.0 started with the concept of mass production, and this revolution witnessed the Second World War, which caused many hiccups in the economy [1]. Science and research played a major role in this revolution, and R&D wings were deployed to invent more efficient ways. Mass production helped in the cost-cutting of the same article (commodity), but any modification in article manufacturing became expensive because of the linear manufacturing process. In Industrial Revolution 3.0, semi-automated systems and programmable computers are used. Automation in processes has made industries more efficient, safe, and accurate. These systems perform simple tasks, but they require human support to get a job done. This revolution kind of prepared the base for all the forthcoming revolutions by incorporating automation, the use of the Internet, connectivity among processes, and the usage of renewable energy resources. The transition from electromechanical devices to digital technology and PLC (Programmable Logic Controller) marked the beginning of Industry 3.0, which first emerged in 1968. Industry 4.0 began in 2011, introducing new expectations and challenges. The main goal of transitioning from Industry Revolution 3.0 to IR 4.0 is to enhance production in manufacturing industries and create smart industries. The main features of Industry 4.0 are smart monitoring*i.e.*, it is possible to have a real-time record of all the processes, ease in information sharing, and smart production. All these things are made possible by using smart IoT and cloud computing technology. This, in turn, helps control industry operations and decision-making.

IMPORTANCE OF DEEP LEARNING FOR INDUSTRY 5.0

Since the last decade, advancements in industrial trends have shown unbelievable improvements in productivity services by adopting the revolutions in Industry 4.0 [10]. Additionally, the industries are bound to use complex, expensive software. ROBOTS are replacing humans in industries, leading to compromised security and an increase in the requirement of more skilled and trained employees for operating intricate processes [11]. So, we need a new industrial model, *i.e.*, Industry 5.0, which promises to provide effective business and consumption models. This model comprises two major actors: manufacturer and consumer. Industry 5.0 brings both humans and machines together to produce efficient employment and output. Machines have significantly enhanced capabilities thanks to various artificial intelligence (AI), machine learning (ML), deep learning (DL), and sustainable computational techniques. AI has contributed significantly to AI search engines, product inventory management, query handling, and customers receiving pop-ups for related searches [12]. Although Industry 4.0 enabled mass production, the industry now requires the capability for high-speed mass personalization of products. Industry 5.0 can offer solutions to all smart industry requirements and is capable of effectively handling dynamic market and consumer needs. Machines carry out tedious tasks, while intricate intelligence is provided by humans themselves. Industries of today look for sustainable ways to enhance their capacity and grow, while also contributing to the environment to create a balance between humans and nature. Whether it is cost-effective production or supply, waste management, or maximum utilization of resources, deep learning has always provided reasonable solutions to industry persons. Various deep learning algorithms with high-end computational devices are used to fabricate a smart and sustainable solution; the best example of this is smart additive manufacturing, which is a sustainable way of smart production. Here, the products are made in different layers, step by step instead of in a single go, using deep algorithms and 3D graphical representations of the design of the product for detailed view and accuracy. Hence, it provides a better product quality for the merchandise. The recent research progress in the domain of deep learning and technologies like cloud computing, AL, big data, and cyber-physical systems has made Industry 5.0 the only way to achieve the benchmark of smart, sustainable, cost-effective manufacturing [13, 14]. Preventive predictive maintenance is another feature of Industry 5.0 to handle anomaly situations beforehand. Various deep learning and AI-based software with preventive model technology perform maintenance actions in place of maintenance tasks in a routine to avoid problematic situations. They are also capable of generating warnings proactively in a situation of threat.

Deep learning is a subset of ML that has the potential to be considered the core component of information processing in Industrial Revolution 5.0. The deep learning concept is extracted from artificial neural networks because of its self-learning behavior from data [12]. Deep learning is performing well in various applications such as health science, crime investigation, text analytics, cybersecurity, visual recognition, *etc* [5, 12]. This learning technique is very popular in current research because of its efficiency, as the data volumes have increased and varied rapidly with time [5].

DEEP LEARNING FOR VARIOUS INDUSTRIES

Deep Learning in Medical and Healthcare

Medical science is advancing day by day. Various research studiesare being conducted on various diseases, involving a lot of data and information flow. This data is applied to various analytical models to derive conclusions, and based on this data, research is carried out further. Handling data and information accurately and at hand whenever it is required is the biggest challenge. The cost of maintenance is also another major concern. The DL and predictive analytics bid on these challenges. A wide range of DL models and methodologies are available that can be modified according to the data applied and problem statement [15, 16].

Medical professionals have been practicing DL and AI techniques in diagnosing the disease of the patient, and with the help of an electronic record management system, the data of the patient and the disease is maintained, ensuring data accuracy, integrity, and privacy. This data, when shared for disease diagnosis, becomes helpful in disease prediction, and treatment can be provided under the supervision of the doctor. But now is the need to make our medical practitioners even smarter and take the diagnosis and treatment practices to a whole new level by using trained COBOTS and providing a personalized experience to the patient by implementing deep learning in personalized medical facilities and personalized treatment provided under the supervision of the doctor. This will help reduce treatment costs and save time, as initial check-ups are performed by autonomous COBOTS before doctors take over for advanced treatment [13].

The digitization of medical data and Industry 5.0 with the discovery of COBOTS and smart wearables like health bands, digital meters, and various mobile health applications has enabled users to be able to access their real-time health data. This data can be shared on the cloud with medical experts in case expert attention is required to the patient, as well as it can be analyzed using DL models to know the health condition of the patient. COBOTs have become highly efficient as they are capable of communicating with doctors to perform critical surgeries, all because of Industry 5.0, which has a strong application of DL concepts [2, 17]. The clinical decision support system (CDSS) comprises a set of intelligent applications that assist medical practitioners in making better medical decisions. The CDSS records implemented using the Industry 5.0 revolution contain machine learning and deep learning algorithms, and software applications like natural language processing and recognition systems make them more effective than earlier [18, 19].

Deep Learning in Education

The word education is a powerful word that means imparting knowledge, learning ability, and good qualities like moral values and emotions to others. Education is very important as it helps spread awareness, acquire discipline, and realize responsibility and social welfare. The traditional approaches to education have evolved from single classrooms to smart classes, providing students with broader exposure. Learning is now done three-dimensionally, which involves converting text into speech with visuals. Industry 5.0 deep learning-based approach has made educators apply DL to personalize education, identify slow learners, enhance ways of teaching, maintain the student records efficiently, analyze student feedback to identify areas of attention, and adopt new ways of learning. Here, the primary goal is to improve the education system and enable the utilization of knowledge-sharing skills of human experts alongside smart computational devices. The education sector with IIoT 5.0 is very flexible for students and teachers. It simply agrees that information spread should have no barriers. The best example of a smart education system was witnessed during the time of the COVID-19 pandemic, which left an impression on human history. In those difficult times, various schools were able to conduct online classes so that the education of the students remained uninterrupted. Fig. (**4**) shows the advantages of DL approaches. DL is applied to analyze the behavior and level of engagement of the students during an online class to make sure that students find the classes interactive and fruitful. These are known as engagement detection techniques using deep learning [20].

Deep Learning in Agriculture

Food is not just a basic commodity of life but a necessity for living. Agriculture is the art and science of cultivation of soil, various crops, and rearing animals. Agriculture is an important factor in the Indian economy and employment. The trading of commodities is done throughout the world to generate revenue. India contributes to 18% of the world's population, and the need for higher production of crops is increasing. Agriculture has become an industry with a total net worth of INR 63,506 billion in 2020 and is expected to grow to INR 125,350 billion by 2026 [21]. The traditional ways of agriculture are no longer effective in producing crops at the required rate. Modern changes in farming style by incorporating techniques of deep learning and data analytics are the need of the hour. Farmers are equally hesitant to use modern techniques because of a lack of knowledge and proper skill training about crop times, soil types, irrigation systems, suitable climate conditions, proper usage of pesticides, *etc*. Industry 5.0 has joined hands together with farming experts, and smart digital technologies like DL algorithms, computer vision, image recognition systems, and other related technologies can be used to overcome all these hurdles. The idea is to enable farmers to know about smart farming techniques and expose them to all the information they require for smart farming so that they can choose the right crops at the right time of the season and gain a high yield of crops. Sensors and actuators are deployed on lands that perceive data like temperature in that area, soil quality, and conditions favorable for crops. Based on that data, a choice of the crops suitable to grow in that area is made. The crops grown accordingly are good quality crops with great nutrition values [22].

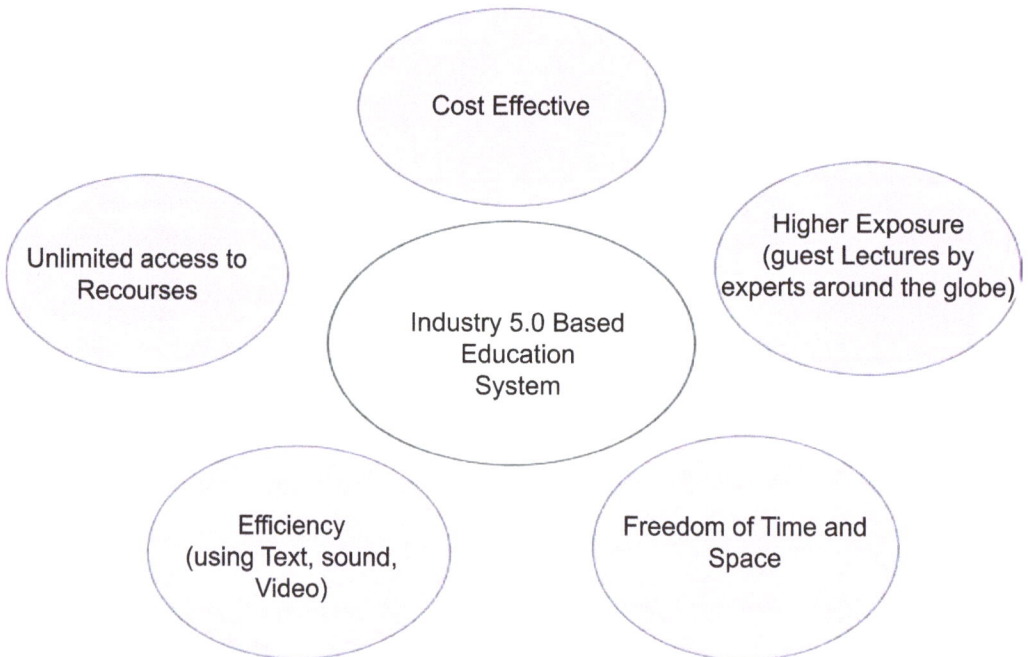

Fig. (4). Advantages of smart education system.

Adopting smart agricultural practices will help farmers maximize crop production and increase profits. The success of AI and DL applications in different genres has made AI most popular in research, and it is being applied to different domains.

As shown in Fig. (**5**), the farmer starts with selecting a crop to grow; the next process is to prepare the land to sow the crop. After that, the seeds of the crop are sowed into the land, then adequate irrigation is timely done, and fertilizers are used at various stages of crop growth; then comes the requirement of pest prevention and maintenance, which include preventing crops from pest and removing growth of unwanted weeds from the land; this is followed by harvesting. The whole process of cultivation is divided into three categories: pre-harvesting, harvesting, post-harvesting [23].

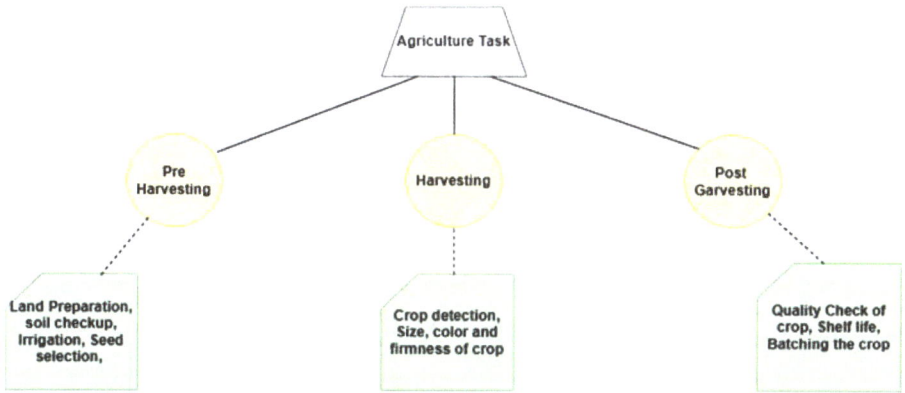

Fig. (5). Agriculture category of tasks and processes.

Deep Learning in Supply Chain Management

Supply chain management is a very crucial sector of an industry; we can call it a backbone that holds up the balance between demand, supply, and production. To meet the rapidly changing consumer demands, every small unit should be in sync with each other to ensure the completion of production and supply activities on time. A minor delay in the processing of a single unit may cause a shutdown of the whole process, causing a major loss to the industry. To avoid such a situation, industries are undergoing a revolutionary change to Industry 5.0 to create a sustainable, predictive, secure, and smart industry environment. Fig. (**6**) shows a traditional industry supply chain [24].

Humans interact with high end digital, sensor-enabled devices that are capable of monitoring multiple activities in real time. These devices continuously share data that is examined thoroughly using data analyzing techniques and data visualizations by extracting required information and applying DL approaches to optimize the tasks being done using the information and ensuring that the industry is able to fulfill the personalized product demand of the consumer in a cost-effective and quick way, which is the main goal of Industry 5.0.

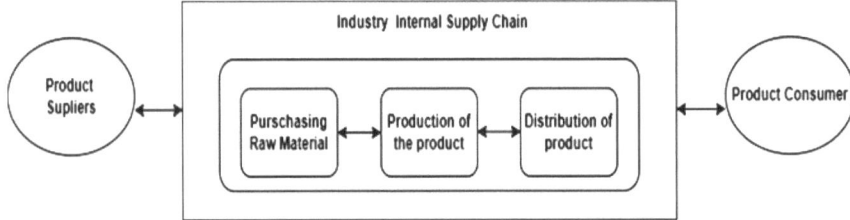

Fig. (6). Industry supply chain.

The concept of a cloud manufacturing ecosystem is possible using digital transformation technology that can create a Digital SCM that contains complete details of factories, suppliers, contract managers, transportation grids, and consumer details like products ordered by them and their location. In this manner, the process of the whole supply chain is carried out virtually [13]. DL models are capable of learning from data shared by sensors, ML, and big data. DL predictive models can predict an anomaly situation and run preventive measures to handle the same.

COBOTS have changed the restriction of working hours as they can work for hours and do monotonous, time-consuming tasks at a constant speed without errors. The tasks of quality check, which require focused attention and a peaceful mind, are done by COBOTS after they are programmed with DL algorithms to perform a task under human workers' supervision, and COBOTS are in touch with the operator throughout the process.

SUGGESTED SOLUTIONS

A new framework for deep Learning in various industries is shown in Fig. (7) [25]. Explained below are all the steps:

STEP 1: "Industry 5.0-based industries are smart industries that utilize various smart technologies and devices to stay ahead. These devices generate large amounts of real-time data streams. This data is crucial for the functioning of these industries."

STEP 2: Data supplied by any source, such as electronic devices, sensors, actuators, COBOTS, other mobile applications, *etc.*, is collected. Data can be present in any form and in any quantity.

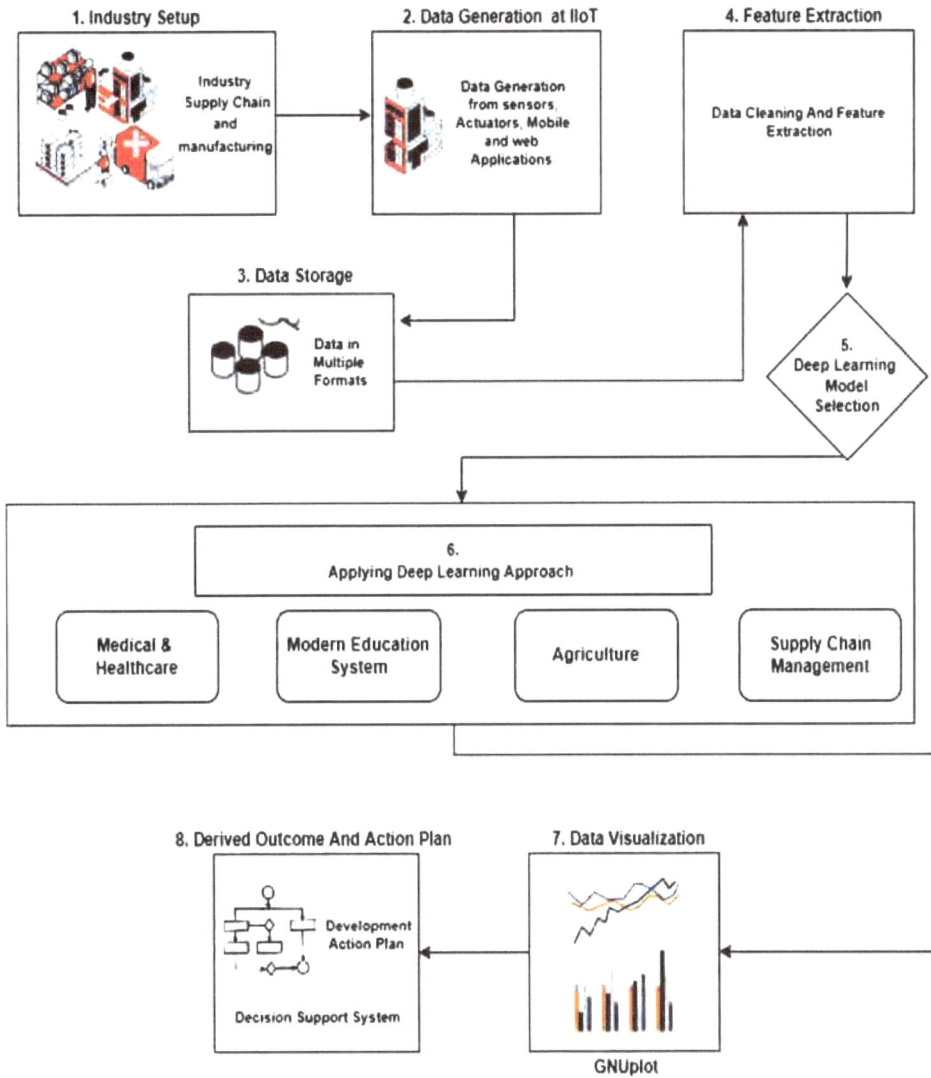

Fig. (7). A deep learning framework for multiple disciplines using IIoT 5.0.

STEP 3: The data is stored either on local servers or shared *via* cloud computing technology for further processing.

STEP 4: The next step is to clean the data using various data extraction techniques for the extraction of useful information.

STEP 5: A deep learning model is selected and applied to the data gathered in the previous step. The deep Learning models are a collection of DL algorithms and techniques that are modified according to the result to be extracted from the data.

STEP 6: Applying a deep learning model to the data.

STEP 7: Representing, visualizing, and analyzing the data using various data visualization techniques and extracting efficient/competent output that can further be used for making various exquisite actions and decisions.

STEP 8: By the results received, the action plan can be made, or any changes to the current processes can be easily done, which will help in optimizing the process.

CONCLUSION

The author thoroughly examined deep earning technology in this book chapter. An overview of all the Industrial revolutions till Industry 5.0 is discussed. The chapter mainly focuses on the applications of Industry 5.0 in traditional industry setups to make them more sustainable and smart. The advantages of using DL and associated technologies in various industry domains are also studied. A deep learning framework for multiple disciplines is also present.

REFERENCES

[1]   A. Sharma, and B.J. Singh, "Evolution of Industrial Revolutions: A Review", *Int. J. Innov. Technol. Explor. Eng.,* vol. 9, no. 11, pp. 66-73, 2020.
[http://dx.doi.org/10.35940/ijitee.I7144.0991120]

[2]   R.A. Khalil, N. Saeed, M. Masood, Y.M. Fard, M.S. Alouini, and T.Y. Al-Naffouri, "Deep learning in the industrial internet of things: Potentials, challenges, and emerging applications", *IEEE Internet Things J.,* vol. 8, no. 14, pp. 11016-11040, 2021.
[http://dx.doi.org/10.1109/JIOT.2021.3051414]

[3]   G. Chhabra, and R. Vasant Varade, Vasant Varade and Pournima, Internet of Things, LAP LAMBERT Academic Publishing, 2021.

[4]   Y. LeCun, Y. Bengio, and G. Hinton, "Deep learning", *Nature,* vol. 521, no. 7553, pp. 436-444, 2015.
[http://dx.doi.org/10.1038/nature14539] [PMID: 26017442]

[5]   I.H. Sarker, "Deep Learning: A Comprehensive Overview on Techniques, Taxonomy, Applications and Research Directions", *SN Comput. Sci.,* vol. 2, no. 6, p. 420, 2021.
[http://dx.doi.org/10.1007/s42979-021-00815-1] [PMID: 34426802]

[6]   Available from: https://in.mathworks.com/ 1994.

[7]   G. Regunath, "Understanding The Difference Between AI, ML, And DL: Using An Incredibly Simple Example," Advancing Analytics Limited, 2021. Available from: https://www.advancinganalytics. co.uk/blog/2021/12/15/understanding-the-difference-between-ai-ml-and-dl-using-an--ncredibly-simple-example

[8]   L. Shahid, M. Driss, W. Boulila, Z.E. Huma, S. Jamal, Z. Idrees, and J. Ahmad, "Deep Learning for the Industrial Internet of Things (IIoT): A Comprehensive Survey of Techniques, Implementation Frameworks, Potential Applications, and Future Directions", *Sensors,* vol. 21, p. 7518, 2021.

[9]   K. Ranjan, G. Y. Reddy. and H. Pathak, "The Understanding of Deep Learning: A Comprehensive Review", *Mathematical Problems in Engineering,* 2021.

[10]   S. Alter, "How Facets of work illuminate sociotechnical challenges of Industry 5.0.," 2020. *European*

Conference on Information SystemsAt: Marrakech, Morocco.

[11]   U. Al Faruqi, "Future Service in Industry 5.0", *Jurnal Sistem Cerdas,* vol. 2, no. 1, pp. 67-79, 2019.
       [http://dx.doi.org/10.37396/jsc.v2i1.21]

[12]   M. Nadimpalli, "Artificial intelligence–Consumers and industry impact", *International Journal of Economics & Management Sciences,* vol. 6, no. 3, p. 03, 2017.

[13]   P.K. Maddikunta, Reddy., Q.-V. Pham., B. Prabadevi., N. Deepa., K. Dev., T. R. Gadekallu., R. Ruby. and M. Liyanage, "Industry 5.0: A survey on enabling technologies and potential applications", *J. Ind. Inf. Integr.,* p. 100257, 2022.

[14]   A. Choudhury, A. Aggarwal, K. Rangra, and A. Bhatt, "The Components of Big Data and Knowledge Management Will Change Radically How People Collaborate and Develop Complex Research", In: *Big Data Governance and Perspectives in Knowledge Management.* IGI Global, 2019, pp. 241-257.
       [http://dx.doi.org/10.4018/978-1-5225-7077-6.ch011]

[15]   A. Muniasamy, T. Sehrish., M. A. Hussain., H. Sultana., V. Muniasamy. and R. Bhatnagar, "Deep learning for predictive analytics in healthcare", *International Conference on Advanced Machine Learning Technologies and Applications,* pp. 32-42, 2019.

[16]   M. Arya, H. Sastry, A. Motwani, S. Kumar, and A. Zaguia, "A Novel Extra Tree Ensemble Optimized DL Framework (ETEODL) for Early Detection of Diabetes", *Frontiers in Public Health,* vol. 9, 2021..

[17]   P. Kumar, R. Chaudhary, A. Aggarwal, P. Singh, and R. Tomar, "Improving Medical Image Segmentation Techniques Using Multiphase Level Set Approach *via* Bias Correction", *Int. J. Eng. Adv. Technol.,* vol. 1, no. 5, pp. 285-289, 2012.

[18]   J. T. Kim, "Application of machine and deep learning algorithms in intelligent clinical decision support systems in healthcare", *Journal of Health & Medical Informatics,* vol. 8, 2018.
       [http://dx.doi.org/10.4172/2157-7420.1000321]

[19]   D.L. Hunt, R.B. Haynes, S.E. Hanna, and K. Smith, "Effects of computer-based clinical decision support systems on physician performance and patient outcomes: a systematic review", *JAMA,* vol. 280, no. 15, pp. 1339-1346, 1998.
       [http://dx.doi.org/10.1001/jama.280.15.1339] [PMID: 9794315]

[20]   P. Bhardwaj, P.K. Gupta, H. Panwar, M. Siddiqui, R. Morales-Menendez, and A. Bhaik, "Application of Deep Learning on Student Engagement in e-learning environments", *Elsevier,* vol. 93, p. 107277, 2021.

[21]   I. Group, "Agriculture Industry in India: Growth and Opportunities," *IMARC*, Available from: https://www.imarcgroup.com/agriculture-industry-in-india [Accessed 25 05 2022].

[22]   S. Kumar, V. Marriboyina, and V. Marriboyina, "Information Extraction From the Agricultural and Weather Domains Using Deep Learning Approaches", *Int. J. Soft. Innov.,* vol. 10, no. 1, pp. 1-12, 2022.
       [http://dx.doi.org/10.4018/IJSI.293266]

[23]   V. Meshram, K. Patil, V. Meshram, D. Hanchate, and S.D. Ramkteke, "Machine learning in agriculture domain: a state-of-art survey", In: *Artificial Intelligence in the Life Sciences* vol. 1. , 2021, p. 100010.

[24]   J. Zhao, M. Ji, and B. Feng, "Smarter supply chain: a literature review and practices", *Journal of Data, Information and Management,* vol. 2, no. 2, pp. 95-110, 2020.
       [http://dx.doi.org/10.1007/s42488-020-00025-z]

[25]   A.I. Khan, A. Al-Badi, "Open Source Machine Learning Frameworks for Industrial Internet of Things", *Procedia Computer Science*, Vol. 170, pp. 571-577. 2020.
       [http://dx.doi.org/10.1016/j.procs.2020.03.127]

CHAPTER 3

IoT-Enabled Smart Production and Sustainable Development

Hitesh Kumar Sharma[1,*]

[1] *Cybernetics Cluster, School of Computer Science and Engineering, University of Petroleum and Energy studies, Dehradun, India*

Abstract: Internet of Things (IoT) technology is a prominent approach for handling present-day issues in various sectors for sustainable development. The agricultural sector is considered the backbone for the sustainability of a nation and plays a vital role in biodiversity sustenance. Precision farming or precision agriculture is the practice of maximizing crop yields and making the agricultural profession more profitable. Precise and timely input of various agricultural parameters through smart and advanced technologies like IoT, AI, image processing, drone-based cameras, computer vision, smart portable devices, GPS, and others provide precision farming a real playground for implementation. The practice of precision farming can boost the efficiency, sustainability, and profitability of farmlands. An automated irrigation system (AIS) is an advanced technology that uses sensors, controllers, and automation to efficiently manage and optimize the watering of plants and crops. While AIS offers numerous benefits, some challenges and problems can also arise, such as in terms of sensor accuracy, connectivity and communication, power supply, maintenance and system updates, cost and implementation, and user understanding and training. Therefore, it is a hard requirement for an intelligent automated system with IoT capabilities that can precisely track and manage water and energy consumption. In today's world, automation dominates human existence. In this chapter, we suggested a comprehensive framework for an IoT-based smart and automated irrigation system to address the drawbacks of conventional systems like drip irrigation and pot irrigation, which cause soil erosion and water wastage. Water is sprayed across the crops in the field by an automated irrigation system to spread it like a downpour. Installing an AIS allows for time- and water-saving water utilization.

Keywords: IoT, Sustainable development, Smart irrigation, Smart farming.

INTRODUCTION

IoT is a system that connects appliances like electrical devices, mechanical devices, computing devices, sensing devices, *etc.*, through the internet to control,

* **Corresponding author Hitesh Kumar Sharma:** Cybernetics Cluster, School of Computer Science and Engineering, University of Petroleum and Energy studies, Dehradun, India; E-mail: hksharma@ddn.upes.ac.in

monitor, and analyze the working of these devices with minimized human interaction. First, the data from devices (like sensors, *etc.*) is transferred to the IoT gateway; the gateway aggregates the data and transfers it to the cloud. Then, the data is monitored, analyzed, and processed. Finally, the result is sent to the user. Everything is somehow connected to the internet. We have always heard of smart city plans. These systems include IoT at some point because we need an internet connection to create a smart environment and make it easy to access and discover a device or app. IoT is a system of related computer devices connected to the Internet. IoT is a network of tangible objects such as buildings, vehicles, and connected furniture to share their data. These items can be identified specifically by their IP address or RFID tag [1, 2].

A descriptive feature of IoT is the idea that an object can be connected to the internet without human contact; for example, a home-sensing sensor will send information to an application on your phone. IoT is a network of embedded objects and electronic devices, software, sensors, and communications so that these objects can collect and exchange data. The IoT system can include a variety of devices, such as smartphones, smartwatches, dynamic trackers, cars, buses, and trains. The idea behind IoT is to connect virtual objects to the internet for monitoring and remote control.

APPLICATIONS OF IOT

The main aim of IoT is to reduce the work load on humans. It is a technology that makes our daily life easier by automating processes, using smarter devices, working faster, reducing cost, *etc.* A few areas or things where IoT is useful are smart watches, smart cars, smart hospitals, smart homes, *etc.*, as depicted in Fig. (**1**) [3].

The detailed description of some major applications of IoT is explained below in the following sub-sections [4, 5].

Industrial Automation

Automated processes save human energy, time, and cost. Tasks that are repetitive or share a similar pattern can be automated so that the system works automatically. Industries use automation in most of their work to scale their business. Industrial robotization is one of the generally huge and normal utilization of IoT. Robotization of machines and instruments empowers organizations to work in a proficient manner with modern software devices to screen and make enhancements for the next process. Industrial robotization further develops precision and proficiency, diminishes mistakes, is simple to control, and is some what open through applications. Machines can work in more brutal conditions than people; mechanization of machines and instruments diminishes labor supply necessities for explicit errands. The connected factory idea is a viable answer for enhancements in every aspect of the activity. Significant parts, such as machines, apparatuses, and sensors, are connected to an organization for simpler administration and access. Outline of cycle stream, screen downtime, status checking of stock, shipment, plan upkeep, stop/stop a specific interaction for further examination, and so on are possible by remotely utilizing industrial IoT arrangements.

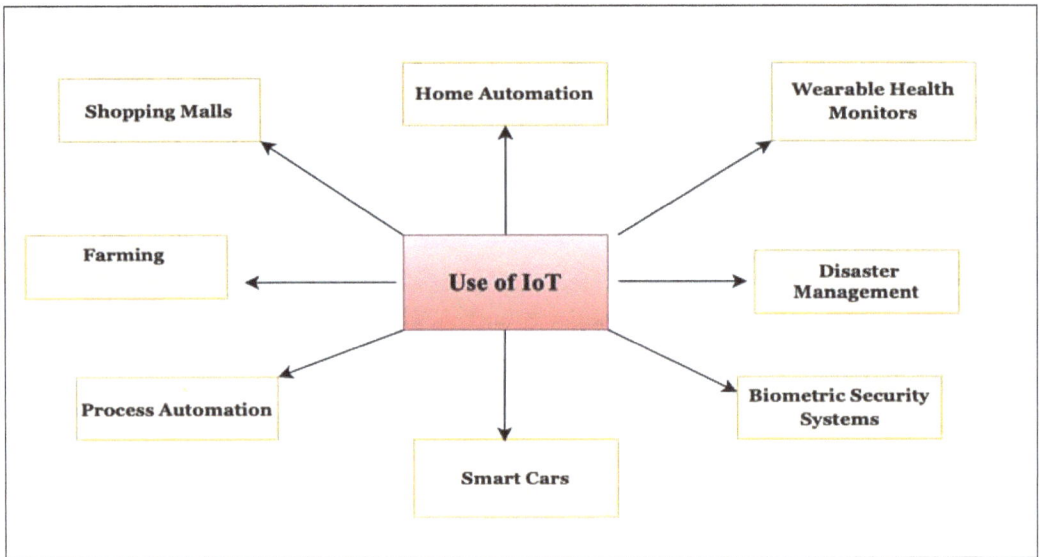

Fig. (1). Application areas of IoT.

Smart Robotics

Many organizations are creating insightful advanced mechanics frameworks for IoT-empowered industrial facilities. Savvy advanced mechanics guarantee the smooth treatment of apparatuses and materials in the assembly line with exactness and proficiency. Predefined particulars can be set for the most extreme accuracy (up to a few nanometers scale for certain applications) utilizing smart, automated arms. The human-machine interface plan will lessen the intricacy of activities, and it will reflect in future IoT-empowered assembling as further developed usefulness. Robots can be modified to perform complex errands with very good quality embedded sensors for constant examination. These mechanical technology networks are connected to a protected cloud for observation and control. A designing group can get to and break down this information to make speedy moves for item upgrades or forestall a surprising disappointment because of a machine issue. Real-time tracking of information, components, *etc.*, helps industries to manage and monitor their work. Delivery-based companies can also keep track of their deliverables by tracking the real-time location. Equipment usage, finances, and other activities can be tracked easily. Many businesses are developing innovative frameworks for enhanced mechanics for industrial facilities enabled by the IoT. Smart, sophisticated mechanics ensure the smooth handling of tools and materials in the assembly line with absolute accuracy and competence. With the help of smart, automated arms, predefined details can be established with the highest degree of accuracy (up to a few nanometers scale for some applications). The complexity of the task will be reduced by the human-machine interface design concept, which will show up as improved utility in future IoT-enabled assemblies. Robots can be programmed to complete complicated tasks and be equipped with high-quality embedded sensors for ongoing inspection. These networks of mechanical technology are linked to a secure cloud for monitoring and management.

Predictive Maintenance

Modern industrial machinery equipped with clever sensors continuously monitors the condition of each important component and can spot any minor issues before the entire structure fails. Smart sensors will alert the integrated framework to the need for maintenance, and alert messages will be sent to alert individuals or groups. Without affecting normal assignments, maintenance designers can analyze the data and make viable plans for plan maintenance. Predictive maintenance is a potent approach to prevent unnecessary breaks in the production process. Unexpected failure of equipment can result in damaged goods, delivery delays, and financial loss for manufacturers.

Integration of Smart Tools / Wearables

The incorporation of intelligent sensors into tools and machinery enables the workforce to carry out the assignment with increased accuracy and competency. Uniquely designed wearables can help employees reduce errors and increase security at the workplace. Innovative wearables can send workers instantaneous warning messages during emergencies like a fire or gas leak. Wearables can continuously monitor a person's health and give feedback if they are unfit for a given task.

Smart Logistics Management

Logistics operations are one of the significant regions in numerous businesses, which needs constant upgrades to help expand requests. Smart sensor innovation is an ideal fit to address a large number of perplexing strategies and activities and oversee products effectively. Retail giants like Amazon utilize robots to convey products to their clients. Trend-setting innovations like robots offer better proficiency, openness, and speed, and they require less labor. Nonetheless, initial speculations are colossal as compared to regular strategies, and execution has impediments.

Enhanced Quality and Security

Acquaintance with IoT innovation in assembling offers improved item quality. Persistent observation and investigation of each stage guarantee better quality by further developing interaction ventures.

The integration of smart devices and software offers a more elevated level of safety. Software-controlled computerization and information assortment from a massive sensor network are connected to a cloud server stage.

ROLE OF IOT IN SUSTAINABLE DEVELOPMENT

This section is about the role of the IoT in smart production and sustainable development. The IoT has a significant impact on smart production and sustainable development because it can improve efficiency and productivity, as well as reduce time to market new products. IoT enables these objects to be monitored and controlled remotely through the internet. IoT enables industrial processes to be automated, and it also helps with energy efficiency. The industrial sector has been using this technology for a while now, but its use in sustainable development is on the rise. IoT can help with energy efficiency by reducing waste and emissions from industrial processes [6]. The IoT is a new paradigm for manufacturing and production. It is a digital transformation of the manufacturing process. IoT is a new way to connect machines, data, and people. It has been heralded as the next industrial revolution that will change the way we produce goods and services. IoT enables manufacturers to be more responsive to customer demand, innovate faster, and improve quality while reducing costs. It brings together sensors, software, actuators, controllers, and human-machine interfaces in order to create a smart manufacturing system that can interact with its environment in real time. The use of IoT is increasing as more and more companies adopt it in their production process. This article discusses how IoT can help companies to improve their sustainability, efficiency, and competitiveness [7].

The IoT will enhance production efficiency, sustainability, and overall quality. The use of IoT can also help reduce the environmental footprint of manufacturing. IoT has many benefits for companies, including increased efficiency in production and an ability to make more informed decisions about their operations. IoT can also provide a way for companies to integrate sustainability into their business model [8].

Requirements such as data management, digitalization, automation, less energy and cost, *etc.*, can be achieved by the usage of IoT in smart production and sustainable development. Artificial intelligence [12], automation, and robotics will help in manufacturing at a faster rate, which will reduce human work. Automated tasks will save time and increase the productivity of the business. Machine learning, data analysis, and monitoring of devices will help in making the business sustainable. On the basis of monitoring and gathering data, necessary decisions will be made related to the business that will increase the chances of success and scaling. IoT will help in connecting devices, manufacturing systems, machines, *etc.*, and will improve the productivity of the business and maintenance of the systems [9].

CHALLENGES FOR IOT IN SMART FRAMING AND SUSTAINABLE DEVELOPMENT

The challenges for IoT in sustainable development are shown in Fig. (**2**).

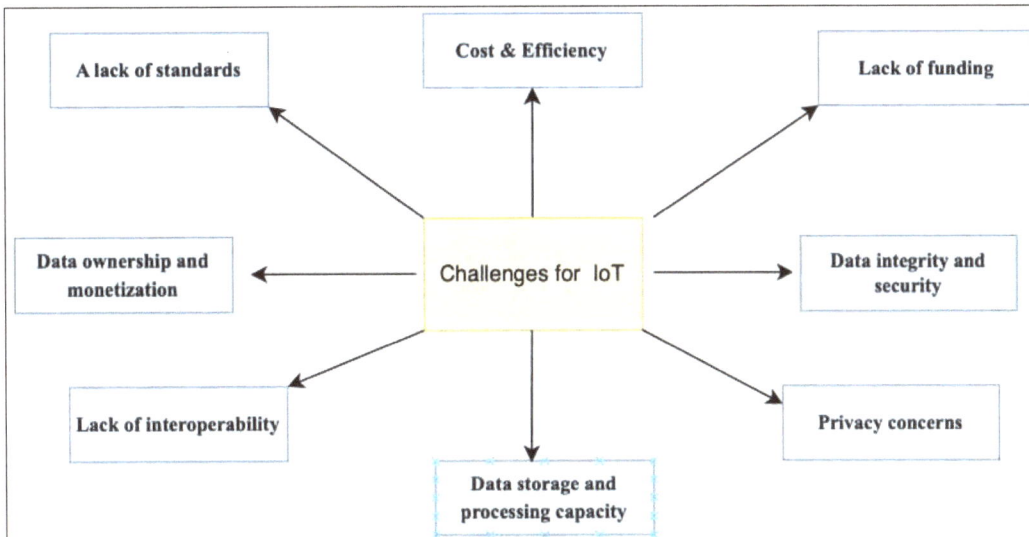

Fig. (2). Challenges for IoT in Sustainable Development.

Some of these major challenges are explained in detail in the following sub-sections:

Lack of Standards and System Failure

A system failure or downtime can cause huge financial loss, damage to devices or machines, injury to human workers, *etc.* An IoT system malfunction is much more dangerous than a commercial IoT system malfunction. So, the system must be preserved or else the industry could face a heavy loss.

Security

Hacking or data breaches can be extremely harmful to industries as important information can be manipulated, destroyed, or leaked. Security attacks can disturb the whole workflow of the system, and as a result, all the tasks can be delayed or sabotaged [10].

Interoperability and Connectivity

As we know there are numerous devices connected together in an IIoT system, so there is a moderate possibility that the devices may not connect. This may be because of the different manufacturers of the devices or because of the network system. Such connectivity problems are a big issue in the IIoT system.

Data Storage and Monitoring networks

Another challenge faced by IoT system-based businesses is the monitoring of the networks. To make sure that the devices are connected properly and the data is visible without any interruption, monitoring is necessary. For this, network engineers are hired to make sure that things are going smoothly for the end user [11].

IMPLEMENTATION OF IOT-ENABLED SMART IRRIGATION SYSTEM

With the use of technical infrastructure, we can manage the irrigation system's water and power usage effectively Fig. (**3**). The system that is being introduced offers a solution in the shape of an AIS that analyzes environmental data to identify where and when proper irrigation is required [11]. The labor of a farmer is greatly simplified and made easy by automation. To automate the irrigation process, the controllers in the system will keep an eye on the actual field site's temperature, humidity, and soil moisture content. IoT, which includes sensors, water pumps, nodeMCU, and other microcontroller devices, is used to implement the system. Generally speaking, hardware requirements are a 2 GHz x86 processor or higher, 256 MB memory (RAM), 100 MB or more of hard drive capacity, a monitor for output, keyboard and mouse for data entry, C-compiler (cc, gcc, egcs), Arduino IDE software requirements, seed, electrician, plumber, PVC pipes, gardener, electricity wirings, agricultural land, fertilizer, *etc.*, as depicted in Fig. (**3**).

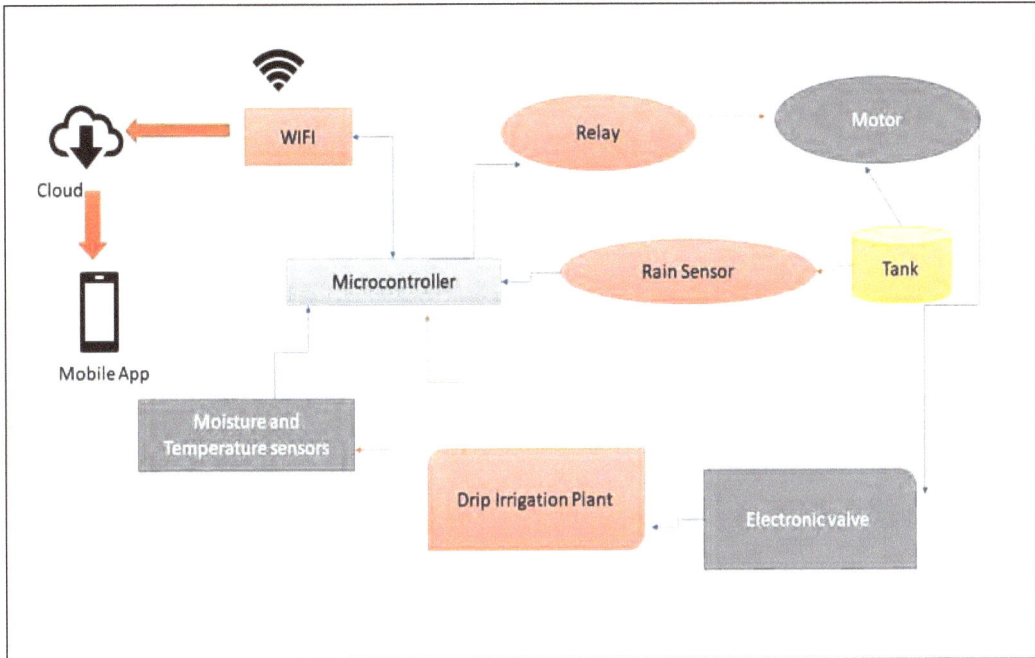

Fig. (3). AIS Component Diagram.

The architecture prototype that was established for this system is already mentioned. As per the mentioned system, there are numerous NodeMCU units linked with Raspberry Pi, which serves as the main controlling system. A temperature, humidity, and moisture sensor is linked to each NodeMCU. The relays that our central controlling system is additionally attached to allow it to transmit an analog signal based on readings from the NodeMCU devices, which are also connected to relays. Depending on the signal the relay has received, pressure valves are automatically turned ON and OFF. The components of AIS are temperature & humidity sensor (DHT 11), pressure pump & motor, relay for water flow, water electric pump, electricity wires and connections, PVC connections, PVC pipes, protoboard/ breadboard, relay board (12V), soil moisture sensor, Node MCU ESP – 8266, rain pipes for sprinkler work, solenoid valve, display screen for pi, and Raspberry Pi 3 kit. Here are definitions of the various devices used in our prototype.

Here, a coil and a few electrical parts make up the modest, straightforward electromechanical device known as a relay. It is an electromagnetic switch that only requires a modest input control signal to regulate a high-voltage source, such as AC mains. The ESP8266 is a low-cost system on a chip, and NodeMCU is based on it. In addition, the Raspberry Pi is a potent, lightweight, ARM-based microprocessor that runs the Linux operating system. It has the input, output, and storage capacity necessary for connections, as shown in circuits in Fig. (**4**).

Fig. (4). AIS Circuit Diagram.

A completely designed and implemented circuit is given in Fig. (**4**). This circuit can be deployed in agricultural land for smart irrigation.

CONCLUSION

By 2030, there will be 9.6 billion people on the planet, and agriculture will be the main source of income in rural regions. As a result, crop yield should be increased without wasting water, which is another vital resource. Even though our nation prides itself on having advanced science and technology, unstable power supply has practically become the norm in recent years. India receives a lot of rain, which offers a vast untapped market for off-grid solar energy. We have included several sensor nodes (such as soil moisture and DHT11) and a control node in our proposed system. The sensor nodes are placed in the field to gather the appropriate values, and the control node subsequently receives the detected data. Based on gathered and sensed environmental data surrounding the crop, the automated system is able to automatically irrigate the field. Additionally, the NodeMCU's Wi-Fi module enables remote monitoring and control of the system. Additionally, wireless network devices use less power and operate more effectively for longer periods of time. For farmers who want to watch their fields remotely, this is a huge benefit. This helps you save lots of time and effort. Additionally, water utilization is optimized. In this way, a water system framework that regulates the stream in accordance with requirements while incorporating computerization into the water system framework is planned, and outcomes are achieved successfully. This instrument is simple to use and can be purchased even by a poor farmer, thanks to the use of low-effort sensors and simple technology. This activity is best suited for locations where water is scarce and needs to be used in small quantities. In this chapter, we attempted to take a little step towards precision farming and offered a low-level application of the concept of smart/précised farming. One element of this comprehensive automated system for smart agriculture is the smart irrigation system.

REFERENCES

[1]   H.K. Sharma, "E-COCOMO: the extended cost constructive model for cleanroom software engineering", *Database Systems Journal,* vol. 4, no. 4, pp. 3-11, 2013.

[2]   S. Kumar, V. Marriboyina, and V. Marriboyina, "Information Extraction From the Agricultural and Weather Domains Using Deep Learning Approaches", *Int. J. Soft. Innov.,* vol. 10, no. 1, pp. 1-12, 2022. [IJSI].
[http://dx.doi.org/10.4018/IJSI.293266]

[3]   G. Bathla, P. Singh, S. Kumar, M. Verma, D. Garg, and K. Kotecha, "Recop: Fine-grained Opinions and Collaborative Filtering based Recommender System for Industry 5.0", *Soft Comput.,* 2021.

[4]   R. Tomar, H. Kumar, A. Dumka, and A. Anand, "Traffic management in MPLS network using GNS simulator using class for different services", *2nd International Conference on Computing for Sustainable Global Development (INDIA Com),* 2015.

[5]   G.D. Singh, S. Kumar, H. Alshazly, S.A. Idris, M. Verma, and S.M. Mostafa, "A novel routing protocol for realistic traffic network scenarios in VANET", *Wirel. Commun. Mob. Comput.,* vol. 2021, no. 1, p. 7817249, 2021.
[http://dx.doi.org/10.1155/2021/7817249]

[6]   P. Kumar, R. Chaudhary, A. Aggarwal, P. Singh, and R. Tomar, Improving Medical Image Segmentation Techniques Using Multiphase Level Set Approach *Via* Bias Correction., *International Journal of Soft Computing and Engineering,* vol. 1, no. 5, pp. 285-289, 2012.

[7]   A. Aggarwal, P. Dimri, and A. Agarwal, "Survey on scheduling algorithms for multiple workflows in cloud computing environment", *Int. J. Comput. Sci. Eng.,* vol. 7, no. 6, pp. 565-570, 2019.

[8]   G. Chhabra, S. Kumar, and P. Badoni, "Automatic gadget charger using coin detection", *1st International Conference on Next Generation Computing Technologies (NGCT),* 2015.
[http://dx.doi.org/10.1109/NGCT.2015.7375261]

[9]   A. Choudhury, A. Aggarwal, K. Rangra, and A. Bhatt, "The Components of Big Data and Knowledge Management Will Change Radically How People Collaborate and Develop Complex Research", In: *Big Data Governance and Perspectives in Knowledge Management.* IGI Global, 2019, pp. 241-257.

[http://dx.doi.org/10.4018/978-1-5225-7077-6.ch011]

[10]   A. Aggarwal, P. Dimri, and A. Agarwal, "Statistical Performance Evaluation of Various Metaheuristic Scheduling Techniques for Cloud Environment", *J. Comput. Theor. Nanosci.,* vol. 17, no. 9, pp. 4593-4597, 2020.
[http://dx.doi.org/10.1166/jctn.2020.9285]

[11]   M. Arya, H.G. Sastry, A. Motwani, S. Kumar, and A. Zaguia, "A Novel Extra Tree Ensemble Optimized DL Framework (ETEODL) for Early Detection of Diabetes", In: *Frontiers in Public Health* vol. 9. , 2021..

[12]   S. Singh, S.K. Jangir, M. Kumar, M. Verma, S. Kumar, T.S. Walia, and S.M.M. Kamal, "[Retracted] Feature Importance Score-Based Functional Link Artificial Neural Networks for Breast Cancer Classification", *BioMed Res. Int.,* vol. 2022, no. 1, p. 2696916, 2022.
[http://dx.doi.org/10.1155/2022/2696916] [PMID: 35411308]

CHAPTER 4

A Suggested Framework for the Prevention of Physical Attacks on IoT Devices

Gaytri Bakshi[1,*] and **Rishabh Kumar**[2]

[1] *Department of Cybernetics, School of Computer Science, University of Petroleum And Energy Studies, Dehradun, India*

[2] *Larsen & Toubro Infotech, Mumbai, India*

Abstract: In today's interconnected world, where most devices are connected to the internet and constantly sharing data, the increasing number of IoT devices presents challenges for large companies to develop secure IoT systems.. With the progression of interconnected systems, the risk of hampering security is also a big concern. In the current scenario, it is very easy for attackers to initiate any kind of security breach. The attack will be either on its software, firmware, or hardware level. This chapter deals with the hardware security of the IoT system, which is also termed physical security. Various security threats related to the physical security of an IoT device are described. Various consequences have been mentioned that can occur due to these attacks. With these physical attacks, a lot of severe loopholes can be created in the current ongoing research and development of these interconnected systems.

Keywords: Hardware security, Internet of things (IoT), IoT attacks, Invasive attack, Non-invasive attack, Physical security, Semi-invasive attack.

INTRODUCTION

With the growing trend of IoT devices in the current market, Gartner Inc. predicted that the number of IoT devices would grow from 5 billion in 2015 to more than 25 billion by 2020 [1]. The term IoT was first quoted by Kevin Ashton in 1999 in his presentation for the P&G (Proctor and Gamble). Before that, the concept of interconnected devices was also in the IT market. As for now, when all the firms, including new startups, are adopting this technology, a mindset needs to be prepared to keep regular checks on the security of these systems. In a recent Gartner study, they mentioned the challenges IoT will face in the upcoming years.

---

* **Corresponding author Gaytri Bakshi:** Department of Cybernetics, School of Computer Science, University of Petroleum And Energy Studies, Dehradun, India; E-mail: gaytri@ddn.upes.ac.in

Sunil Kumar, Silky Goel, Gaytri Bakshi, Siddharth Gupta & Sayed M. El-kenawy (Eds.)

'Security' and 'privacy' topped the list as the most severe challenges, and by 2023, most of these security hazards will be shielded [2]. But this will only happen if we put our effort into identifying these problems in the current systems. The glitches in the current systems include immature protocols, ever-changing threats, complex vendor landscape, and lack of skills. IoT security is not a technical problem that needs to be resolved, but it is a complete concept that needs to be revised for a proper understanding of its security problems. This paper is divided into four sections. The first section introduces the reader to the IoT (Internet of Things) and its growing influence. Section two depicts various aspects of IoT security. Section three describes various security attacks, out of which the focus of this paper is on the attacks related to hardware and its security. The reader gets a deep insight into how the glitches within the architecture lead to the downfall of both hardware and, eventually, the entire system.

IOT SECURITY

IoT attacks [3] can be used for different purposes depending on the goals. Some of the most prominent reasons are data and the impact on the services of the service provider. They try to steal secrets from the device either to produce a competitive product or to steal data and services. Some of the major threats are:

Data Security

In an IoT ecosystem, data is the most important asset and the most vulnerable component. Important and valuable data can be stolen from IoT devices (hardware components) and can be used to develop competitive products or to steal data from them.

Denial of Service (DoS Attack) [4, 3]

In this attack, the intruder/hacker puts malicious code into the device's firmware or software component. Also, it can be injected into the hardware, which can damage the product because the vendor must face the damage cost. Also, a DoS attack involves flooding data to the server to crack it or to increase its response timing.

Brute Force Attack [3]

Random attempts of keys to overpass the authentication process is what brute force is all about. To overcome the attack, companies use various cipher algorithms. Multiple levels of authentication are applied to reduce the chances of hitting and trial. Various malwares are developed to implement brute force attacks. One of them is Morsi botnet malware, which came into the picture in

2016. Constantinos kolias *et al.* [5] have stated how these malware tools have exploited the IoT system.

Distributed Denial of Services (DDoS [3])

In a DoS attack, the intruder/malicious attacker tries to bypass the security to use or consume the resources and manipulate the work. Such an attack that compromises numerous nodes and gateways is called a DDoS attack. Some of the DDoS attacks involve sending or transmitting data (malicious) to the server from various modes to affect its services. Some of the prominent DDoS techniques are UDP, FLOOD, KMP/ANG FLOOD, SYN FLOOD, Ping of death, and zero-day DDoS. Krushang Sonar *et al* [6]. have stated various attacks of DDoS on various levels of IoT architecture.

IP Address Piracy

IoT technology is all about a heterogeneous network of connected devices *via* their IPs. If an IP can be attacked by a malicious user, it can access the entire data of IoT devices as well as the entire system and can also affect its data traffic. Most of the IP piracy takes place at the protocol level (Network layer). RPL (routing protocol for low power and lossy networks) has recently been standardized as the widely used protocol for IoT. It works on IPV6 protocol, so it supports various protocols like 6lowPAN and CoAP. RPL can be implemented on Contiki OS (IoT's most known OS) to implement data nodes and IP stacks. Various attacks include selective-forwarding attacks, sinkhole attacks, Hello flood attacks, and worm mole attacks. Walgreen Linus *et al.* [7] have highlighted various IDS implementation and RPL attacks in an IoT environment.

Cloning And Overbuilding [8]

One of the biggest challenges is cloning. It is a scenario in which, without putting any effort, opponent companies try to copy the product. With this, they make a profit and increase their sales. Cloning a device is just reverse engineering. Also, sometimes companies put their claim on some other companies' products as their own. These are not attacks but a challenge that will come into the picture with the growth of the IoT market.

CATEGORIES OF ATTACK

IoT is a technology that is ubiquitous, popular, and widely adopted by the world. It is based on WSN and data gathering. It is a technology that does not have any technological restrictions and has the capability to be implemented in every sector. The wide scope of IoT makes it more vulnerable [9] than any other technology in the entire world. IoT architecture [3] comprises three main components (based on the architecture of devices).

- Hardware.
- Firmware and Protocols.
- Software and Network.

All these three components have their own vulnerabilities and flaws. Intrusion at any of these components can impact the entire system.

Software and Network Security Threat

IoT is nothing but a connection of devices with the internet, which is a network of networks. Millions of connected nodes lead to enormous loopholes. This makes the network vulnerable to attacks along with the nodes connected to it. Various inefficiencies that lead to such attacks are:

- Setup of weak passwords.
- No consistent updating of software.
- Vulnerable interfaces.
- Inefficient methods to protect data.
- Incompetent methods to manage IoT devices.

If regular checks are maintained, the software or network threats can be prevented.

Firmware and Protocols Security Threats

Firmware plays an essential role in an IoT system. Vulnerabilities within the firmware can lead to the entire system being broken. If the attacker gets hold of the IoT system by targeting a firmware attack, it can lead to the following:

- Transform and damage the hardware.
- The attacker can target the operating system.
- Gain access to software such as applications.

IoT protocols deal with IoT architecture. Glitches within the architecture layers can lead to vulnerabilities within the system.

Hardware Security Threats

Hardware architecture varies from manufacturer to manufacturer. The design of each development board varies from the purpose of its development to the design of the ICs. But the things that remain common irrespective of the design are the 'functional blocks', which are responsible for the functioning of the board. All these functional blocks, except the few naming complex structures, are vulnerable to threats related to their security. The first threat is obviously on the chips, which are intended to store data and control the device. According to S.P. Skorobogator *et al.* [10], physical attacks and temper resistance are classified based on their level of impact and resistance which is well depicted by Fig. (**1**). They are categorized into 6 parts, from least severe to highly severe attacks. These classifications are based on factors such as cost, operation, and type of technology used.

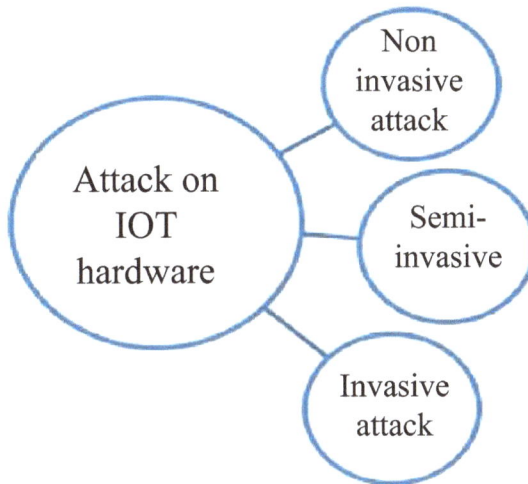

Fig. (1). Types of physical attacks [10].

Non-invasive Attacks [11]

These types of attacks are based on software. They do not involve any chipset or any other device to be interfaced [12]. It does not even demand to let any device undergo testing to detect any flaw in its structural preparation. It is reverse engineering where the attacker can study the data sheet of the chip or realize the structural logic of the chip by dissembling it through the software.

Further, noninvasive attacks are classified into two parts based on their approach.

- Passive Attacks.
- Active Attacks.

In passive attack [13], the study of the signals and clock cycles takes place with the electromagnetic emission. These parameters are usually analyzed for passive attacks. Examples are power analysis, timing attacks, *etc.*

In active attacks [13], the attacker creates a flaw in the circuit using some specifications, such as manipulation of signals, which in turn leads to the failure of the device and breaks the entire system. This can be done by fluctuating the power supply of the devices by manipulating the signals while sending and receiving them. All these attacks come under the category of brute force attacks. This can be explained well by considering a device that gets activated and generates an interrupt at 00101. If an attacker manipulates the signal and manages to generate the sequence, the device can start sending the signals.

If the circuitry logic of any system is well perceived by any attacker, it is easy for him to find the loopholes. He can study the current flow, such as spikes and surges, and then manage the device's activities during an ongoing operation. The attacker can create a short circuit by manipulating the drivers at the receiver end at both data and address bus levels. This strategy would carry heavy charges and completely damage the device.

Another method to steal data from the device is called data remanence [14]. In this technique, the chip is disassembled to extract the stored information; this takes place in SRAM/EEPROM of the devices where the data remains stored in the device after the power supply is disconnected. Lowering the temperature below a specific threshold also results in the freezing of the SRAM (nonvolatile) memory.

Invasive Attacks [15]

The chips in a microcontroller are nothing but a tiny combination of different gates (logic gates) combined and fabricated beneath a passivation layer. The attacker, in this case, must reach that layer to get access to various information. In this kind of attack, it is mandatory to contact the internal components of the controller. In the case of an IoT development board microcontroller, the board needs to be completely disassembled to get to the internal chips and ICs. This requires ionizing the upper layers or using various imaging techniques to get access to the core. This involves various levels of testing and is quite expensive to perform. The cost of testing depends upon the complexity of the chip. As the size of the chip decreases, its complexity increases, and it will require expensive equipment to perform its testing.

There are various reverse engineering [16] methods that can be used to open the layers of ROM and read data from it. To perform an invasive attack, the upper layer of the chips is removed, and then various probings and modifications are performed, such as:

Microprobing [17, 18]

This technique is used to get inside the core of the chip and perform various injection attacks on the test points. As the chip is exceedingly small and cannot be easily viewed from a normal eye, it requires five components to perform the tasks.

- Microscope.
- Device test socket.
- Micromanipulators.
- Stage.
- Probe tip.

The quality of the microscope depends on the kind of magnification required to get inside the inner components and test points of the chip. The cost to perform this attack depends upon the size and chip complexity.

Deprocessing [19]

It is the process in which the inner layer of the chip is removed to understand its internal structure. As an example, Fig. (**2**) shows the Atmel AMTGA 328p IC, which can be integrated with the Arduino board. The IC is fabricated and contains its entire structure in it. In DE processing, the outer layer of fabrication is removed to get inside the internal structure of the chip.

Fig. (2). Integrated circuit at mega 328p.

This helps the attacker in two ways:

- It can perform microprobing easily.
- It can understand the chip's internal structure.

DE processing the chip is a chemical method to remove the fabrication layer of the ICs. It is performed in three ways:

- Plasma etching: Plasma etching is a form of plasma processing used to fabricate integrated circuits. It involves a high-speed stream of glow discharge of an appropriate gas mixture being shot at a sample.
- Chemical etching.
- Mechanical polishing.

Reverse engineering [16]

This technique requires understanding the internal structure inside a semiconductor device to perform various tasks. Understanding the structure helps in gathering information regarding the different interconnection gates and transistors inside the chip. This requires knowledge of VLSI and chip designing because the attacker must remove all the layers of the chip. It will help the attacker to connect any other component to the chip for its specific function. Also, rival companies sometimes use this method to understand and copy the chip.

Semi-Invasive Attacks

The attacks which do not fall under the category of invasive and noninvasive attacks are categorized as semi-invasive attacks. According to S.Skorobogator *et al.* [20], semi-invasive attacks can be performed in processors, which enables them to store the data even after the power supply is disconnected. For example, Arduino, ES8266, 8085 processors, *etc.*, all have one common thing attached to them. This common thing is EEPROM or SROM. EEPROM (electrically erasable programmable read-only memory) is used to store data even after the power supply is lost. The size of the EEPROM is fixed in each controller. Earlier, UV rays were used to disable the security fuses inside the EEPROM. But these days, most microcontrollers are so designed that they can cope with this attack. So, nowadays, various other techniques have come into the picture to perform semi-invasive attacks.

UV Attacks

OTP and EPROM microcontrollers can be accused of using this technique. This is one of the oldest methods and was used in the late 70's on microchips. Nowadays, manufacturers of controllers use various techniques to counter this method. EEPROM and fused memory chips have been introduced, but they do not let the attacker understand the structure inside the chip.

Advanced Imaging

In this method, various imaging devices, like microscopes, are used to understand the structure of the chips and know about their components like EEPROM, SROM, processors, logic gates, *etc.* These components are later used in reverse engineering the chips. But nowadays, there is a limitation to this. As the size of the chip decreases, its structure becomes more complex. The number of transistors is also increasing, and their size is also decreasing to nanometer. This has made it difficult to understand the structure.

Optical Fault Injection Attack

An incredibly old vulnerability that was in trend in the 1990's was when microcontrollers were attacked using probing techniques and power analysis attacks. Now, this attack has become more advanced. This attack is used to manipulate the behavior of the controller at minimal cost, just using a laser pointer in some cases. This can be used to manipulate the bits present inside the SROM. Also, it can create multiple errors inside the device's cryptographic algorithms and protocols. The things/components that were thought to be more secure to UV ray attacks are more sensitive to this attack, like EEPROM and hash memory cells as shown in Fig. (**3**) [21]. This attack can cause a change in the state of components from '1' to '0' or either '0' to '1' in most cases.

Flash Memory Bumping Attacks

Cryptographic hardware and embedded systems workshop mentioned bumping attacks on embedded devices, which can be used to extract sensitive data, algorithms, and cryptographic keys from the chips.

Optical Enhanced Position Lacked Analysis

It is a technique by which the current pulse through an IC is visible in the current trace. It is a power analysis method that involves measuring the power consumption of the entire chip. After that, laser beams are used on the specific areas of the chip to examine the logic states of transistors. It is a combination of a semi-invasive attack and an invasive attack.

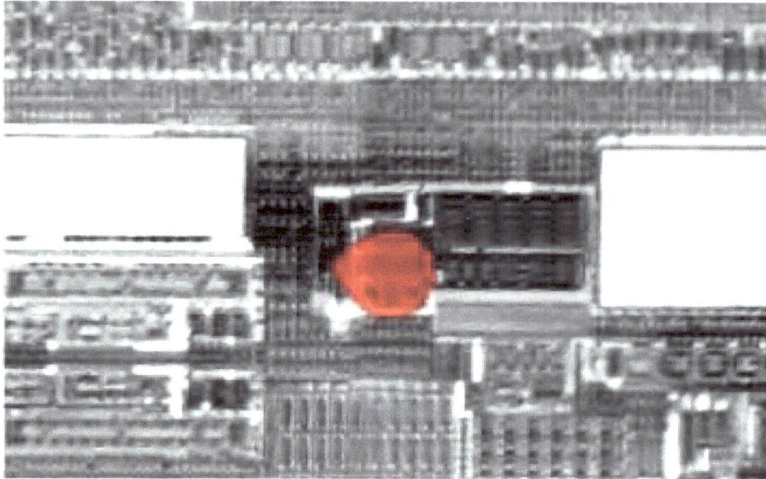

Fig. (3). Optical fault injection [21].

DEFENSIVE METHODOLOGIES

Hardware is an integral part of IoT and its environment. Preventing and protecting it is the foremost work that needs to be incorporated in this brewing technological era. When Industrial IoT adopts the IoT architecture, the physical layer is the first primary layer where both aspects, hardware and software, work hand in hand to create connectivity. Considering the hardware and the severe types of attacks, it is the chief component in the entire system that needs to be made secure from any type of physical attack. Defensive methodologies have been adopted in the domain of networks where data transmission takes place. The three major categories of attack, invasive, non-invasive, and semi-invasive, focus on breaching the hardware component of the IoT either on the host side or on the network side. Many algorithms have been generated to work in these aspects, but the most promising ones are the machine learning models.

Machine learning concepts incorporate learning techniques that make the machine or the system self-sustained enough to learn and predict the outcomes. There are three types of learning methodologies such as:

- Supervised Learning: This type of learning requires supervision. In other terms, if supervised learning is adopted, the model is trained with the labeled data. The efficiency of the model is checked with unlabelled data.
- Unsupervised learning: In this type of learning, the data on which the model is trained is unlabeled, and the computational complexity of the algorithm is high.
- Reinforcement Learning: In this learning methodology, the algorithm learns and corrects it according to the trial and error methods.

Using these learning techniques, Ml models are implemented to produce defensive methdoldogies [22]. There are many aspects upon which these defensive methodologies can be adopted, such as:

Authentication

In an IoT environment, many sensors exist within a network. According to the IoT network architecture, the IoT nodes lie in the physical layer. To protect IoT devices, authentication is a necessity. It distinguishes the source node from the rest of the network to protect the other devices from attacks such as Sybil attack [23].

In an IoT system, the most fundamental devices to work are sensor nodes, which communicate to other devices within a network in the physical layer, which is usually done with the radio channels and transmitters. To study the attacks that can happen, learning-inspired authentication methods are adopted to protect the nodes. The features involved in this learning are received signal strength, channel state information, values indicated by the received signal strength indicator, radio channels' impulse responses, and the MAC address of the node.

The machine-learning model with these features is trained on the radio signals received by the transmitter and tests the system under threshold conditions. To opt for an accurate threshold for authentication is difficult due to the radio environment. By applying reinforcement learning, the system can decide the threshold value for authentication [24].

Another reinforcement learning, Q learning, can be used to improve authentication accuracy. This learning is based on the RSSI value and helps the user to opt for an appropriate threshold for accuracy. Considering the location of an IoT device as one of the factors for physical attack, a learning technique such as IGMM can be applied, which works on the factor of proximity and hides the actual location of the IoT device.

To improve the authentication accuracy, a deep neural network [25] can be applied. A deep neural network identifies the channel state information of the network signals and senses a spoofing attack.

Access Control

In an IoT network, many different devices with different working platforms relate to each other. This makes it a heterogeneous environment where each device needs to be protected to stop any upcoming attack. IoT nodes contain sensors that are mostly deployed in an outdoor environment. Their computation is mostly restricted with limited resources, which makes it an arduous task to detect an occurring anomaly. In such a situation, a machine learning algorithm can be used to design an access control system for IoT devices, which would preserve energy and maintain the life of the IoT devices [26].

Many times, the received signal strength of Wi-Fi is susceptible to reflection, refraction, interference, and noise in the channel that can lead to abnormality in signal strengths. This abnormality obstructs the detection of any unidentified node within a network. To solve this issue [27, 28], an outliner detection technique is developed with the help of machine learning techniques such as I Forest, SVM, K-nearest neighbor, and random forest. By using these techniques, the outsider nodes are removed, which helps in increasing the localization of indoor nodes within a closed network of IoT devices.

Attackers can cause an attack on an entire IoT site by compromising one IoT node. In such an attack, the entire network is affected by one node when it is in its operational state, and the network works normally when the node is in sleeping mode. This conceals the attacker and does not come to notice. To protect the entire system from one default node [29], a detecting technology protects the industrial IoT networks from an on-and-off attack. To detect the anomaly caused by such an attack, the detecting mechanism uses a machine learning algorithm that calculates the trust of the neighboring nodes within a routing strategy.

Offloading

In an IoT network, after the data has been taken by the sensory node, it goes for offloading to the cloud. The data acquired is computationally analyzed, and the results are presented to the user. So, in this process of offloading, the IoT network faces problems related to the physical layer and the MAC layer, such as data traffic jamming, eaves dropping, DDOS, *etc*.

Malware attack: Some of these attacks can have the potential to harm the hardware as well.

To protect the system from such attacks, quality learning, which is reinforcement learning, can be implemented. It does not require a model but learns the upcoming actions by arbitrarily picking the stochastic transitions. Based on a study [30], the system can implement the offloading strategy on quality learning and protect the system from attacks.

Another methodology, deep quality learning [31], is used to implement CNN (Convolutional Neural Networks) to elect a radio frequency, reduce traffic jamming, and increase the signal-to-interference-plus-noise ratio of the signal that is received.

CRITICAL ANALYSIS AND SUGGESTIVE FRAMEWORK

Various machine learning methodologies adopted by the researchers are reviewed in their work. The scenario of the building's secure system is mostly based on the study of radio frequency, which is mostly based on the deep study of the physical layer inthe architecture. This study revolves around how the software part, including communication, electronic connection, and transmission fusion, can lead to hardware damage. The protection methodologies using machine learning against physical attacks of blowing out or tampering with the nodes within a network are still left out.

To counter the attack of tampering, a framework can be built using machine learning, which can be divided into the following modules:

- Topology design: Under this section of the module, the deployment of the sensor node should be done according to some topology whose design should be implemented using the machine learning approach. The route of the data packets within a network should be tracked. And if any node gets damaged, it should be excluded from the network.
- Image capture: Each sensor node needs to have a nano camera and a PIR sensor installed. As the camera is so small, it is not visible to the intruder. If anyone tries to damage the node, the sensor can raise an alarm, and the face of the intruder can be captured and stored in logs.
- Alarm notification: This module should send a notification to the network admin if anyone comes close to the node, and if, in some condition, the intruder succeeds in damaging the node, the notification should reach the administrator to rule out the defaulter node within a network.

Such a framework can work well where a lot of sensors need to be implemented in an IoT site.

CONCLUSION AND FUTURE WORK

So, as it is said, privacy is a myth; there is no such thing that does not have any vulnerability into it and cannot be breached. The vulnerability will be in the internal design of the other components of the device, and we must take care of all the parameters. We must examine hardware as the software components of the device to make it secure. And in the Internet of Things, embedded devices play the biggest role. In this case, these components pose the biggest threat to security. Also, in IoT, most of the hardware is deployed to the client, so it is quite easy to temper and manipulate the machine's functionalities. So, to protect the device from such kind of threat, secure hardware with secure software is most demanded in the current IoT environment.

REFERENCES

[1]   Gartner, "Analysts to Explore How IoT Will Accelerate Digital Transformation Initiatives" *Gartner IT Symposium/Xpo*, Barcelona, Spain, 3-7, 2019.

[2]   Gartner, "Analysts Explore the Future of Privacy", *Virtual Gartner Security & Risk Management Summit,* pp. 14-17, 2020.

[3]   G. Bakshi, "IoT Architecture Vulnerabilities and Security Measures", *Security Incidents & Response Against Cyber Attacks Springer, Cham,* pp. 199-215, 2021.

[4]   L. Liang, K. Zheng, Q. Sheng, and X. Huang, "A denial of service attack method for an iot system", *8th international conference on Information Technology in Medicine and Education (ITME),* pp. 360-364, 2016.
[http://dx.doi.org/10.1109/ITME.2016.0087]

[5]   K. Sonar, and H. Upadhyay, "A survey: DDOS attack on Internet of Things", *International Journal of Engineering Research and Development,* vol. 10, no. 11, pp. 58-63, 2014.

[6]   P. Kannadiga, and M. Zulkernine, "DIDMA: A distributed intrusion detection system using mobile agents", *Sixth International Conference on Software Engineering, Artificial Intelligence, Networking and Parallel/Distributed Computing and First ACIS International Workshop on Self-Assembling Wireless Network,* pp. 238-245, 2005.
[http://dx.doi.org/10.1109/SNPD-SAWN.2005.31]

[7]   L. Wallgren, S. Raza, and T. Voigt, "Routing attacks and countermeasures in the RPL-based internet of things", *Int. J. Distrib. Sens. Netw.,* vol. 9, no. 8, p. 794326, 2013.
[http://dx.doi.org/10.1155/2013/794326]

[8]   S. McNeil, "Solving today's design security concerns", *Xilinx white paper,* vol. 1, no. 2, p. 365, 2012.

[9]   R. Chaudhary, P. Singh, and A. Agarwal, "A security solution for the transmission of confidential data and efficient file authentication based on DES, AES, DSS and RSA", *Int. J. Innov. Technol. Explor. Eng.,* vol. 1, no. 3, pp. 5-11, 2012.

[10]   S. P. Skorobogatov, "Semi-invasive attacks-A new approach to hardware security analysis", *computer laboratory: Technical report.* University of Cambridge, 2005.

[11]   A. Ukil, "Embedded security for Internet of Things", *2nd National Conference on Emerging Trends and Applications in Computer Science,* pp. 1-6, 2011.

[12]   B.M.S. Bahar Talukder, F. Ferdaus, and M.T. Rahman, "Memory-Based PUFs are Vulnerable as Well: A Non-Invasive Attack Against SRAM PUFs", *IEEE Trans. Inf. Forensics Security,* vol. 16, pp. 4035-4049, 2021.
[http://dx.doi.org/10.1109/TIFS.2021.3101045]

[13]   S. Skorobogatov, "Physical attacks on tamper resistance: progress and lessons", *Proc. of 2nd ARO Special Workshop on Hardware Assurance.* Washington, DC., 2011.

[14]   Y. Kai, Z. Xuecheng, Y. Guoyi, and W. Weixu, "Security strategy of powered-off SRAM for resisting physical attack to data remanence", *J. Semicond.,* vol. 30, no. 9, p. 095010, 2009.
[http://dx.doi.org/10.1088/1674-4926/30/9/095010]

[15]   Singh, N., & Chhabra, G. "Cryptography and Steganography Techniques" In *Information Security and Optimization*, Chapman and Hall/CRC, pp. 79-91, 2020.
[http://dx.doi.org/10.1201/9781003045854-6]

[16]   O. Shwartz, Y. Mathov, M. Bohadana, Y. Elovici, and Y. Oren, "Reverse engineering iot devices: Effective techniques and methods", *IEEE Internet of Things Journal,* vol. 5, no. 6, p. 4965-4976, 2018.

[17]   Q. Shi, N. Asadizanjani, D. Forte, and M.M. Tehranipoor, "A layout-driven framework to assess vulnerability of ICs to microprobing attacks", *IEEE International Symposium on Hardware Oriented Security and Trust (HOST),* pp. 155-160, 2016.
[http://dx.doi.org/10.1109/HST.2016.7495575]

[18]   S. Skorobogatov, "How microprobing can attack encrypted memory", *Euromicro Conference on Digital System Design (DSD),* pp. 244-251, 2017.
[http://dx.doi.org/10.1109/DSD.2017.69]

[19]   S. Moein, and F. Gebali, "Quantifying overt hardware attacks: Using ART schema", In: *Computer Science and its Applications.* Springer: Berlin, Heidelberg, 2015, pp. 511-516.
[http://dx.doi.org/10.1007/978-3-662-45402-2_76]

[20]   S. Skorobogatov, "Flash memory 'bumping'attacks", In: *International Workshop on Cryptographic Hardware and Embedded Systems* Springer: Berlin, Heidelberg, 2010, pp. 158-172.

[21]   R.R. Singh, M. Thakral, S. Kaushik, A. Jain, and G. Chhabra, "A blockchain-based expectation solution for the internet of bogus media", In: *Intelligent Data Communication Technologies and Internet of Things.* Springer: Singapore, 2022, pp. 385-397.
[http://dx.doi.org/10.1007/978-981-16-7610-9_28]

[22]   L. Xiao, X. Wan, X. Lu, Y. Zhang, and D. Wu, "IoT security techniques based on machine learning: How do IoT devices use AI to enhance security?", *IEEE Signal Process. Mag.,* vol. 35, no. 5, pp. 41-49, 2018.
[http://dx.doi.org/10.1109/MSP.2018.2825478]

[23]   Chithaluru, P., Tanwar, R., & Kumar, S. "Cyber-Attacks and Their Impact on Real Life: What Are Real-Life Cyber-Attacks, How Do They Affect Real Life and What Should We Do About Them?". In *Information Security and Optimization*, Chapman and Hall/CRC. pp. 61-77, 2021.

[24]   L. Xiao, Y. Li, G. Han, G. Liu, and W. Zhuang, "PHY-layer spoofing detection with reinforcement learning in wireless networks", *IEEE Trans. Vehicular Technol.,* vol. 65, no. 12, pp. 10037-10047, 2016.
[http://dx.doi.org/10.1109/TVT.2016.2524258]

[25]   C. Shi, J. Liu, H. Liu, and Y. Chen, "Smart user authentication through actuation of daily activities leveraging WiFi-enabled IoT", *Proc. ACM Int Symposium on Mobile Ad Hoc Networking and Computing (MobiHoc),* pp. 1-10, 2017.
[http://dx.doi.org/10.1145/3084041.3084061]

[26]   J.W. Branch, C. Giannella, B. Szymanski, R. Wolff, and H. Kargupta, "In-network outlier detection in wireless sensor networks", *Knowl. Inf. Syst.,* vol. 34, no. 1, pp. 23-54, 2013.
[http://dx.doi.org/10.1007/s10115-011-0474-5]

[27]   M.A. Bhatti, R. Riaz, S.S. Rizvi, S. Shokat, F. Riaz, and S.J. Kwon, "Outlier detection in indoor localization and Internet of Things (IoT) using machine learning", *J. Commun. Netw. (Seoul),* vol. 22, no. 3, pp. 236-243, 2020.
[http://dx.doi.org/10.1109/JCN.2020.000018]

[28]   Ambika Agarwal, and Neha Bisht, *International Journal Of Science & Technoledge,* vol. 4, no. 1, pp. 132-136, 2016.

[29]   R. Sharma, P. Madan, S. Upadhyay, P. Singh, and G. Chhabra, "Track Your Parking Lot with the Help of Sensors," *International Journal of Innovative Technology and Exploring Engineering*, vol. 8, no. 11, pp. 4269–4274, Sep. 2019.

[http://dx.doi.org/10.35940/ijitee.K2467.0981119]

[30]   M. Hasan, A. Venkatanarayan, I. Mohan, N. Singh, and G. Chhabra, "Comparison of Various DoS Algorithm", *Int. J. Inf. Secur. Priv.,* vol. 14, no. 1, pp. 27-43, 2020.
       [http://dx.doi.org/10.4018/IJISP.2020010103]

[31]   G. Han, L. Xiao, and H.V. Poor, "Two-dimensional anti-jamming communication based on deep reinforcement learning", *IEEE Int'l Conf. Acoustics, Speech and Signal Processing,* pp. 2087-2091, 2017.
       [http://dx.doi.org/10.1109/ICASSP.2017.7952524]

Machine Learning and Collaborative Technologies

CHAPTER 5

Use of Artificial Neural Network in Segmenting Clinical Images

Amit Verma[1,*]

[1] *School of Computer Science, UPES, Dehradun, Uttarakhand, India*

Abstract: Inaccurate detection of tumors, fractures, and breast cancer in clinical images has become one of the major issues in the medical field. Variations or errors in medical reports caused by operators, machines, or the environment become a common cause of delay or incorrect diagnosis. Therefore, correct segmentation of areas of interest in clinical images like X-rays and MRIs is highly required. To solve this problem, many researchers have provided various state-of-the-art automatic or semi-automatic methods of segmentation. Artificial neural networks play a significant role in increasing the accuracy of clinical image segmentation. In this chapter, the workings of ANN and the difference between gradient and stochastic gradient descent are discussed. Also, the application of ANN in tumor, fracture, and breast cancer segmentation is discussed using authentic and publically available datasets. This chapter mentions the results and confusion matrix of some state-of-the-art methods. This chapter will help readers know about ANN, the use of gradient and stochastic gradient descent, the application of ANN in segmenting clinical images, and the confusion matrix.

Keywords: ANN, Clinical images, Deep learning, Segmentation, Tumor segmentation.

INTRODUCTION

In the past few decades, a lot of work has been done in various medical fields. Most of the work is related to increasing accuracy in predicting tumor size, cancerous tissues, and fractures. MRIs [1] and X-rays [2] play a pivotal role in predicting the affected area. The manual detection or segmentation of these clinical images is a lethargic and time-consuming process, majorly in the segmentation of tumor size and cancerous tissues. Manually segmenting the MR images depends on the experience of machine operators. Therefore, reports may vary depending on machine operator experience and other parameters as these reports are paramount for doctors to start the diagnosis of the patient. Therefore,

* **Corresponding author Amit Verma:** School of Computer Science, UPES, Dehradun, Uttarakhand, India;
E-mail: amit.verma@ddn.upes.ac.in

Sunil Kumar, Silky Goel, Gaytri Bakshi, Siddharth Gupta & Sayed M. El-kenawy (Eds.)

the uniformity and accuracy of these reports are essential. To overcome the mentioned problem, many researchers proposed various state-of-the-art methods of segmenting MR images with high accuracy. Most of the research in the area of medical imaging is shifting from machine learning to deep learning, majorly to artificial neural networks [3 - 6]. ANN [7 - 9] provides very high accuracy in segmenting the infected area in MR images and predicting the tissue class. In this chapter, we majorly discuss the segmentation of brain tumors, lung cancer, and breast cancer based on MR images.

Brain Tumor Segmentation

A tumor is an abnormal division of cells that grows in an uncontrolled way [10]. Based on the growth of the tumor, it can be distinguished as benign (noncancerous) and malignant (cancerous) [11]. During the segmentation of MRIs, only the malignant part is considered. Brain tumor segmentation is basically carried out for segmenting the core, enhancing, and completing the tumor [12]. Most of the researchers use a deep learning-based ANN approach to provide a fully automated method for brain tumor segmentation using a publically available BraTS dataset.

Lung Cancer Segmentation

Lung cancer is considered the second largest disease that causes maximum mortality [13, 14]. The disease spreads at a high rate, as observed by comparing year-on-year data [15]. Cancer tissue segmentation in the early stage is most important for better diagnosis of the patient. Accurate segmentation of cancer tissue helps doctors to provide better medication to the patient. However, the manual segmentation of medical images requires a lot of effort and time. Further, the accuracy of manually segmented images depends on the expertise and experience of the radiologist. This raises a great demand for some automated approaches to perform lung cancer segmentation with high accuracy. A neural network [16, 17, 18], which mimics the human brain, can be used for the classification of cancer tissues with high accuracy.

Many researchers proposed various methods for lung cancer segmentation using the ANN approach.

Breast Cancer Segmentation

According to the data provided by WHO, breast cancer is one of the most common causes of death in women [19, 20]. Timely and accurate detection of MCs (Micro calcifications) plays a vital role in the proper treatment of breast cancer [21]. However, due to the small and nonuniform shape of MCs, their detection is a challenging and time-consuming task. Due to these difficulties, manual detection of MCs can easily be prone to errors. Therefore, an accurate and automated approach for the detection and segmentation of breast cancer is very much required. Many researchers have given various state-of-the-art works for breast cancer detection [22, 23]. It has been found that the ANN approach provides significant accurate results in the classification of breast cancer tissues. ANN is a collection of artificial neurons connected with each other using synopsis, where information travels from the input layer to the output layer, with multiple hidden layers in between.

ARTIFICIAL NEURAL NETWORK (ANN)

It is a network of connected artificial neurons that mimic the human brain. ANN has one compulsory input and output layer with a variable number of hidden layers in between.

The Neuron

The concept of deep learning is to mimic the human brain [24]. Neurons are brain tissues that are connected in some structure to receive information from various sensors of the human body and to provide an output signal to perform various tasks. A structure with a single main neuron in terms of machine/deep learning is shown in Fig. (**1**), where some neurons in the input layers are connected with the main neuron in the center.

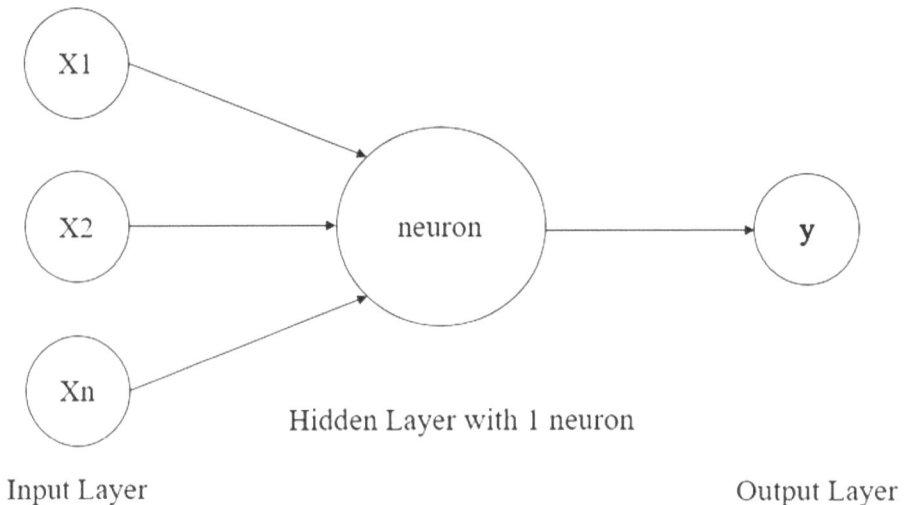

Fig. (1). Simple network with input/output layer and single neuron in the hidden layer.

The main neuron is further connected with the output layer, providing the output value. According to Fig. (**1**), the first layer is the input layer, having three neurons; each neuron provides information to the hidden layer. Each neuron in the input layer represents the independent variable in the dataset. Further, the input layer data is passed to the hidden layer. In the case of deep learning [25 - 27], it is required to standardize or normalize the input values. That is, all the input values should lie in a particular range. It makes the calculation fast and easy for neural networks. The hidden layer processes the input and provides the predicted value to the output layer. The output of the neural network can be a continuous value, binary output, or categorical output. In the case of continuous value or binary output (yes/no or 0/1), there will be a single output, as shown in Fig. (**1**). However, in the case of categorical output, there can be more than one output, as shown in Fig. (**2**).

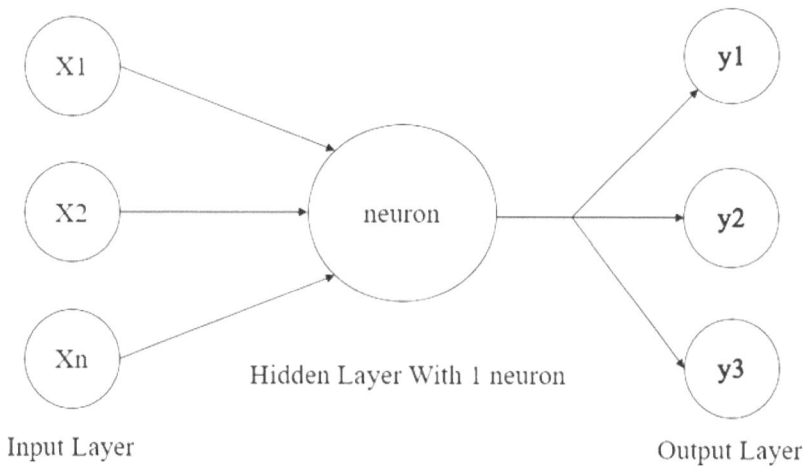

Fig. (2). Output layer for categorical output.

Categorical output means when there can be more than one output value. One point to remember is that as the input layer represents the single row in the table (or dataset), in the same way, output y also represents the corresponding truth value of that row (Fig. **1**).

Synopsis is the connecting line between the input layer and the hidden layer. Each synopsis is assigned weights, as shown in Fig. (**3**). These weights play a vital role in the learning process of neural networks. Weights are adjusted to improve accuracy, reduce errors in the neural network, and increase or decrease the impact of a particular input to train the network. Gradient descent and backpropagation process used for adjusting weights will be discussed in the upcoming topics in this chapter.

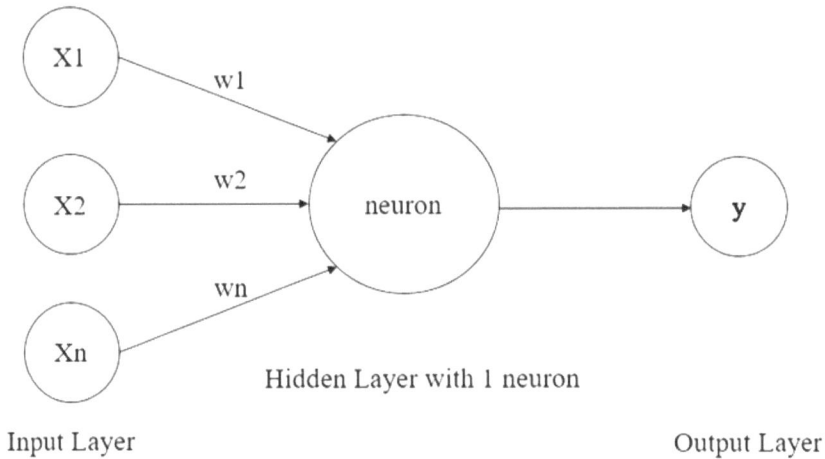

Fig. (3). Synopsis with weights in simple neural network.

Working of ANN

To understand the working of neural networks, we can consider a network with multiple neurons in the hidden layer, as shown in Fig. (**4**). However, a single hidden layer is considered to keep things simple and understandable. The actual network can have a lot more hidden layers. The input layer is fully connected with all the neurons in the hidden layer. According to the below figure, all neurons in the input layer (x1, x2, and x3) are connected to every neuron in the hidden layer. If we consider that equal weights are assigned to the entire synopsis, then it means that all the input neurons or values are equally important for all the neurons in the hidden layer to train the model. However, this will not be the correct way to train a machine. Weights are adjusted accordingly, and some weights remain very close to zero for hidden layer neurons. That means not all neurons in the input layer remain equally important for neurons in the hidden layer. Therefore, (Fig. **4**) is redrawn as (Fig. **5**), in which some of the synopsis was removed from the network.

Gradient and Stochastic Gradient Descent

In the case of any neural network, to increase the accuracy or to train the machine, it is very important to adjust the weights repeatedly. Backward propagation is used to adjust the weights assigned on synopsis. These propagations around the neural network are connected to reduce the difference between the predicted ($\hat{y}$) and the actual value (y). Difference or loss represented by a cost function C is shown in Eq. **1**.

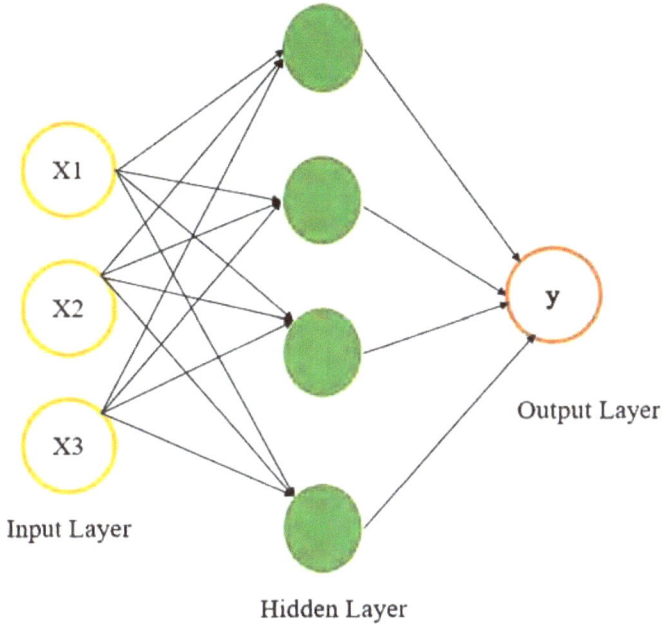

Fig. (4). Neural network with multiple neurons in the hidden layer.

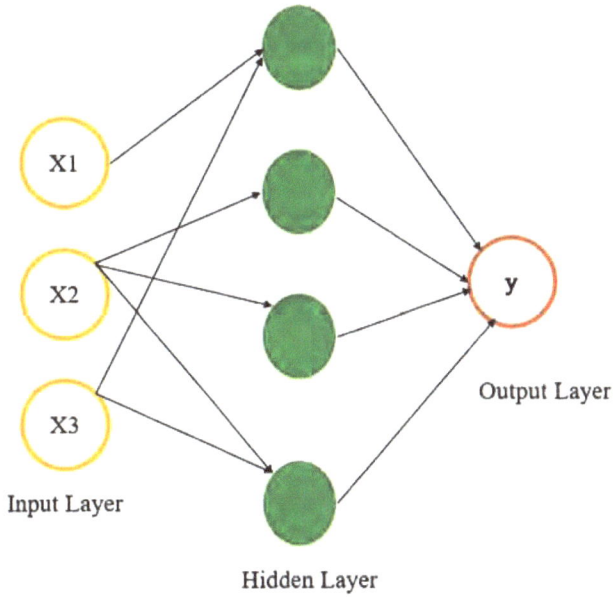

Fig. (5). Not all input layers neurons contribute equally to training the model.

$$C = \sum \tfrac{1}{2}(\hat{y} - y)^2 \tag{1}$$

To minimize this difference or cost function, one way is to take a large number of values to adjust the weights. Values can be considered in a range of very small to big values with very small differences. These steps were plotted on the graph, as shown in Fig. (**6**). In the figure below, we can see that after bypassing a certain point, the loss starts increasing, and that point is known as the point of convergence.

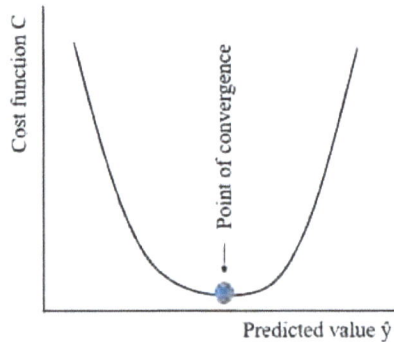

Fig. (6). Point of convergence.

Cost function C is minimum at the point of convergence. Therefore, the ultimate goal is to achieve the corresponding weights according to this point. However, it is not feasible to consider a large number of values to adjust the weights until convergence. Therefore, to solve this problem, the gradient descent method [28, 29] is used to achieve the point of convergence. In this method, instead of considering a very small difference between the weight values, relatively larger differences are considered to get the converging point early. Starting from a certain point, the slope is calculated to find the direction of movement. Negative and positive slopes are calculated according to the angle of inclination. If the angle of inclination is acute (less than 90 degrees), then the slope will be positive, and if the angle of inclination is obtuse (greater than 90 degrees), then the slope will be negative, as shown in Fig. (**7**).

If the slope is negative, we adjust the weights to move in the right direction, which is downwards, as shown in Fig. (**8**) below. At another point 2 in Fig. (**9**), the calculated slope is positive, so we move left, which is downwards.

With this continuous process, we reach the point of convergence where the cost function will be minimum. The movement of the point depends on the learning rate alpha. As shown Fig. (**10**), at point 6, we get the point of convergence. Now, considering a practical example, we will examine the working of gradient descent. Table **1** shows columns dictating the number of hours students study and the percentage of marks achieved. Here, the independent variable x is the number of hours, and the truth value y is the percentage of marks achieved. Now, all values of variable x are given as input to a network to predict the corresponding predicted values, that is ŷ (first epoch), as shown in Table **2**. Calculating ŷ for all rows in one go is known as 1 epoch.

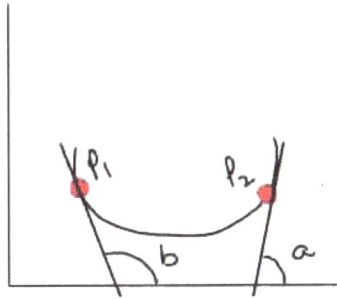

Fig. (7). b and a are the angles of inclination.

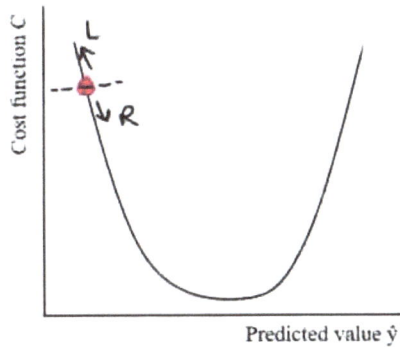

Fig. (8). Negative slope of the starting point, L & R showing left and right side.

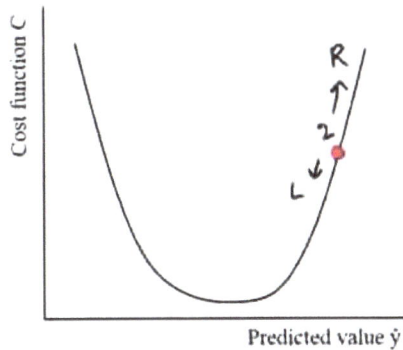

Fig. (9). Positive slope at point 2, so move downwards (left side).

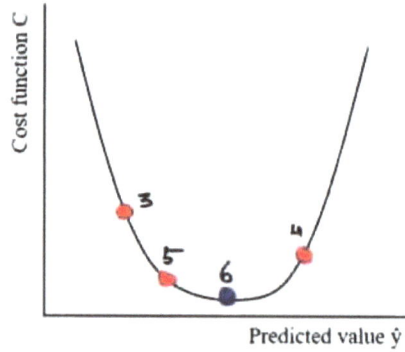

Fig. (10). Point of convergence at point 6.

Table 1. Provided dataset.

Number of Hours (x)	Percentage of Marks Achieved (y)
4	67
6	77
5	78
2	44
3	56
0	23

Table 2. Predicted values ŷ with the first epoch.

Number of Hours (x)	Percentage of Marks Achieved (y)	Predicted Value with First Epoch (ŷ)
4	67	55
6	77	65
5	78	70
2	44	55
3	56	50
0	23	34

Then, cost function C is calculated using equation 1, as shown in Figs. (**11** - **13**) [28, 29]. As the value of C is quite large, weights are adjusted accordingly, and another epoch is carried out. This process continues until the value of C gets minimized.

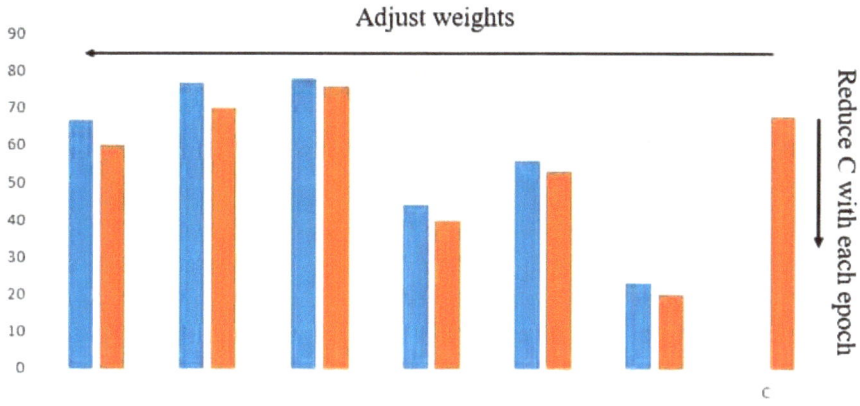

Fig. (11). Result of first epoch.

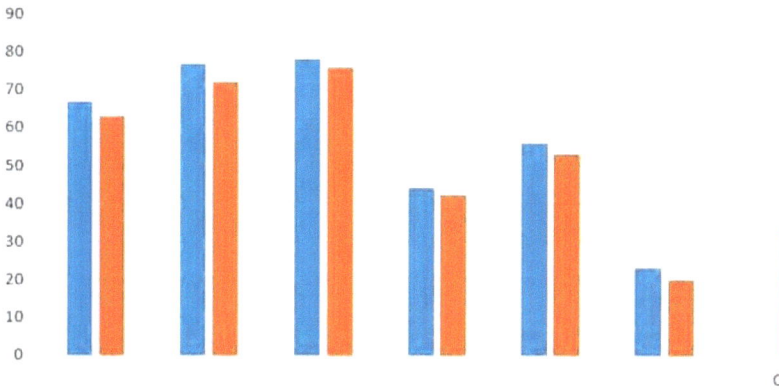

Fig. (12). Result of second epoch.

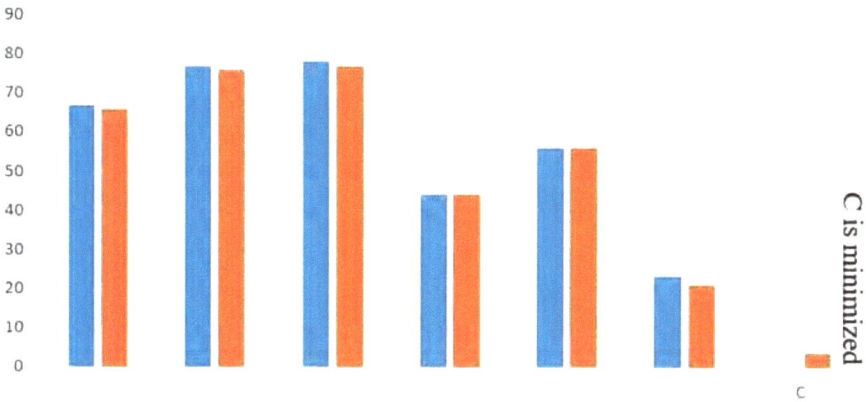

Fig. (13). Result after n^{th} epoch.

There is one major difference between the working of gradient and stochastic gradient descent. In the case of gradient descent, all rows of the dataset are given as input to the neural network at once, and the aggregate cost function (C) is calculated. After that, weights are adjusted to minimize the value of C. However, in the case of stochastic gradient descent [30, 31], one row of the dataset is given as input to the neural network, and C is calculated for the same. Then, the weights are adjusted to minimize C. Similarly, the same process is carried out for another row of the dataset. After completion of all the rows for the very first time, this one complete process is known as a single epoch in the case of stochastic gradient descent. The same process continuesuntil the value of C is minimized.

APPLICATION OF ANN

Artificial neural networks mimic the human brain. ANNs have a compulsory input layer having neurons equal to the total features (columns) in the dataset. Neurons in the output layer depend on the total classes in the dataset. The middle part of the ANN comprises variable number of hidden layers, which depends on the type of application. There are vast application areas of neural networks [32]; neural networks are applicable in almost every area. In this chapter, we have focused on the application of ANN in medical imaging and segmentation. Mainly, three areas of application are discussed in detail.

Brain Tumor Segmentation

Today, MRI can be considered one of the most important methods of capturing the internal structure of the human body. MRI plays a pivotal role in image acquisition of brain tumors. Based on the MRIs, various automated approaches are developed using machine and deep learning for accurate segmentation of tumor size and shape. However, the deep learning-based ANN approach proves to be one of the better ways to solve the problem with high accuracy. In a study [33], the author has given a method for automated segmentation of brain tumors using a fuzzy C-mean clustering approach. Gabor and ANN are used for feature extraction. The Gabor filter proposed by Dennis Gabor is a linear filter used for image texture analysis. The model is trained and tested using 60 MRIs and achieves an accuracy of 85%. Parra *et al.* [34] implemented ANN on a brain tumor dataset from McConnell Brain Imaging Center [35]. The proposed segmentation approach used MRIs with T1 and T2 modalities for the segmentation process. The application of ANN using MRIs gives much better accuracy in segmenting the tumor tissues as compared to phantom images. In another study [36], the author used ANN over an MRI dataset of brain tumors. Before creating the neural network, data is pre-processed by enhancing the MR images for better segmentation. Thereafter, features are extracted from the images.

Haralick's method [37] is used for the feature extraction process based on the grey level dependence matrix of images [38]. Experimental results of the proposed model show great accuracy of 99% and sensitivity of 97.9% in brain tumor segmentation. In a study [39], the author used 65 MR images of which 50 images were used for training the model and 15 images for testing. The grey level co-occurrence matrix (GLCM) and grey code run length matrix (GCRLM) were used for the feature extraction process [40 - 43]. These featured datasets were used to train the neural network model for brain tumor segmentation. Experimental results show an accuracy of 98%.

Lung Cancer Segmentation

With the invention of ANN by Geoffrey Hinton, researchers broadly accept the application of ANN in lung cancer segmentation as compared to the other machine learning approaches. With the high accuracy of ANN, multiple researchers have proposed various methods for cancer detection and segmentation. In another research study [44], the author used ANN for lung cancer segmentation. The detection of participating neurons and the number of layers in the hidden network of the ANN model are based on various experimental results. The author also stated the best suitable backpropagation training approach [45, 46] for the model. With the experimental results, it has been found that the model performance is much better than the various already existing methods. Nautiyal *et al.* [47] developed a method for early detection of lung cancer. The method is divided into two parts: firstly, pre-processing the data and secondly, designing a neural network for the classification model. In pre-processing, the author used a region growing method for segmenting the area of interest. Various features were extracted from the segmented area. Finally, featured data was used for training and testing the classification model. The ANN-based classification approach gives better results for lung cancer cell classification. In a study [48], the author has presented a method for the classification of lung cancer using CT images in Dicom format. Before training the model, a non-local mean filter [49, 50] is used to remove the Gaussian noise [51, 52] from the CT images, and the lung area is segmented with the threshold method [53]. Textural and structural features are extracted to build a featured dataset from the given CT images. After the pre-processing of the data, ANN, SVM, and k-NN [54 - 56] are used for training the classification model.

Breast Cancer Segmentation

For decades, breast cancer has been a common cancer disease in women. Early detection of breast cancer can be the most helpful step for doctors to provide a better diagnosis to the patient. The manual detection of breast cancer by radiologists using MR images or any other medical imaging technique is very tedious and time-consuming, and it also requires good knowledge and experience. Due to all these drawbacks, it is highly required to have an automated approach for the classification of breast cancer with higher accuracy. Many researchers have proposed various methods to automate the process of breast cancer detection. In another study [57], the author has proposed a method using ANN with a gradient descent backpropagation approach [58, 59] to train the model. The Wisconsin dataset is used to train the model and experiment. The achieved experimental results for the classification of breast cancer are very high (99.37%).

In another study [60], the author has shifted the focus from the accuracy of the model to correctness in decision-making. The decision-making power of the ANN model is unfolded in the presented method. The author has used both supervised and unsupervised learning methods with ANN to build a model with better decision-making. The main objective of the method is to minimize the misclassification cost. Saad *et al.* [61] proposed a method with two major parts. Firstly, the area of interest segmented from the mammogram, and secondly, the segmented area dataset used to train the model for breast cancer classification. Experimentally, it has been found that ANN has shown more accuracy but lacks sensitivity as compared to neural networks with Adaboost [62]. Overall accuracy and sensitivity shown are 98.68 and 80.15%, respectively. In a research work [63], to provide an efficient way for the detection of breast cancer, various image enhancement and breast segmentation techniques are explored. Bayesian neural network [64, 65] is used to train the model for classification of cancerous tissues in breast mammograms and ultrasound medical images.

CONCLUSION

Accurate and timely detection of cancerous tissues is the most important and challenging task for better diagnosis of the patient. Today also, the radiologist prepares the report of medical images like CT scans, mammograms, and MRIs manually. Therefore, chances of manual error or non-uniformity remain in the reports as per the experience and knowledge of the radiologist and other parameters. So, it is very much required to have a better-automated approach for accurate and uniform segmentation of cancerous tissues in various parts of the body. Considering the above problem, an artificial neural network is discussed in detail, which is nowadays used by many researchers for the classification of malignant tissues. Moreover, the applications of ANN are highlighted and discussed, mainly for the classification of brain tumors, lung cancer, and breast cancer segmentation. By reading the chapter, readers will get clear and complete knowledge about the training and working of ANN with its wide applicability.

REFERENCES

[1]   Westbrook, Catherine, and John Talbot. MRI in Practice. *John Wiley & Sons*, 2018.

[2]   Warren, Bertram Eugene. X-ray Diffraction. *Courier Corporation*, 1990.

[3]   Neeraj Sharma, and Lalit M. Aggarwal, "Automated medical image segmentation techniques", *Journal of medical physics/Association of Medical Physicists of India,* 2010.
[http://dx.doi.org/10.4103/0971-6203.58777]

[4]   G. Margi, and B. Talati, "Automated medical image segmentation using RBF ANN", *International Conference on Information, Communication, Instrumentation and Control,* 2017.
[http://dx.doi.org/10.1109/ICOMICON.2017.8279052]

[5]   Lay Khoon Lee, Siau Chuin Liew, and Weng Jie Thong, "A review of image segmentation methodologies in medical image", *Advanced computer and communication engineering technology,* pp. 1069-1080, 2015.
[http://dx.doi.org/10.1007/978-3-319-07674-4_99]

[6]   R. Merjulah, and J. Chandra, "Segmentation technique for medical image processing: A survey", *International Conference on Inventive Computing and Informatics,* 2017.
[http://dx.doi.org/10.1109/ICICI.2017.8365301]

[7]   S. Agatonovic-Kustrin, and R. Beresford, "Basic concepts of artificial neural network (ANN) modeling and its application in pharmaceutical research", *J. Pharm. Biomed. Anal.,* vol. 22, no. 5, pp. 717-727, 2000.
[http://dx.doi.org/10.1016/S0731-7085(99)00272-1] [PMID: 10815714]

[8]   J. Zupan, "Introduction to artificial neural network (ANN) methods: what they are and how to use them", *Acta Chim. Slov.,* vol. 41, pp. 327-327, 1994.

[9]   S.B. Maind, and P. Wankar, "Research paper on basic of artificial neural network", *Int. J. Recent Innov. Trends Comput. Commun.,* vol. 2, no. 1, pp. 96-100, 2014.

[10]   T.L. Whiteside, "The tumor microenvironment and its role in promoting tumor growth", *Oncogene,* vol. 27, no. 45, pp. 5904-5912, 2008.
[http://dx.doi.org/10.1038/onc.2008.271] [PMID: 18836471]

[11]   K. Hosseinzadeh, and S.D. Schwarz, "Endorectal diffusion□weighted imaging in prostate cancer to differentiate malignant and benign peripheral zone tissue", *J. Magn. Reson. Imaging,* vol. 20, no. 4, pp. 654-661, 2004.
[http://dx.doi.org/10.1002/jmri.20159] [PMID: 15390142]

[12]   S. Pereira, A. Pinto, V. Alves, and C.A. Silva, "Brain tumor segmentation using convolutional neural networks in MRI images", *IEEE Trans. Med. Imaging,* vol. 35, no. 5, pp. 1240-1251, 2016.
[http://dx.doi.org/10.1109/TMI.2016.2538465] [PMID: 26960222]

[13]   M.B. Schabath, and M.L. Cote, "Cancer progress and priorities: lung cancer", *Cancer Epidemiol. Biomarkers Prev.,* vol. 28, no. 10, pp. 1563-1579, 2019.
[http://dx.doi.org/10.1158/1055-9965.EPI-19-0221] [PMID: 31575553]

[14]   T. Vavalà, M. Rigney, M.L. Reale, S. Novello, and J.C. King, "An examination of two dichotomies: Women with lung cancer and living with lung cancer as a chronic disease", *Respirology,* vol. 25, no. S2, pp. 24-36, 2020.
[http://dx.doi.org/10.1111/resp.13965] [PMID: 33124087]

[15]　Manuela M. Bergmann, "Validity of self-reported cancers in a propsective cohort study in comparison with data from state cancer registries", *American journal of epidemiology,* vol. 147, no. 6, p. 556562, 1998.
[http://dx.doi.org/10.1093/oxfordjournals.aje.a009487]

[16]　S-C. Wang, "Artificial neural network", In: *Interdisciplinary computing in java programming.* Springer: Boston, MA, 2003, pp. 81-100.
[http://dx.doi.org/10.1007/978-1-4615-0377-4_5]

[17]　H. Abdi, "A neural network primer", *J. Biol. Syst.,* vol. 2, no. 3, pp. 247-281, 1994.
[http://dx.doi.org/10.1142/S0218339094000179]

[18]　Y.H. Hu, J-N. Hwang, Ed., *Handbook of neural network signal processing.,* 2002, pp. 2525-2526.

[19]　Ganesh N. Sharma, "Various types and management of breast cancer: an overview", *Journal of advanced pharmaceutical technology & research,* p. 109, 2010.
[http://dx.doi.org/10.4103/2231-4040.72251]

[20]　E.J. Watkins, "Overview of breast cancer", *JAAPA,* vol. 32, no. 10, pp. 13-17, 2019.
[http://dx.doi.org/10.1097/01.JAA.0000580524.95733.3d] [PMID: 31513033]

[21]　P. Cowin, T.M. Rowlands, and S.J. Hatsell, "Cadherins and catenins in breast cancer", *Curr. Opin. Cell Biol.,* vol. 17, no. 5, pp. 499-508, 2005.
[http://dx.doi.org/10.1016/j.ceb.2005.08.014] [PMID: 16107313]

[22]　Flavio S. Fogliatto, "Decision support for breast cancer detection: classification improvement through feature selection", *Cancer Control,* 2019.
[http://dx.doi.org/10.1177/1073274819876598]

[23]　M. Karabatak, "A new classifier for breast cancer detection based on Naïve Bayesian", *Measurement,* vol. 72, pp. 32-36, 2015.
[http://dx.doi.org/10.1016/j.measurement.2015.04.028]

[24]　M. Fullan, J. Quinn, and J. McEachen, "Deep learning", *Engage the World Change the World. London/Ontario: Corwin/Principals' Council,* 2018.

[25]　I. Goodfellow, Y. Bengio, and A. Courville, "Deep learning", *MIT press,* 2016.

[26]　D. Learning, "Deep learning", *High-Dimensional Fuzzy Clustering,* 2020.

[27]　Yan, Le Cun, B. Yoshua, and H. Geoffrey. "Deep learning." *Nature,* 2015: 436-444.

[28]　F. Guély, and P. Siarry, "Gradient descent method for optimizing various fuzzy rule bases", *Second IEEE International Conference on Fuzzy Systems,* IEEE, 1993.
[http://dx.doi.org/10.1109/FUZZY.1993.327570]

[29]　C. Samir, P-A. Absil, A. Srivastava, and E. Klassen, "A gradient-descent method for curve fitting on Riemannian manifolds", *Found. Comput. Math.,* vol. 12, no. 1, pp. 49-73, 2012.
[http://dx.doi.org/10.1007/s10208-011-9091-7]

[30]　L. Bottou, "Stochastic gradient descent tricks", In: *Neural networks: Tricks of the trade.* Springer: Berlin, Heidelberg, 2012, pp. 421-436.
[http://dx.doi.org/10.1007/978-3-642-35289-8_25]

[31]　N. Ketkar, "Stochastic gradient descent", In: *Deep learning with Python.* Apress: Berkeley, CA, 2017, pp. 113-132.
[http://dx.doi.org/10.1007/978-1-4842-2766-4_8]

[32]　O. Omidvar, J. Dayhoff, Ed., *Neural networks and pattern recognition.* Academic Press, 1998.

[33]　B. Amarapur, "An automated approach for brain tumor identification using ANN classifier", *International Conference on Current Trends in Computer, Electrical, Electronics and Communication,* 2017.

[34]   C.A. Parra, K. Iftekharuddin, and R. Kozma, "Automated brain data segmentation and pattern recognition using ANN", *The Proceedings of the Computational Intelligence, Robotics and Autonomous Systems (CIRAS),* 2003.

[35]   http://www.bic.mni.mcgill.ca/brainwebBrainWeb: Simulated Brain Database. McConnell Brain Imaging Centre. Montreal Neurological Institute, McGill University.

[36]   H.E.M. Abdalla, and M.Y. Esmail, "Brain tumor detection by using artificial neural network", *2018 International Conference on Computer, Control, Electrical, and Electronics Engineering,* 2018. [http://dx.doi.org/10.1109/ICCCEEE.2018.8515763]

[37]   A. Porebski, N. Vandenbroucke, and L. Macaire, "Haralick feature extraction from LBP images for color texture classification", *First Workshops on Image Processing Theory, Tools and Applications.,* 2008.

[38]   G. Sen, W. Liu, and H. Yan, "Counting people in crowd open scene based on grey level dependence matrix", *International Conference on Information and Automation,* 2000.

[39]   E. Abbadi, Nidahl K., and N.E. Kadhim., "Brain cancer classification based on features and artificial neural network", *Brain,* vol. 6, no. 1, pp. 123-134, 2017.

[40]   P. Mohanaiah, and P. Sathyanarayana, "Image texture feature extraction using GLCM approach", *International journal of scientific and research publications,* pp. 1-5, 2013.

[41]   N. Zulpe, and V. Pawar, "GLCM textural features for brain tumor classification", *International Journal of Computer Science Issues (IJCSI),* p. 354, 2012.

[42]   Tang, Xiaoou., "Texture information in run-length matrices", *IEEE Trans. Image Process.,* vol. 7, no. 11, pp. 1602-1609, 1998. [PMID: 18276225]

[43]   X. Sun, "Automatic diagnosis for prostate cancer using run-length matrix method", In: *Medical Imaging 2009: Computer-Aided Diagnosis.* vol. 7260. International Society for Optics and Photonics, 2009.

[44]   M.S. Sharif, M. Abbod, A. Amira, and H. Zaidi, "Artificial neural network-based system for PET volume segmentation", *Int. J. Biomed. Imaging,* vol. 2010, no. 1, p. 105610, 2010. [http://dx.doi.org/10.1155/2010/105610] [PMID: 20936152]

[45]   Hao Yu, and Bogdan M. Wilamowski, "Levenberg-marquardt training", *Industrial electronics handbook,* 2011. [http://dx.doi.org/10.1201/b10604-15]

[46]   A. Reynaldi, S. Lukas, and H. Margaretha, "Backpropagation and LevenbergMarquardt algorithm for training finite element neural network", *Sixth UKSim/AMSS European Symposium on Computer Modeling and Simulation,* 2012.

[47]   R. Nautiyal, P. Dahiya, and A. Dahiya, "Different approaches of ann for detection of cancer", *Int. J. Recent Technol. Eng,* vol. 7, no. 6c, pp. 88-93, 2019.

[48]   P. Naresh, and D.R. Shettar, "Early detection of lung cancer using neural network techniques", *Int Journal of Engineering,* vol. 4, pp. 78-83, 2014.

[49]   J. Yang, J. Fan, D. Ai, X. Wang, Y. Zheng, S. Tang, and Y. Wang, "Local statistics and non-local mean filter for speckle noise reduction in medical ultrasound image", *Neurocomputing,* vol. 195, pp. 88-95, 2016. [http://dx.doi.org/10.1016/j.neucom.2015.05.140]

[50]   A. Ben Said, R. Hadjidj, K. Eddine Melkemi, and S. Foufou, "Multispectral image denoising with optimized vector non-local mean filter", *Digit. Signal Process.,* vol. 58, pp. 115-126, 2016. [http://dx.doi.org/10.1016/j.dsp.2016.07.017]

[51]   P. Bergmans, "A simple converse for broadcast channels with additive white Gaussian noise

(Corresp.)", *IEEE Trans. Inf. Theory,* vol. 20, no. 2, pp. 279-280, 1974.
[http://dx.doi.org/10.1109/TIT.1974.1055184]

[52] P.M. Djuric, and M. Petar, "A model selection rule for sinusoids in white Gaussian noise", *IEEE Trans. Signal Process.,* vol. 44, no. 7, pp. 1744-1751, 1996.
[http://dx.doi.org/10.1109/78.510621]

[53] X. Xu, S. Xu, L. Jin, and E. Song, "Characteristic analysis of Otsu threshold and its applications", *Pattern Recognit. Lett.,* vol. 32, no. 7, pp. 956-961, 2011.
[http://dx.doi.org/10.1016/j.patrec.2011.01.021]

[54] V. Sapra, L. Sapra, J.K. Sandhu, and G. Chhabra, "Biomedical Diagnostics through Nanocomputing", In: *Nanotechnology.* Jenny Stanford Publishing, 2021, pp. 443-460.
[http://dx.doi.org/10.1201/9781003120261-13]

[55] William S. Noble, "What is a support vector machine?", *Nature biotechnology,* 2006.
[http://dx.doi.org/10.1038/nbt1206-1565]

[56] S. Singh, S.K. Jangir, M. Kumar, M. Verma, S. Kumar, T.S. Walia, and S.M.M. Kamal, "[Retracted] Feature Importance Score-Based Functional Link Artificial Neural Networks for Breast Cancer Classification", *BioMed Res. Int.,* vol. 2022, no. 1, p. 2696916, 2022.
[http://dx.doi.org/10.1155/2022/2696916] [PMID: 35411308]

[57] P. S, F. Al-Turjman, and T. Stephan, "An automated breast cancer diagnosis using feature selection and parameter optimization in ANN", *Comput. Electr. Eng.,* vol. 90, p. 106958, 2021.
[http://dx.doi.org/10.1016/j.compeleceng.2020.106958]

[58] V. Sapra, L. Sapra, Y. Bansal, G. Chhabra, and R. Tanwar, "Machine Learning Approach for Identifying Survival of Bone Marrow Transplant Patients", In: *Emerging Technologies for Computing, Communication and Smart Cities.* Springer: Singapore, 2022, pp. 31-40.
[http://dx.doi.org/10.1007/978-981-19-0284-0_3]

[59] S.K. Lenka, and A.G. Mohapatra, "Gradient descent with momentum based neural network pattern classification for the prediction of soil moisture content in precision agriculture", *IEEE International Symposium on Nanoelectronic and Information Systems,* 2015.
[http://dx.doi.org/10.1109/iNIS.2015.56]

[60] R. Jafari-Marandi, "An optimum ANN-based breast cancer diagnosis: Bridging gaps between ANN learning and decision-making goals", *Applied Soft Computing,* vol. 72, pp. 108-120, 2018.

[61] Saad, Ghada, Ahmad Khadour, and Qosai Kanafani, "ANN and Adaboost application for automatic detection of microcalcifications in breast cancer", *Egypt. J. Radiol. Nucl. Med.,* vol. 47, no. 4, pp. 1803-1814, 2016.

[62] M.M. Baig, M.M. Awais, and E.S.M. El-Alfy, "AdaBoost-based artificial neural network learning", *Neurocomputing,* vol. 248, pp. 120-126, 2017.
[http://dx.doi.org/10.1016/j.neucom.2017.02.077]

[63] M.H-M. Khan, "Automated breast cancer diagnosis using artificial neural network (ANN)", *Iranian Conference on Intelligent Systems and Signal Processing,* 2017.
[http://dx.doi.org/10.1109/ICSPIS.2017.8311589]

[64] P. Kumar, R. Chaudhary, A. Aggarwal, P. Singh, and R. Tomar, Improving Medical Image Segmentation Techniques Using Multiphase Level Set Approach *Via* Bias Correction., *Int. J. Eng. Adv. Technol.,* 2012. [IJEAT].

[65] P. Izmailov, "What are Bayesian neural network posteriors really like?", *International Conference on Machine Learning,* 2021.

CHAPTER 6

Role of Artificial Intelligence (AI) and Industrial IoT (IIoT) in Smart Healthcare

Hitesh Kumar Sharma[1,*]

[1] *Cybernetics Cluster, School of Computer Science and Engineering, University of Petroleum and Energy studies, Dehradun, India*

Abstract: Information technology has shown its presence in every sector that requires automation and intelligence. Traditional healthcare is a major sector in which lots of advancements are needed. AI and IIoT are two main IT-based advanced technologies that are required in many phases to convert traditional healthcare to smart healthcare. The two major requirements of a smart healthcare system are data collection and data analysis, and both of these requirements can be fulfilled by AI and IIoT technologies. IIoT can help collect healthcare data in an automated way using various sensors and other hardware devices. The use of AI-based algorithms and software to replicate human cognition in the analysis, display, and comprehension of complicated medical and healthcare data is referred to as artificial intelligence in healthcare. Artificial intelligence can be utilized to perform the same tasks in a more efficient and cost-effective manner. It is always preferable to prevent a disease than to cure it. Artificial intelligence-based apps can assist users in leading a healthy lifestyle and being proactive. When customers realize they have power over their own health, they are more motivated to live a healthy lifestyle. This chapter describes the role of artificial intelligence (AI) and the Industrial Internet of Things (IIoT) in smart healthcare and telemedicine.

Keywords: Artificial intelligence, E-hospital, Industrial IoT, Smart healthcare, Telemedicine.

INTRODUCTION OF INDUSTRIAL IOT (IIOT)

The Industrial Internet of Things is the extended version and evolution of the Internet of Things in industries. It lays a focused emphasis on big data, machine learning, and m2m (machine to machine) communication that, in turn, helps improve efficiency and reliability in the operations of industries and enterprises. The IIoT includes robotics, medical devices, software production processes, and

[*] **Corresponding author Hitesh Kumar Sharma:** Cybernetics Cluster, School of Computer Science and Engineering, University of Petroleum and Energy studies, Dehradun, India; E-mail: hksharma@ddn.upes.ac.in

industrial applications [1]. Industrial IoT (Industrial Internet of Things) is an extension of the Internet of Things that focuses on connecting devices to a network and then collecting and analyzing data. Industrial IoT is still in its infancy and has not yet reached its full potential [2]. However, it will continue to develop as more industries adopt it. It will enable many new business models, such as predictive maintenance, asset tracking, and automated control systems. Industrial IoT is a network of physical objects, sensors, and actuators that are linked to the internet and share data. Industrial IoT has been around for decades, but it was not until recently that it has become mainstream. It is now being used in manufacturing and production to reduce costs and increase productivity. Industrial IoT is the connection of physical objects to the internet. These physical objects can be anything from a car and a pacemaker to a coffee cup. The advantage of these devices is that they can connect and communicate with each other without human intervention. The future of Industrial IoT is in the convergence of AI and IoT. AI will be able to provide data-driven insights into how these devices interact with each other and their surroundings [3].

Some major applications of IIoT are given in the following points [4, 5].

1. It is used in the mining industry. With the help of IIoT, we can make such a device that can sense any type of harmful gases and can alert the authorities out there so that any harm can be avoided.

2. In mining, any small fire can trigger large damage to the mines and, in severe cases, can bring the whole mining cave down, so to avoid this, IIoT can play a major role.

3. Sensor's network comprises different gas sensors.

4. RFID tags of tracking miners.

5. It is also used in the healthcare industry. Traditionally, it is not possible for doctors to monitor patients continuously; the doctors need to visit the patient and then only he/she can monitor the health conditions of the individual.

6. But now, with the advent of IIoT, this process is made a lot easier with the use of sensors. Nowadays, doctors can monitor patients continuously, and alerts can be generated frequently to avoid any severe cases or the death of patients even after reaching them on time.

7. Connectivity of the healthcare devices to the internet helps in locating each device and also knowing the status of the connected devices.

INTRODUCTION OF ARTIFICIAL INTELLIGENCE (AI)

AI stands for artificial intelligence. Just as human intelligence is the intellectual capability of humans to learn, adapt, or understand situations in one's environment, artificial intelligence is the ability of machines, stimulated by human intelligence, to understand technology and programs according to the technical situations that can make any task faster and easier. AI or machine learning systems are fueled by such a vast amount of data that they can provide services to humans anytime and anywhere. From auto-correcting any word in one's mobile to helping any handicapped with his daily life, AI has acted as the most useful innovation for world change. Moreover, advanced AI is helping the world of scientists to explore more of the Universe through satellites surrounding outer space, which is eventually helping all of us to know about the happenings of past, present, and the near future [6, 7]. The evolution of artificial intelligence (AI) is likely to become more pandemic in various fields, for example, education, healthcare, fraudulent acts, *etc.*, to monitor and detect situations for actions. (Fig. **1**).

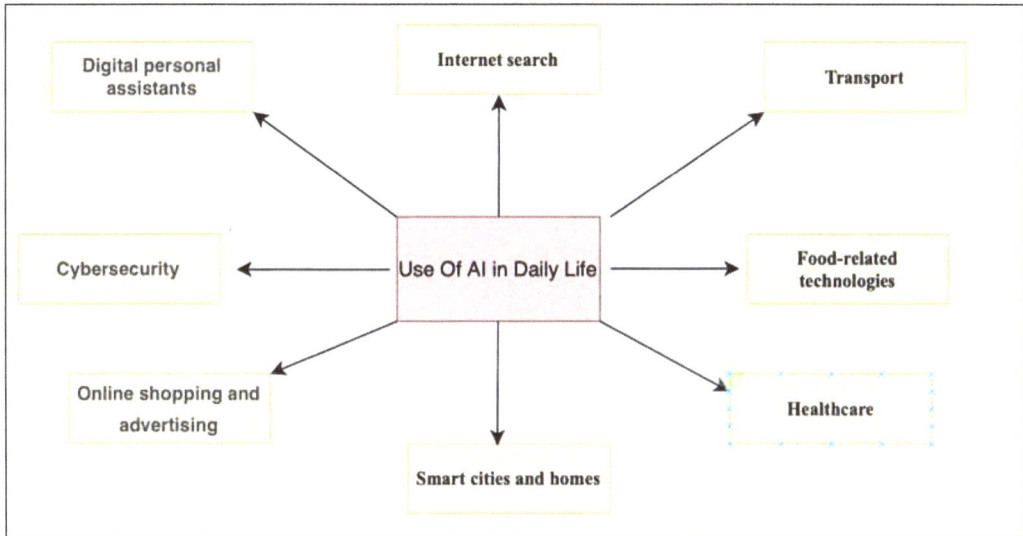

Fig. (1). Applications of AI.

ROLE OF AI IN INDUSTRIAL IOT (IIOT)

IIoT is a network of physical devices, vehicles, buildings, and other items that are connected to the internet. It is used to collect and analyze data from these devices. The use of AI in IIoT is expected to increase in the next few years [8 - 10].

The benefits of AI in IIoT are:

• Increased efficiency.
• Reduced human error.
• Improved accuracy.
• Reduced downtime.

The IIoT is all about the use of sensors and other technologies to automate physical processes. This automation has allowed for more efficiency in many industries. There are many ways that AI can be applied in the IIoT, such as predictive maintenance, real-time monitoring, and predictive analytics. Predictive maintenance is when a company uses AI to predict when a machine will break down based on its usage. This allows the company to schedule necessary repairs before they happen, which saves time and money.

Smarter Machines

Data analysis and processing can be easily dealt with AI; hence, the workload on humans is reduced, and the devices work on their own in an efficient and faster way. Real-time managing, monitoring, implementing, and decision-making become easier.

Maintenance

IIoT maintains and keeps track of the business's workings, and with the help of AI, we get precise and qualitative outcomes. AI helps to achieve better energy utilization, asset tracking, sustainable business, less human dependency, *etc.*

Automation

With the help of AI, many IIoT processes can be automated so that the system works on its own efficiently; otherwise, it would require highly skilled humans to perform the task.

Improved Customer Services

Customer satisfaction is the most important aim of a business, and with the help of AI and IIoT, customer demands can be accomplished much more easily. For example, AI can help translate languages while a customer is using a website that is in a different language than his native language.

Scalability and Analytics

AI and IoT can handle retail analytics and estimate the business's future. This will help in the financial growth of the business.

Self-driving Cars

Tesla's self-driving cars are the best examples of IoT and AI working together.

Retail Analytics

Retail analytics includes various informative elements, from cameras to sensors, to notice clients' development and to anticipate when they will arrive at the checkout line. Thereby, the framework can propose dynamic staffing levels to diminish the checkout time and expand the usefulness of the clerks.

Robots in Manufacturing

Manufacturing is one of the enterprises that generally accepts new innovations like IoT, artificial intelligence, facial recognition, profound learning, robots, and more.

Better Risks Management

Pairing AI with IoT helps organizations understand and predict a wide range of risks and automate for a prompt response, allowing them to better address financial loss, employee safety, and cyber threats.

Real-time monitoring is when companies use AI to keep track of their production lines in real time so that they can identify any problems or malfunctions before it becomes too difficult or expensive to fix them. Predictive analytics is when companies use data collected from their machines to predict how well they will run.

The applications of AI in IIoT can be seen in the following ways:

- Optimizing energy use by smart homes.
- Monitoring supply chains for inventory levels.
- Enhancing customer service by answering customers' questions.
- Data analytics: Analysis of data collected from connected devices.
- Predictive maintenance: Prediction and prevention of equipment failures.
- Process automation: Automation for repetitive tasks.

The implementation of artificial intelligence makes devices smart and intelligent on various levels. Some major levels are shown in Fig. (**2**).

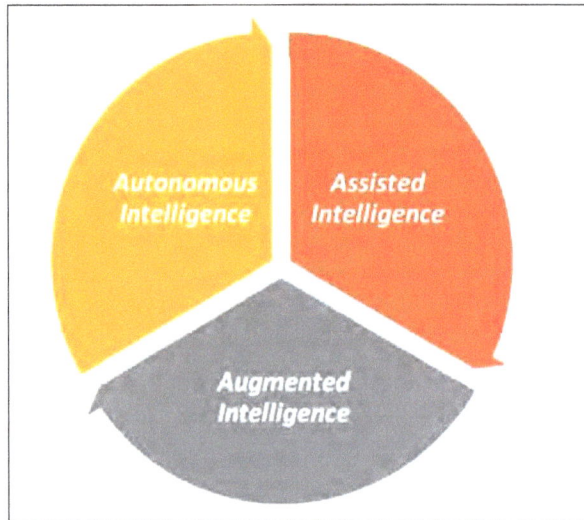

Fig. (2). AI in smart devices.

Assisted Intelligence

At this level, AI allows the identification of errors and gives companies the ability to predict breakdowns. They can monitor their machines in real-time, prevent downtime conditions, and thus increase overall efficiency.

Augmented Intelligence

At this level, AI offers machines the intelligence to make self-decisions and warn humans about the potential disadvantages.

Autonomous Intelligence

Machines gain the skills or expertise to identify errors and can hence take necessary actions at this level of intelligence. They learn new ways to do things and hence contribute an important role in maximizing the production rate of the company. Based on the level of intelligence they want to inculcate in their machines, industries can use AI to process the data transmitted from IoT devices.

CHALLENGES OF AI IN INDUSTRIAL IOT (IIOT)

The IIoT is a vast field, and it is difficult to predict the challenges that will arise because of AI. However, there are some common challenges faced by all companies that are adopting AI into their company. One of the most significant challenges is maintaining data quality. As more and more data gets collected, it becomes increasingly difficult for companies to keep track of what data they have already collected and what data they still need. This leads to wasted time spent on collecting the same information over and over again. Another challenge is how to make sure that AI will not be biased in its decision-making process due to its lack of experience or human input. One way companies can avoid this problem is by using human input as much as possible when training the AI system so that it can learn. The challenges of AI in IIoT are that there are many different types of sensors and data sources that generate huge amounts of data. The challenge is not only to collect this data but also to make sense of it all. The challenges of AI in IIoT are not limited to the lack of security, privacy, and data ownership. The biggest challenge is that the AI must be able to learn from its mistakes. The more it learns, the more it can improve. The IIoT is an industry that will be heavily impacted by AI. The industry has high standards for accuracy and consistency, which are difficult to achieve with humans alone. AI can help with these standards by analyzing data and providing insights without bias. The challenges of AI in IIoT are numerous. The most common challenge is the lack of public datasets for training the algorithms. Another issue is the lack of a good enough model to learn from and make decisions [4, 11, 12,].

The following are some of the challenges that companies will need to address. (Fig. **3**).

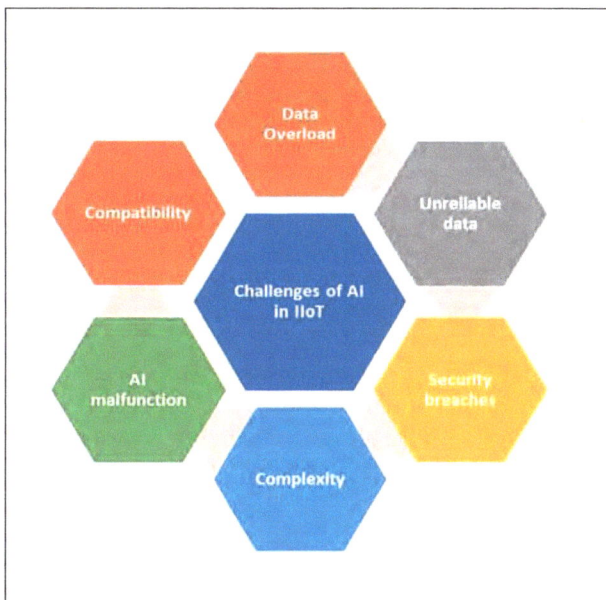

Fig. (3). Role of AI in IIoT.

Data Overload

IoT devices generate a lot more data than traditional systems, which makes it difficult to analyze the data in a timely manner.

Unreliable Data

Due to the presence of sensors in IoT, there is an increased risk of inaccurate or faulty data being generated by these devices. This can lead to incorrect decisions being made by the system and may even result in loss of life or property damage.

Security Breaches

With all this new IoT data being generated, there is also an increased risk that hackers will find their way into these systems.

Complexity

The complex algorithms and working of AI-based devices are difficult to understand. Technical expertise is required while dealing with such tools.

AI Malfunction

The AI may misunderstand the information, which can lead to problems in the further stages or processes. This may happen when the AI system is not smart enough to handle the situation or the issue occurred is out of its programmed range.

Compatibility

To make the AI and IIoT systems work efficiently, we need to manufacture or program the devices such that they can be connected to each other *via* a network system and the workflow can progress without any interruptions.

As a CTO who works with programming modelers and heads of specialty units supporting and orchestrating IoT game plans, it is conspicuous there is a capability between our vision of AI and what is genuinely occurring in the business at this moment. While there are enthralling appraisals and entrancing use cases - for instance, unscrupulously skillful plans - machines and robots are not meandering around us. AI can help update and maintain plant tasks, but before that, we need to address four specific challenges. The first challenge is connecting devices. Currently, many devices like lights and temperature sensors use Bluetooth or ZigBee, which are not compatible with the internet. More advanced equipment may use OPC or proprietary communication protocols, but they are still unable to connect to the internet due to their complexity. The second challenge is obtaining data. Although many devices are connected to the internet, some companies are not yet fully utilizing the data that these devices are generating. A machine perpetually streaming data about voltage, temperature, battery, and contact is not critical if the information is not visible (and to be seen, information should be composed so it very well may be set into an understood district model). Furthermore, the information is senseless without the capacity to perceive the result [13]. This proposes we need information on how machines genuinely bite the dust before we can set up for what's happening. Straightforwardly following connecting gadgets and sending data to an information lake, we truly need relief to see what occurs. Here, we can use trained professionals, as they may give us more data. For instance, a machine with a great deal of vibration will soon fizzle [14, 15]. Whenever we gather satisfactory information using AI, we enter a status stage. This is uncommon for each machine, tending to factors like the particular model, kinds of information, and potential results. With this data, we can then utilize a real system to track down associations among bits of reactions and results. No single model is unprecedented for all use cases; information researchers need to attempt different models and see what works.

CONCLUSION

Artificial intelligence is constantly changing and evolving, so it is hard to predict the future of AI development. Various apps have also been developed that can scan and read the text on its own, recognize the faces of individuals, and identify the products and denominations of currency notes. One thing we know for sure –is that AI will have an impact on our lives in every way possible. Artificial intelligence using IoT devices is available in the market for a variety of reasons. One of its applications is to track the login and log-out of individuals working in various companies by making use of physical features such as face identifiers, thumbprint scanners, *etc.* It enhances cybersecurity by preventing irregular activities and dirty practices.

In this chapter, we have discussed the importance of IIoT and the role of AI in making IIoT a more advanced and useful technology for sustainable development.

REFERENCES

[1]   A. Aggarwal, P. Dimri, and A. Agarwal, "Statistical Performance Evaluation of Various Metaheuristic Scheduling Techniques for Cloud Environment", *J. Comput. Theor. Nanosci.,* vol. 17, no. 9, pp. 4593-4597, 2020.
[http://dx.doi.org/10.1166/jctn.2020.9285]

[2]   A. Aggarwal, P. Dimri, and A. Agarwal, "Survey on scheduling algorithms for multiple workflows in cloud computing environment", *Int. J. Comput. Sci. Eng.,* vol. 7, no. 6, pp. 565-570, 2019.

[3]   A. Aggarwal, P. Dimri, A. Agarwal, M. Verma, H.A. Alhumyani, and M. Masud, "IFFO: An Improved Fruit Fly Optimization Algorithm for Multiple Workflow Scheduling Minimizing Cost and Makespan in Cloud Computing Environments", *Math. Probl. Eng.,* vol. 2021, pp. 1-9, 2021.
[http://dx.doi.org/10.1155/2021/5205530]

[4]   S. Singh, S.K. Jangir, M. Kumar, M. Verma, S. Kumar, T.S. Walia, and S.M.M. Kamal, "[Retracted] Feature Importance Score□Based Functional Link Artificial Neural Networks for Breast Cancer Classification", *BioMed Res. Int.,* vol. 2022, no. 1, p. 2696916, 2022.
[http://dx.doi.org/10.1155/2022/2696916] [PMID: 35411308]

[5]   A. Aggarwal, P. Dimri, A. Agarwal, and A. Bhatt, "Self adaptive fruit fly algorithm for multiple workflow scheduling in cloud computing environment", *Kybernetes,* 2020.

[6]   M. Arya, H.G. Sastry, A. Motwani, S. Kumar, and A. Zaguia, "A Novel Extra Tree Ensemble Optimized DL Framework (ETEODL) for Early Detection of Diabetes", *Frontiers in Public Health,* vol. Vol. 9, 2021.

[7]   G. Bathla, P. Singh, S. Kumar, M. Verma, D. Garg, and K. Kotecha, "Recop: Fine-grained Opinions and Collaborative Filtering based Recommender System for Industry 5.0", *Sot Computing,* 2021.

[8]   A. Bhatt, P. Dimri, and A. Aggarwal, "Self-adaptive brainstorming for jobshop scheduling in multicloud environment", *Softw. Pract. Exper.,* vol. 50, no. 8, pp. 1381-1398, 2020.
[http://dx.doi.org/10.1002/spe.2819]

[9]   S. Goel, S. Gupta, A. Panwar, S. Kumar, M. Verma, S. Bourouis, and M.A. Ullah, "Deep Learning Approach for Stages of Severity Classification in Diabetic Retinopathy Using Color Fundus Retinal Images", *Math. Probl. Eng.,* vol. 2021, pp. 1-8, 2021.
[http://dx.doi.org/10.1155/2021/7627566]

[10]   S. Kumar, G.H. Sastry, V. Marriboyina, H. Alshazly, S.A. Idris, M. Verma, and M. Kaur, "Semantic Information Extraction from Multi-Corpora Using Deep Learning", *Comput. Mater. Continua,* pp. 1-17, 2021.

[11]   S. Kumar, V. Marriboyina, and V. Marriboyina, "Information Extraction From the Agricultural and Weather Domains Using Deep Learning Approaches", *Int. J. Soft. Innov.,* vol. 10, no. 1, pp. 1-12, 2022. [IJSI].
[http://dx.doi.org/10.4018/IJSI.293266]

[12]   G.D. Singh, M. Prateek, S. Kumar, M. Verma, D. Singh, and H.N. Lee, "Hybrid genetic firefly algorithm-based routing protocol for VANETs", *IEEE Access,* vol. 10, pp. 9142-9151, 2022.
[http://dx.doi.org/10.1109/ACCESS.2022.3142811]

[13]   G.D. Singh, S. Kumar, H. Alshazly, S.A. Idris, M. Verma, and S.M. Mostafa, "A Novel Routing Protocol for Realistic Traffic Network Scenarios in VANET", *Wirel. Commun. Mob. Comput.,* vol. 2021, no. 1, p. 7817249, 2021.
[http://dx.doi.org/10.1155/2021/7817249]

[14]   H.K. Sharma, "E-COCOMO: the extended cost constructive model for cleanroom software engineering", *Database Systems Journal,* vol. 4, no. 4, pp. 3-11, 2013.

[15]   R. Tomar, H. Kumar, A. Dumka, and A. Anand, "Traffic management in MPLS network using GNS simulator using class for different services", *2nd International Conference on Computing for Sustainable Global Development (INDIACom),* 2015.

CHAPTER 7

Deep Learning and Machine Learning Algorithms in the Industrial IoT

Rahul Nijhawan[1], Neha Mendirtta[2], Arjav Jain[3], Arnav Kundalia[3] and Sunil Kumar[4]

[1] *Thapar University, Patiala, India*

[2] *Chandigarh University, Punjab, India*

[3] *University of Petroleum and Energy Studies, Dehradun, India*

[4] *Chitkara University Institute of Engineering and Technology, Chitkara University, Punjab, India*

Abstract: One of the latest industrial revolutions is deep transformation and human progress, which has led to the "Automation of Everything". The physical world, along with digital interfaces and data analysis, is connected *via* an interconnected network of computers. This change holds the key to unlocking trillions of opportunities in the coming ten years. Productivity has improved greatly in digital and physical industries, which leads to improved quality of life and sustainability. There are loads of challenges due to the massive amount of data being collected by sensors in the current world of IIoT. This chapter aims to review the various deep learning and machine learning technologies, algorithms, and their effect on IIoT. Several applications of machine learning in gaining useful insights from IoT data are also discussed in this chapter.

Keywords: Analytics, Deep learning, Industrial IOT, ML.

INTRODUCTION

Industries such as healthcare, transportation, manufacturing, and energy, which rely heavily on operational technology, are forced to change due to the Industry 4.0 revolution. Fog and edge computing technologies were previously needed [1] by IIoT for proper connectivity within Industry 4.0. However, there is one more interconnected element that is crucial for IIoT analytics.

---

* **Corresponding author Rahul Nijhawan:** Thapar University, Patiala, India;
E-mail: rahulnijhawan2010@gmail.com

Sunil Kumar, Silky Goel, Gaytri Bakshi, Siddharth Gupta & Sayed M. El-kenawy (Eds.)

Deep learning and machine learning not only add value but also improve the analytics of IoT platforms and big data. There are three types of data in Industrial IoT. 1) Raw data (data that is unstructured and unprocessed), 2) Metadata (data pertaining to data), and 3) Transformed data (data that is transformed). The algorithms listed below use each of the three types of data for identification, categorization, and decision making. When combined with big data analytics, deep neural networks can be used for drawing useful information for decision making. In the areas of real-time analytics and streaming data associated with edge computing networks, the use of artificial neural networks is essential for effective decision-making.

There are many applications of IIoT in healthcare, retail, automotive, and transport. Production, customer satisfaction, and reliability can be improved in many industries with the use of IIoT. The initial goal of IIoT was to improve current processes and augment the existing infrastructure, but later, completely new and improved services and products were created.

The impact of IoT is well-known in many industries. The Internet of Things (IoT) creates many opportunities for improved operations, new and improved services and products, and progressive business models. Deep learning and ML algorithms will have a great impact on the satisfaction, production, and reliability of customers that will depend on incorporating applications, devices, software, and key technologies. Anything that requires vigilant integration and orchestration needs a great deal of technology.

Equipment, machinery, intelligent devices, and automation embedded systems that perform simple as well as complex tasks without the help of humans are made smarter by the use of these technologies [2, 3]. It should also be noted that smartness in the enterprise should also include enhancements in areas such as cognitive automation, smart data discovery, the workplace, and many others.

A digital twin is a copy of any process or a physical thing like a wind turbine. It is often referred to as a product of IoT that has exponentially expanded these types of devices and also a similar amount of data that can be used to look up the design, efficiency, and a lot more factors. It is necessary for a digital twin to update continuously and "learn" about any changes. There have been a lot of changes in the industry marketplace due to IoT and its solutions.

This chapter compares a variety of ML and DL techniques and their applications in analytics solutions, which are being rapidly adopted in industrial and enterprise data applications. Assessment of various new business models and their solutions is also done, along with forecasting for revenue and unit growth for IIoT and analytics. This chapter particularly pivots on the challenges that come along with real-time performance, interoperability, security, and energy efficiency. An overview of potential research directions and other research efforts done to solve challenges associated with IIoT is also provided in this chapter.

IIOT ANALYTICS OVERVIEW

The Industrial Internet of Things is primarily divided into four components:

Things- The machines and systems that are used in numerous industries are constantly monitored and are used as a source of data.

Intelligent Edge Gateway- **The** edge gateway acts as the intermediate step between the industrial machinery and the IoT cloud platforms.

IoT Cloud- Data analytics, deep learning, ML algorithms, and various artificial intelligence techniques require extremely large amounts of data. The IoT cloud is the core Internet of Things platform. All the data that flows in an IoT device is handled by the cloud itself. Some of the important capabilities of the IoT cloud are event processing, big data processing stream analytics, and extremely powerful machine learning capabilities. Various services such as authentication, platform APIs, and various SDKs are also offered by the cloud.

Business Integration and Applications- These systems work on the backend and integrate several IT systems to make sure that the necessary data is received by the machines to complete all the processes. ERP, QMS, planning, and scheduling are some examples of such systems (Fig. **1**).

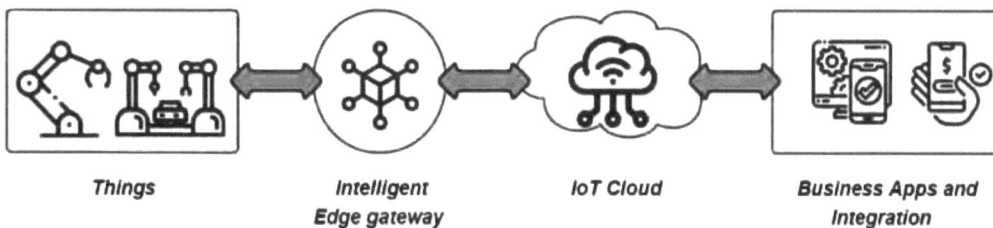

| Things | Intelligent Edge gateway | IoT Cloud | Business Apps and Integration |

Fig. (1). Industrial Internet of Things architecture.

Depending on the type of outcome and the end product generated, data analysis may be roughly classified into three categories: predictive analysis, descriptive analysis, and prescriptive analysis (Fig. **2**).

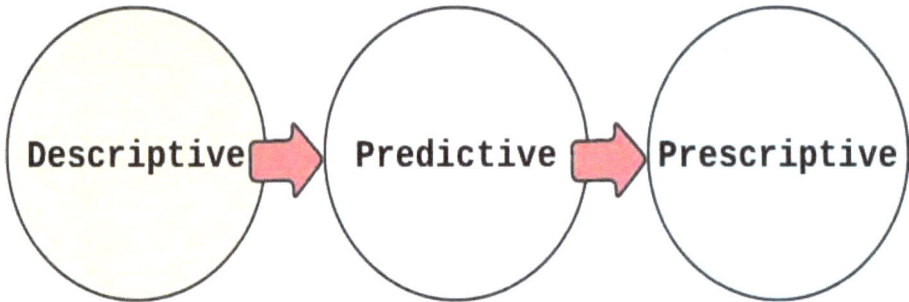

Fig. (2). Different types of analysis.

Descriptive data analysis is used when we have to gather insights into the current operating conditions. This analysis defines what is happening or has already happened. No inferences are drawn from the sample provided in descriptive analysis; we only summarize, organize, and describe the data.

The predictive analysis predicts the problems that could arise in the future. Predictive analysis is a type of progressive analytics method. It is also used to create useful predictions regarding unknown future occurrences. The predictions are carried out by analyzing the data using the available techniques from data mining and modeling, statistics, and ML.

A step above predictive analysis is prescriptive analysis. It suggests solutions for upcoming issues that might come up in the future. The prescriptive analysis provides decision options and showcases the implications of each of the decisions made while also mitigating a future risk at the same time. To improve the accuracy of its predictions, prescriptive analysis automatically analyzes fresh data.

TYPES OF DATA

Sometimes, we do not get any insightful information from the data. However, if we combine data from different places, we can create new and useful observations. There are three categories of data that can be used either directly or indirectly by IoT devices.

Structured Data

Structured data is defined by a schema or architecture, which determines how the data is handled in the form of a table. It is often seen in computer systems.

Data that is structured is usually stored in the form of a relational database, and the data is either provided by humans or generated by machines. The queries generated by us are used to obtain useful information from the data. Structured data is usually found in credit card numbers, stock information, and banking activities.

Unstructured Data

This type of data follows no specific logical schema that could distinctly recover useful data through traditional programming methodology. No known data models are capable of processing and are not able to fit unstructured data. It can be non-textual, such as images, videos, textual, like emails or messages, or even human-generated data.

Semi-Structured Data

Sometimes, data shares the properties of both structured data and unstructured data; this kind of data is typically known as semi-structured data. It often adheres to a specific format and consistency and is used to reduce the amount of space taken and increase data clarity. Examples of semi-structured data are XML documents. All semi-structured data is managed using the NoSQL database (Fig. **3**).

Fig. (3). Structured, unstructured, and semi-structured data.

All three types of data are generated by industrial IoT machines. Because structured data is already architectured in a self-defined framework, it is simple to maintain and handle. On the contrary, a few data analytics tools are required for the preprocessing and management of unstructured and semi-structured data. In IIoT, the perspective data analysis from the edge devices provides us with network data that is constantly in motion, such as file transfers and emails; this data can further be filtered and processed either in a data center or sometimes in the same network. A real-time data analysis software sends an appropriate response back to the IoT devices.

OBSTACLES IN IIOT

Security

IoT faces security obstacles because of two reasons. Firstly, the devices are constrained in IoT, and secondly, the scale. A constrained device is a device that has restricted CPU processing power, battery, memory, and bandwidth. Given the limited capabilities of these devices, they cannot protect themselves. The other constraint is the standard interfaces they use for management. These devices are easy targets for DDoS (Distributed denial-of-service) attacks and need support from external sources.

Interoperability

Due to the sheer number of devices used in IoT, every device must use the same type of encodings and protocols. The problems can also be solved by an IoT environment that is interoperable.

It is essentially a system with multiple layers and a stack of communication protocols amongst components. The usage of interoperability may potentially boost the economic value of IoT markets.

Interoperability is also required for purchasing IoT services and products.

Real-time Response

Real-time response is required for many applications, *e.g.*, controlling the temperature of a boiler. As the IoT infrastructure is still evolving, it further increases the difficulty for non-developed countries to be connected continuously to the cloud. IoT applications should be able to work even if there is no connection to the cloud.

Readiness for the Future

IoT is a volatile field that is continuously changing, and thus, the current systems should be able to work with future applications and different service providers. The potential of possible innovation on the pre-existing infrastructure is a big measure of success for IoT deployments. Context-awareness is the biggest element that needs to be implemented using ML to overcome the problems mentioned and to improve edge computing capabilities.

CONTEXTUAL ANALYSIS AND ITS NEED IN IIOT

According to authors [4 - 6], The combination of operational technology (OT) and traditional information and communication technologies has resulted in the creation of IIoT. There is a lack of understanding of the difference between conventional enterprise ICT systems and cyber-physical systems based on the traditional approach. On the other hand, some assessments [7] of the security problems faced by IoT devices figured out some constraints of the devices. It specified that current security mechanisms, based on "traditional public-key infrastructures, will almost certainly not scale to accommodate the IoT's amalgam of contexts and devices."

The author accounted for the limitations of IIoT devices, *e.g.*, RFID tags and sensors that are not able to use strong encryption because of processing power and economic restraints. Additionally, there is a disparity due to the shorter lifespan of some devices and the relatively long lifespan of other devices, which are often expected to have a lifespan much greater than their alternatives.

The focus of the previous section was the problems with IoT devices, such as replacing/recharging a drained battery or issues preventing proper communication. It is expected from an industrial device to have no issues during real-time responsive analysis, but there are certain caveats. For example, if we attach a tracking device to mobile agricultural equipment such as a tractor, the tracking device will most probably use GPS technology to get the location of the tractor. But a downside of GPS is that it does not work properly indoors. Now, if only the last known location is displayed in the UI, the GPS location will be wrong if the tractor is inside some building, and it will not indicate the reallocation of the tractor and will cause confusion.

In this situation, the device has no issues. Furthermore, the contextual state of the device is necessary for the functioning of the system. To classify the tractor into a state (here, "indoors"), we need contextual data. Contextual data provide useful information so that there is no confusion when the tracker is unable to track the position with great accuracy indoors. Every appliance is aware of the fact that the

GPS signal is weak and unreliable, and therefore, an accurate location cannot be achieved. This section inspects the various parts of the management of contextual devices using ML and IoT contextually for buying, building, or implementing big-scale solutions based on IoT.

MACHINE LEARNING FOR CONTEXTUAL ANALYSIS

ML is one of the most important components in contextual analysis in Industrial IoT. Over time, it may be valuable in making a system more resilient in assessing and identifying difficulties with IoT devices.

The following machine learning algorithms can be created:

- Models for prediction.
- Models for detection of anomalies.
- Models for recommendation.

RCA, also known as root cause analysis, is a process that intends to identify the fundamental cause of any issue extremely accurately by analyzing the logs and past events.

Finding the root cause of an IoT device is vital since no crucial system can be down for an extended period of time. Manually identifying the problem can take hours on end; however, using machine learning-based RCA takes only a few minutes or even seconds. The machine operates on not only dynamic data but data logs as well and improves with time as it recognizes patterns and sees the relationship between them and the root cause. This is a very effective strategy for improving the manageability and versatility of IoT distributions.

One of the very first steps of getting into the ML field is rule-based analysis. Creating a rules engine is one of the most important steps, which can be separated from the implementation at a deeper level. IoT system users can introduce new rules to enhance the system. This is possible because of decoupling.

Security models can be implemented based on the above concepts and can be used to find hidden and future threats in an IoT environment. The context feeds back to itself using past data and patterns, resulting in self-learning. To obtain more accurate predictions and suggestions, these systems must be trained for contextual analysis over a vast number of networks and deployment settings.

ROLE OF ANALYTICS IN IIOT

While working with big data, it is extremely important to have an analytics system to create useful reports and heat maps that can be used to make decisions. The high-level user-visible requirements in an analytics system are as follows:

1. Using data correlation to determine the actual outcome.

2. SCAP (Security Content Automation Protocol) or an NBI feed in JSON format for adopters can be used to consume the data, resulting in better adoption and reporting.

3. It should be capable of data segmentation, funnels, and filters so that the data can be sliced or diced if needed.

4. Data analytics for unstructured and structured data should be provided by the systems; this is extremely vital as information about security violations and threats can come in any form.

Furthermore, ML aids in the contextual analysis of the system, which, in turn, makes the system more secure.

Machine Learning Algorithms

Applying ML in IIoT can be extremely effective as it provides improved performance and reduces the time taken at a very low cost. Recently, we have all seen the advantages of ML techniques in our daily lives, from streaming services with recommended titles based on our previous watching patterns to predicted search results that appear on search engines. Machine learning algorithms are capable of handling vast and complicated amounts of data in order to deduce meaningful patterns or trends, such as data anomalies. When the threshold is reached, machines must evaluate information and make conclusions efficiently. The numerous machine learning algorithms listed in Table **1** provide us with better data analysis and predictions in IIoT systems.

K-nearest Neighbor Algorithm

KNN [8] is an algorithm that classifies an unseen data point by observing the K data points in the training data set that is closest to the feature space. We can find the K nearest neighbors of the new data point. This can be done by using the Euclidean distance or any other similar distance metric. X represents the new vector, $Nk(x)$ represents its K nearest neighbor, y represents the predicted labels, and the discrete random variable is denoted by t.

Table 1. Different algorithms of machine learning.

Algorithm	Type of Task
K-Nearest Neighbour	Classification
Naive Bayes	Classification
Support Vector Machine	Classification
Linear Regression	Classification / Regression
Random Forest	Classification / Regression
K-means	Clustering
Principal Component Analysis	Feature Extraction and Dimensionality Reduction
Canonical Correlation Analysis	Feature Extraction
Neural Networks	Classification / Regression

NAÏVE BAYES ALGORITHM

A naive Bayes classifier is a group of probabilistic classifiers that classify an input vector $z = (z_1, z_2, ..., z_m)$ based on Bayes' theorem along with the "naive" assumption that the features (attributes) in z are independent given a class variable t. It only requires a few data points to be trained, can work with data points having high dimensionality, and is fast and easily scalable [9]. These algorithms are most popularly used for filtering spam [10], categorization of text, and medical diagnosis [11].

SVM

Support vector machine is a technique based on the concept of probability that performs binary classification and finds a hyperplane that divides the classes in the data set (used in training) with the greatest difference possible. The label of an unknown data point can be estimated using ML algorithms for IoT use cases. SVM is used in applications like smart environment, traffic prediction, anomaly detection, smart traffic, and finding anomalies in power datasets [12 - 14].

REGRESSION

It is a simple technique for determining the value of a dependent variable Y based on multiple independent variables XP. Generally, there are p different predictors. The regression models then take the form:

$$y = \beta 0 + \beta 1\ x1 + \beta 2\ x2 + \varepsilon\ (1)$$

RANDOM FOREST

Random forest [15] is a classification algorithm that uses ensemble learning. A large number of decision trees are built during training, and the output is either a mode of class labels (classification) or an average of prediction (regression). It works efficiently on large datasets and can work with high-dimensional data.

K-MEANS CLUSTERING

The objective of this technique [16] is clustering or grouping the unlabeled dataset into K clusters, where each cluster must have similar data points. Classically, the distance between the points is the measure of similarity. Thus, in K-means clustering, we find a set of K cluster centers {s1, s2, …., sk}, such that there is a minimum distance between the points and the data points. The algorithm has limitations due to the fact that it uses Euclidean distance for measuring similarity. Also, the selection of types of data is limited. Furthermore, outliers can have a great effect on the cluster centers. K-means has been used [17] in event processing in real-time and clustering of sensor data for analysis.

PCA (PRINCIPAL COMPONENT ANALYSIS)

One of the most popular algorithms used for feature analysis is PCA (Principal Component Analysis). In health analytics, PCA is widely used for appropriate feature extraction. For example, if we are aware that some symptoms are particularly prevalent in predicting Type 1 diabetes patients, specialists must also know the specific features. PCA is used to decrease the number of features and the feature recommendation tractable [18]. PCA does not have any effect on the original features.

To generate an efficient data mining outcome, the data is sorted into various clusters; data that is widely away from each other in Euclidean distance is generally picked. The centroid is the center of the cluster. A data point is assigned to a cluster on the basis of how similar its features are to those of the centroid. To find the best solution for all data points, PCA reduces the distance between each of the data points and its corresponding centroid iteratively.

CCA (CANONICAL CORRELATION ANALYSIS)

Canonical correlation analysis is used to reduce the dimensionality of the model. It is analogous to principal component analysis; CCA takes two or more variables at a time, whereas principal component analysis only considers one variable. The basic goal is to locate a corresponding pair of strongly cross-correlated linear subspaces, where each component is correlated inside each subspace and also with one component from another subspace. Solving the generalized eigenvector problem will give the optimal solution [19]. Failures in indoor environments have been detected by authors [20, 21] by combining PCA with CCA.

NEURAL NETWORKS

A great amount of computational power is required for high-dimensional data, and there is great difficulty in selecting parameters to input data. Neural networks work by trying to copy the working of the human brain; for example, humans can detect certain objects or entities from a given scene. Quite a few types of neural networks exist, each with its own applications and use cases.

There are mainly three types of DNNs (Deep Neural networks):

1. Deep Belief Network.

2. Convolutional Neural Network.

3. Recurrent Neural Network.

DL is basically an extended approach to ML and shows its robustness when a model extracts the features on its own, for example, a specific color from a large data set made up of voices, images, *etc.* Generally, features are selected manually on the basis of trial and error and with the guidance of experts in machine learning. However, deep learning provides the provision of automatic feature extraction as well as classification and inference with high accuracy. The field of artificial intelligence has grown immensely due to machine learning.

This development of AI over the years has led to various industries applying artificial intelligence to IIoT use cases. For example, artificial intelligence models are being used in communication support systems where the needs of people are recognized through the use of images and voices. Deep learning has also been applied to Industrial IoT. The use of deep learning for IIoT has been expanded to increase the accuracy and speed in the analysis of data utilizing cumulative knowledge and experiences from various other industrial applications.

Apart from image and voice data, other types of data that are collected by various sensors installed in industrial products and equipment are also analyzed by ML and DL using learning, action, and inference. It improves the quality of service and products along with the business operations of the customers.

DL has also immensely contributed to the digital twin concept. For example, a drone-based system for inspection and monitoring of electricity and power infrastructure, made possible in collaboration with Toshiba and Alpine

Electronics, Inc., works on the basis of image detection. Deep learning is used for image recognition, and it finds any deterioration of the transmission lines. This system has led to the detection of damaged parts swiftly and accurately by using the images taken by the aerial drone.

Dynamic Rules Using ML and DL

The scenario set in the real world, which arises on the basis of the current environment, is called context. The rule is just a set of conditions for the context.

Based on the rules, suitable action is taken, given a context for the real-world scenario. The required decisions are made by the user depending on the rules, and the action is triggered in real time. However, the decision can be automatic as well. As soon as the model exists or is created after some time frame, and the context is compliant with it, it is quite simple to make a decision based on rules. Out of many ways, one way is to build a model over a period of time and then define a baseline. Then, every data point can be compared using the baseline. A few requirements related to machine learning for a system where they are very relevant are as follows:

1. Using multiple rules, correlation of data must be possible using the system.

2. Depending on the requirement, there should be a provision for working with multiple levels of analytics by the system.

3. The system should be able to detect anomalies, which is useful when a data point deviates from the model. In a traditional approach, such input is disregarded. A system based on ML, on the other hand, should at least try to figure out what is causing the abnormality. This can provide a wealth of information about the situation in which these skills can intervene.

4. Such a system should also be capable of performing predictions based on historical data. This feature will make the system capable of dealing with forthcoming scenarios, which can include a threat or a problem that demands immediate observation.

5. The trend must be visible over time in the system.

Domain intelligence using ML and DL

The working of deep and machine learning can be classified into two parts; the first is at the edge where data is both collected and processed locally or processed on a gateway. In the other type, a central processing unit like the cloud is used.

We can divide intelligence into four domains depending on where the data is processed.

MONITORING

Data on an Internet of Things device is analyzed based on conditions, which include environmental characteristics like temperature, humidity, or the presence of carbon dioxide; among others, ML algorithms are employed to monitor, allowing us to spot failures as soon as possible.

BEHAVIORAL CONTROL

Behavioral control works in conjunction with monitoring. Along with the supplied set of parameters, a threshold value is defined. Machines learn on the go and indicate when there are anomalies detected.

OPTIMIZATION

Along with the numerous above-mentioned systems, deep neural networks are employed to determine a chemical composition at a specific temperature. The main objective of this design is to maximize the outcome.

SELF HEALING

Closed-loop is one of the popular approaches in deep learning, especially in neural networks. The systems are termed self-healing when they can optimize operations and also evaluate and combine new parameters dynamically. These systems are also capable of executing further optimizations.

CONCLUSION

With the emergence of the IIoT, data is increasing fast, and in order to obtain further data, technological improvements are necessary. These improvements help us to clean the information and retrieve critical data and values contained within it. Data can be extracted in huge chunks while also detecting patterns and certain trends within it. The cleaned data can also be used to predict future outcomes using ML algorithms. IIoT decision-making would provide a larger benefit in terms of properly controlling and managing their assets. The machine learning algorithms help us in preventing the assets from malfunctioning while at the same time anticipating demand. This helps in enhancing the overall performance of the firm. Bringing in all the given features, as well as more on digital twins, might provide major benefits.

REFERENCES

[1]   M. Aazam, and E-N. Huh, "Fog computing micro datacenter based dynamic resource estimation and pricing model for IoT", *29th International Conference on Advanced Information Networking and Applications,* pp. 687-694, 2015.
[http://dx.doi.org/10.1109/AINA.2015.254]

[2]   L. Atzori, A. Iera, and G. Morabito, "The internet of things: a survey", *Comput. Netw.,* vol. 54, no. 15, pp. 2787-2805, 2010.
[http://dx.doi.org/10.1016/j.comnet.2010.05.010]

[3]   C. Cecchini, M. Jimenez, S. Mosser, and M. Riveill, "Architecture to support the collection of big data in the internet of things", *World Congress on Services,* pp. 442-449, 2014.

[4]   K. Steenstrup, "Predicts 2017: IT and OT Convergence Will Create New Challenges and Opportunities", *Gartner,* 2016.

[5]   C. Hertzog, "Smart Grid Trends to Watch: ICT Innovations and New Entrants", *OECD Publishing,* 2012.

[6]   N. Shah, "IT and OT Convergence—The Inevitable Evolution of Industry", *IoT for All,* 2017.

[7]   R. Roman, P. Najera, and J. Lopez, "Securing the internet of things", *Computer,* vol. 44, no. 9, pp. 51-58, 2011.
[http://dx.doi.org/10.1109/MC.2011.291]

[8]   T. Cover, and P. Hart, "Nearest neighbor pattern classification", *IEEE Trans. Inf. Theory,* vol. 13, no. 1, pp. 21-27, 1967.
[http://dx.doi.org/10.1109/TIT.1967.1053964]

[9]   A. McCallum, and K. Nigam, "A comparison of event models for naive Bayes text classification", *AAAI-98 Workshop on Learning for Text Categorization,* vol. 752, pp. 41-48, 1998.

[10]   V. Metsis, I. Androutsopoulos, and G. Paliouras, "Spam Filtering with Naive Bayes which Naive Bayes?", *CEAS,* pp. 27-28, 2006.

[11]   G.I. Webb, J.R. Boughton, and Z. Wang, "Not so naive Bayes: aggregating one dependence estimators", *Mach. Learn.,* vol. 58, no. 1, pp. 5-24, 2005.
[http://dx.doi.org/10.1007/s10994-005-4258-6]

[12]   P. Chugh, and G. Chhabra, "Application of Machine Learning in Agricultural Automation", *Biotica Research Today,* vol. 2, no. 7, pp. 538-540, 2020.

[13]   M. Shukla, Y. Kosta, and P. Chauhan, "Analysis and evaluation of outlier detection algorithms in data streams", *International Conference on Computer, Communication and Control (IC4),* pp. 1-8, 2015.
[http://dx.doi.org/10.1109/IC4.2015.7375696]

[14]   S.K. Ramakuri, P. Chithaluru, and S. Kumar, "Eyeblink robot control using brain-computer interface for healthcare applications", *International Journal of Mobile Devices, Wearable Technology, and Flexible Electronics,* vol. 10, no. 2, pp. 38-50, 2019. [IJMDWTFE].
[http://dx.doi.org/10.4018/IJMDWTFE.2019070103]

[15]   P. Kumar, R. Chaudhary, A. Aggarwal, P. Singh, and R. Tomar, Improving Medical Image Segmentation Techniques Using Multiphase Level Set Approach *Via* Bias Correction.,

[16]   S. Singh, S.K. Jangir, M. Kumar, M. Verma, S. Kumar, T.S. Walia, and S.M.M. Kamal, "[Retracted] Feature Importance Score-Based Functional Link Artificial Neural Networks for Breast Cancer Classification", *BioMed Res. Int.,* vol. 2022, no. 1, p. 2696916, 2022.
[http://dx.doi.org/10.1155/2022/2696916] [PMID: 35411308]

[17]   H. Home, D. Le Phuoc, and M. Serrano, "Real-time analysis of sensor data for the inter-net of things by means of clustering and event processing", *International Conference on Communications (ICC),* pp. 685-691, 2015.

[18]   A. Naik, HTTPS:// sites.google.com/site/dataclusteringalgorithms/k-means-clustering-algorithm

[19]   G. Chhabra, A. Prasad, and V. Marriboyina, "Future trends of artificial intelligence in human biofield", *Int. J. Innov. Technol. Explor. Eng.,* vol. 8, no. 10, pp. 3809-3814, 2019.
[http://dx.doi.org/10.35940/ijitee.J9987.0881019]

[20]   Ambika Agarwal, and Neha Bisht, *International Journal Of Science & Technoledge,* vol. 4, no. 1, pp. 132-136, 2016.

[21]   D.N. Monekosso, and P. Remagnino, "Data reconciliation in a smart home sensor network", *Expert Syst. Appl.,* vol. 40, no. 8, pp. 3248-3255, 2013.
[http://dx.doi.org/10.1016/j.eswa.2012.12.037]

Designing and Testing the System in IIoT: Case Study

CHAPTER 8

Adoption of IoT in Healthcare During Covid-19

Silky Goel[1,*] and **Snigdha Markanday**[1]

[1] *School of Computer Science, University of Petroleum and Energy Studies, Dehradun, India*

Abstract: COVID-19 has shattered existence and implemented a change in the strategies, priorities, and activities of people, organizations, and governments. These progressions are the momentum for the advancement of technology. In this chapter, the discussion is about the pandemic's effect on the reception of the Internet of Things (IoT) in different areas, specifically healthcare, smart cities, smart buildings, smart homes, transportation, and industrial IoT. Industrial IoT (IIoT) healthcare has essentially decreased the expenses for monitoring and safeguarding individuals at home by helping to improve human healthcare quality. Despite its significant convenience and advantages, it faces challenges related to security and protection from the perspective of bilateral fine-grained access control as well as the genuineness and tamper resistance of shared health information.

Keywords: COVID-19, Healthcare, Internet of things, Industrial internet of things, Smart healthcare devices.

INTRODUCTION

IoT assists in supplying physical items with Internet access and data transmission and reception capabilities. The IoT concept has evolved into and through a variety of technologies, including embedded systems, AI, machine learning, and sensors. It relates to the idea that hospitals would get smarter over time, with various fixed or wireless Internet devices. When the information is being gathered by smart devices, the necessary task can be completed. Smart cities, cars, gadgets, theatre sets, residences, and related healthcare are all receiving IoT applications. The use of IoT in the healthcare industry depends on a variety of medical devices, sensors, artificial intelligence (AI), imaging, and diagnostic tools. These devices can be improved based on their quality and productivity both in established businesses and in emerging ones.

The Internet of Things (IoT) enables the movement of information over or across the Internet by connecting all computational, mechanical, and digital systems

* **Corresponding author Silky Goel:** School of Computer Science, University of Petroleum and Energy Studies, Dehradun, India; E-mail: silkygoel90@gmail.com

without the need for human involvement. This technology is seeing a boom in terms of surveillance during the COVID-19 pandemic medical services. Currently, a lot of people pass away because of inaccurate health information. This technology uses sensors to quickly warn users of any health-related issues in real time. All COVID-19 patient-related data is stored on the cloud. This technology records a person's actions and issues warnings about various health issues.

There is a basic requirement for the necessary tools to ensure a successful operation in the medical industry. IoT has a high capacity for performing effective activities and analyzing recovery from surgery. During the COVID-19 pandemic, the IoT improved patient care. With the Internet of Things, continuous monitoring efficiently prevents numerous diabetic complications, cardiovascular breakdown, pulse, and other fatalities. To seamlessly transfer the anticipated health data to the doctor, smart medical equipment is connected *via* a smartphone. These devices also collect information on oxygen levels, blood pressure, weight, and the quantity or amount of sugar, among other things.

Body temperature, heart rate, and saturation levels are the main parameters that are watched at the hospital to ensure that patients recover quickly. The use of IoT applications for monitoring various parameters enables the technology to be used for the COVID-19 patient's quick recovery. It is also helpful for the hospital to observe patients who are placed under observation. The IoT device transmits the health parameters it collects to the cloud, where any specialist can access them to review the patient's medical history. IoT provides emergency services in addition to monitoring health parameters. These services include dispatching an ambulance from the closest clinic to the patient, tracking the location (GPS) of the patient by the hospital, and establishing communication between the patient and the doctor. Different biosensors are attached to various boards, including Node MCU, Android, and Raspberry Pi, to check this parameter. Similarly, we can activate a warning system for the patient to remind him to keep an eye on health indicators that will be transmitted to the clinical administrators and the local health station. The BH1790GLC optical sensor monitor, pulse rate sensor, BM-CS5R heart rate monitor, and wearable heart monitoring inductive sensor from ROHM are used to detect the pulse in IoT-based system applications [1]. The IoT-based medical services application uses the LM 35, MAX30205, GTPCO-033, NTC indoor regulators, and RTD sensors, among other IoT-checked metrics, to measure body temperature [2]. An Internet of Things (IoT) application was developed to collect data on healthcare that uses the ontology method. In order to treat the patient in a remote location, doctors will put together the ontology. All the doctors in need of a quick solution found this method to be simple. This data may be stored on the cloud for additional examinations by doctors. With the help of the Internet of

Things, we can provide emergency services like ambulances, blood, and specialists who are available to come to work. The use of IoT is significant in this pandemic. The Internet of Things (IoT) is a developing technology that assists in the discovery of new drugs and clinical treatments. IoT builds networks of devices like sensors and boards that enable the management of medical services [2]. The data that is uploaded to the cloud is protected. As it gathers the patient's data and information without human interaction, the accuracy rises. When deciding a patient's treatment in an emergency, this knowledge is useful.

The Internet of Things, in other words, is the arrangement of interconnected devices and processes that accept all network components, including hardware, software, and network connectivity (IoT). IoT is more than just a concept; it underpins a fundamentally good architectural framework that, at long last, makes integration and effective information flow between the person in need and the service providers possible. The ineffective reachability to the patients is currently the second-biggest obstacle after the invention of a vaccine, and it is the root of a considerable portion of the problems. The IoT concept makes patients more accessible, which makes it easier to give them serious consideration in the hope that they can beat this sickness. In light of the current pandemic situation, where the number of infected individuals is increasing daily worldwide, it is crucial to make use of the appropriate and coordinated services offered by the Internet of Things system. Additionally, where the Internet of Healthcare Things (IoHT) or Internet of Medical Things (IoMT) are linked to the current issues, IoT has been employed proactively to satisfy needs in a number of domains. Updated and improved data on settled cases can be found by upholding the

IoHT/IoMT rules. The Internet of Things (IoT) offers several benefits during the COVID-19 pandemic. It helps ensure that individuals who have come into contact with the virus are promptly placed in quarantine. It is seclusion that is beneficial for a foundation for observation. The web-based network allows for efficient monitoring of all high-risk patients. Biometric readings, including heartbeat, blood pressure, and glucose levels, are taken using this technique. The clinical staff's productivity has increased as their duties have grown, thanks to the successful implementation of this innovation. The comparison may be more useful and less expensive now that COVID-19 is widespread. Processes related to IoT for COVID-19 are creative, novel ways to combat the COVID-19 pandemic and solve significant problems in a lockdown situation. Continuous information and other crucial patient data can be collected with the help of this innovation. IoT is used in COVID-19's initial steps to gather health data from various organs of the afflicted patient and deal with using the virtual administration framework for all the information. This invention aids in information control and completes the report cycle. Concerns about the overall influence of IoT on COVID-19 settings, including contact tracking, group recognizable proof, and consistency of isolation, have been raised [3].

The COVID-19 pandemic-recommended IoT method will make it possible to monitor patients effectively in this way. By encouraging an informed group about a related network, the group's identity can be substantially established. It is also possible to develop a specific mobile application to help the less fortunate. The regulators, such as experts, doctors, and guardians, should be promptly informed of the adverse effects and recovery and so forth to shorten the overall quarantine period. Innovative developments are being made globally to promptly identify COVID-19 patients [4]. As a result, the public authority of India has sent out a cell phone application called Arogya Setu, which is intended to foster a connection between the sizable Indian population and organizations that provide healthcare services in order to make the general public more aware of the COVID-19 pandemic. Taiwan also quickly mobilized and launched explicit protocols for any prospective COVID-19 case, as well as provided ID, concealment, and asset arrangements to monitor the security of the nearby region. Taiwan supplied and organized its public health insurance coverage to promote the production of massive volumes of data for inquiry.

To help with case-distinguishing evidence, data concerning movement vestiges and clinical side effects was collected, an index was taken, and continuing warnings were established during a clinical appointment. They also used this latest technology, which involves reading QR codes and relatedly disclosing trip records, to identify the tainted ones. The COVID-19 pandemic relies on IoT applications that leverage many linked devices to build a smart network for the proper functioning of the board system. To increase the patient's safety, it gives alerts and monitors every disease [5]. It meticulously records the patient's information and data with essentially little human participation. This information is also helpful for suitable dynamic involvement. IoT adoption provides numerous major benefits in combating COVID-19 as a pandemic.

Applications of IoT for the COVID-19 Pandemic

- **Web-connected clinic :** A single united network inside the clinic's walls is required for the IoT to help with the influenza-like COVID-19 pandemic.
- **Inform the concerned clinical staff in the case of a problem:** This cooperation allows the staff and patients to respond more quickly and effectively when necessary or requested.
- **Transparent COVID-19 treatment:** Patients can benefit from the advantages provided and practically presented without favoritism or favors.

- **Automated treatment process:** To cure patients appropriately, it is necessary to ascertain treatment plans.
- **Telehealth conference :** By using teleservices, even the poor living in remote locations can conveniently get care.
- **Wireless medical care organizations recognizing COVID-19 patients :** This improves the accuracy and productivity of the ID method [6].
- **Smart pursuit of contaminated patients:** The successful patient follow-up eventually strengthens specialized cooperatives, enabling them to handle the cases with even greater care.
- **Real-time data during the spread of this disease:** As technologies, locations, and other factors have advanced over time, data may beshared in real time, emphasizing the importance of precision care.
- **Identify creative arrangements:** The main goal is to look for oversight. It has achieved a great deal by making a variety of ground-level improvements [7].
- **Connect all medical devices and equipment to the internet:** IoT interfaces clinical instruments, gadgets, and machines to make smart data frameworks according to individual COVID-19 patient prerequisites.

It adopts an alternate interdisciplinary strategy to augment efficiency, quality, and information about forthcoming diseases. IoT innovations recognize changes in crucial patient information for deciding important data. IoT advances have exceptionally affected great clinical gadgets, which assist with meeting customized arrangements during the pandemic. These advancements can catch, store, and examine the information carefully [8]. All the patient records are kept carefully, and with the assistance of web offices, patient information and data are handily partaken in crisis cases, and specialists are made to work efficiently. By utilizing smart sensors, we accomplish a superb ability to screen and control each one of the fundamental necessities of clinical temperature, sugar level, circulatory strain, and data in regard to COVID-19 patient health. The software plays a fundamental role in the most ideal way of correspondence and observation. All records are put away secretly for experiencing the treatments at their best levels later on. Man-made reasoning upgrades specialists' and specialists' exhibitions to accomplish precision, productivity, and dependability in treatment. Applying this innovation can decrease the patient's agony and quickly distinguish proof of imperfect bone formation for giving out appropriate medicine. Various actuators present the movement and control of the physical object. The augmented simulation is the best innovation of IoT to work on the nature of arranging ongoing data. IoT-empowered medical services provided support during the pandemic. IoT has a beneficial outcome on medical care to work on the existence of millions of people groups. It recognizes infection and completely screens the medical care framework [9]. It gives modified regard for individuals for their advantages.

Technologies utilized in IoT can include reminder arrangements, practice checks, carbohydrate levels, pulse, illness condition, and substantially more data during the pandemic. In the clinical field, IoT has an alternate application to make advancements during the pandemic. Following patients and staff in this way reduces waiting time, making it the most effective approach. It acquaints a few gadgets to make the patient agreeable. With smart gadgets like blood gas analyzers, thermometers, hospital beds, glucose meters, ultrasound, and X-rays, there is an improvement in long-term care. IoT is appropriate to supplant the organic part or upgrade the natural structure. Its applications are in clinical gear, such as associated imaging, clinical tasks, drug conveyance, patient checking, research facility tests, and medicine given during the pandemic [10]. IoT helps specialists and wellbeing experts to provide the best treatment for the patient. It brings together a data framework in an emergency clinic where movements of every sort are put away carefully, and different data investigations can likewise be used for the utilization of critical thinking during the pandemic. Without much of a stretch to screen patient's well-being, the innovation pursues an exact choice during cases that seem much more complex to solve. By keeping a consistent check on the well-being status, it alarms about any forthcoming illnesses and answers to its counteraction. It is useful in the recognition of asthma and a sign of a drug on schedule.

There are three essential objectives of the chapter. Right off the bat, we give a broad yet aggregate audit of the utilization of the advancements in the field and domain of IoT for various applications like the early findings, far-off quiet checking, quarantine observing, food and medication conveyance, and so on, on the side of preventive estimates like maintaining social distancing and severe lock-down, comparable with the pandemic circumstance [11].

In the end, the chapter directs an itemized writing audit. It leads to a point web quest to distinguish the creative applications for which arrangements in the IoT have been utilized. We discuss different intriguing applications, for example, involving specific and related thermometers for the early findings, keeping a remote check, utilizing wrist groups for isolation, and observing preventive measures.

Furthermore, researchers propose a start-to-finish IoT design for working with everyday social and expert exercises during the pandemic emergency with a mix of:

• Transient reactions for actuating preventive alarms promptly after recorded body boundaries drop out of reach.

- Long haul methodology incorporating an assortment of essential boundaries after some time, such as distant meetings, contact following, quarantine checking, food and medication conveyance, far-off conduct observing, and crisis reaction, if necessary.
- Researchers propose explicit conventions on each layer of the IoT design for working with the applications that are more related to the pandemic [12]. To accomplish that, they have surveyed the existing conventions working on different IoT layer designs; in the illumination of discoveries, they have the proposed conventions for the utilization of each layer (5G (URLLC), LTE-M, Bluetooth, and LoRa for MAC layer). Conventional ideas are being made based on the necessities of climate and application.

During the global pandemic, remote monitoring using IoMT became a reality for the management of healthcare facilities. In addition, the remote consideration of utilizing IoMT can decrease the gamble of openness for the weakest populaces, for example, old people with pre-conditions [13]. Along these lines, it is crucial to utilize remote screens and analytic apparatuses to upgrade the consideration conveyance while limiting the actual collaboration to the least.

In addition to monitoring physical activity, the Internet of Medical Things (IoMT) can also provide support from various angles. For instance, it can help people adhere to their medication schedules by tracking the usage of medication bottles and encourage physical activity by monitoring movement and heart rate [14].

HOW TO GET AWARE OF COVID-19?

Quarantine Monitoring

Mobile apps can also be used as IoT devices by specialists to keep track of the people who are quarantined, especially those with a history of migration. Specifically, GPS trackers are implanted with IoT devices that can supply location information to specialists who can make appropriate moves to manage the progression of infected individuals [15]. Smart devices are currently being employed in various areas of the world to ensure social distancing is maintained by the people.

Smart wearable GPS beacons are currently being used. Various varieties of bright wristbands contain GPS chips and have the ability to pair with clients' PDAs to track their locations and progress.

Creating Preventive Cautions

Since the rise of IoT gadgets in the medical services sector, it has been assumed that wearable sensors have the potential to reduce therapeutic costs through early detection and avoidance [16].

In recent years, wearable sensors have also been seen as a means of maintaining social separation and, as a result, slowing the spread of COVID-19. A smart band called I Feel-You is being developed by an Italian institute to measure interior heat levels and deliver alarms. An alarm can be triggered if a client's temperature rises to or exceeds 37.5°C. Furthermore, the smart band distinguishes a person's physique. When a smart band detects the existence of another smart band in a certain radio range, both vibrate to alert the clients about friendly separation. Despite the fact that the smart band's frequency is similar to that of Bluetooth, residents in other countries have worn wristbands and other wearable devices. Immune touch is another smart wristband [17]. The bracelet has an accelerometer that records the movement of the hand many times per second. The vibration in the wristbands may prevent consumers from coming into touch with their faces, lowering the risk of COVID-19 transmission.

Cleaning

Hospital cleanliness is one of the most fundamental cycles that should be mechanized to stay away from infections that can spread easily. The spread of pandemics can, to a great extent, be prevented by cleaning and sanitizing the office premises, especially those lodging the patients on analysis. IoT buttons have been used to send out cautions to the experts for maintaining cleanliness and upkeeping concerns of the public offices. The buttons are known as Wanda Quick Touch. The significance of the functionalities and elements of the buttons is that they require no framework and are worked once when they are charged by the battery [18]. The cautions are sent by the staff of the offices like nursing homes, bathrooms, and rooms where the patients are kept for observation to tell the administration or cleaning staff right away. Besides, the buttons can be combined with versatile applications to assist the administration with exercises related to cleanliness, reaction of the staff, and so forth.

Contact Tracing

Contact tracking is vital to restrict the spread of COVID as an individual can be a transporter of the infection even much earlier than he fosters the normal side effects of having fever or dry hack. The gamble of getting the disease quickly is the most noteworthy for individuals who have been in contact or near vicinity with the patient inside the nearness of 1.5-2 m for 10-15 min. Consequently, it is expected to distinguish the individual contacts analyzed or reported as positive.. Temperature, proximity, GPS, and GIS are examples of sensors that can be used for this purpose. A few IoT arrangements have been presented for proactive contact, which might raise the most frequent method of isolating people in danger [19].

A creative arrangement of wearables has been created that does not just monitor the strength of the client but can likewise assume a pivotal part in contact tracking. The "verification of well-being" wearable gadgets include GPS area detection [20]. When necessary, manual controls are also provided to work with manual differences in the client's health status. The device uses proximity sensors to keep track of the people with whom the user interacts. Aside from being stored on the wearable, the log is also kept up on a uniform dashboard that can be shared with the administration. If a person is found to be positive for COVID-19 and chooses to have his health status assessed, the device sends an alert to everyone with whom he had previously communicated. These wearables are cost-effective and provide timely assistance.

In Australia, the government has released a PDA application called "COVID Safe," which assists health officials in identifying people who may be at high risk of COVID-19 as a result of contact with a tested patient [21]. The data provided by the application can be accessed by the health authorities in order to comply with the protection rules.

In China, patients were encouraged to fill out vital data online before visiting the short-term divisions. This information reflects the history of home visits for areas previously afflicted, the history of interaction with those who reside there, the history of contact with persons who have been identified as having COVID-19, and the history of contact with those who have had COVID-19 in the previous three weeks. This information assists professionals in tracking contacts if a positive COVID-19 case is identified in the short term.

Restaurants and retailers have also made extensive use of Quick Response (QR) codes for contact information, following up on, as well as assisting with, the request setup and installment selection [22]. Customers were instructed to use their PDA cameras to scan the QR codes that were posted in public spaces across China. It was possible to follow contact based on the general setting data using this data from the client's device.

To gain access, they must show their QR health codes [23]. Bluetooth signals have also been introduced in places such as trams, taxis, restaurants, and retail outlets. These instructions send arbitrary identifiers that are kept on clients' smart devices and then used for contact tracking. It has been challenging for users of specific Apple and Google devices to track contacts across different countries.

Medicine and Food Delivery to COVID Patients

The proposed IoT engineering provides the end clients with the providers for requesting important supplies or prescriptions while staying away from the need for actual contact. First and foremost, the web innovations coordinated with site pages and versatile applications permit the end clients to put in their requests. Besides, different propositions are made to utilize robots to convey provisions to suffering or isolated individuals to guarantee social isolation [24]. Home robotization advancements, for example, shrewd entryway locks, reconnaissance cameras, movement indicators, and video telephones, permit the protected and contactless requesting of provisions. In this vein, COVID-19 is expected to follow in the footsteps of the home robotization sector.

Safety at Workplace

Work environment well-being can likewise be guaranteed by utilizing straightforward IoT gadgets. For instance, portable applications can be given to the representatives, which serve as a reminder for clean-up. Reach sensors may be utilized to keep workplace public spaces like bathrooms or containers separated. As recently referenced, Estimate has fostered the verification of well-being sensors to guarantee the security of workers through quick contact.

Essentially, one more form of contact following wearable [25] gadgets or keychains has been created by Microshare and Kerlink, which are resource-following organizations. Organizations either do not permit their representatives to possess cell phones or workers themselves do not have them. The representatives approach one another, and the workers' IDs, alongside the encoded codes, can be put away. The contact information is also transmitted over the received and consolidated dataset through the low power wide area network (LoRaWAN), which helps experts track the point of contact of employees who test positive or develop symptoms. Notwithstanding contact tracing, IoT devices at work can also ensure that people do not come into physical contact with facilities, thereby reducing the risk of contaminating them. For instance, the work environment can be made more secure by sending IoT arrangements, for example, shrewd water containers, brilliant registration frameworks, smart indoor regulator controls, savvy access controls, and brilliant administration of the offices. A large portion of these arrangements depend on voice, signal, or versatile application control.

IoT frameworks related to the work environment and board programming have additionally been utilized to make advanced floor plans. The workstations are considered inaccessible in light of the social separating prerequisite utilizing area data. The refreshed floor plans are passed on to the representatives utilizing contact focuses as well as versatile applications. Workers are checked for disrupting social separating norms utilizing the picture and movement information namelessly. Besides, the information produced by IoT sensors is communicated through dashboards.

Smart Metering

Smart meters provide energy providers with a fantastic opportunity to charge customers and provide standard inventory while maintaining a safe barrier between agents and customers. Smart meters [26] can also notify specialists if any changes are made, which could help with navigation in terms of separation of administration. According to the shopper's point of view, shrewd meters give ongoing information about the utilization designs, which could assist buyers in controlling their bills during the pandemic when monetary requirements have become extreme. In this way, by utilizing savvy metering, the specialists would have no need to truly peruse the meters, send the month-to-month bills to the buyers, or visit the areas to really look at altering. Despite the positive traits of brilliant meters, developing nations like Pakistan, India, Bangladesh, and so forth still do not have access to them. Coronavirus circumstances can be viewed as a chance to send the brilliant meters to such nations.

Lifestyle

Coronavirus has had a significant impact on people's lives from one side of the globe to the other, with detrimental consequences on individual and family health. The three domains of physical well-being and wellness, emotional well-being, and homegrown pressure and viciousness are covered in this section. To combat the spread of COVID-19 [27], recreation centers, wellness centers, and active work communities have been closed all across the world. During the interval, IoT devices can also be used to assist clients in their wellness initiatives. IoT devices can also be used to detect people's anxiety and communicate with their loved ones *via* advanced administration devices, thereby lowering the risk of depression and other serious health risks.

Social separation reduces the risk of the spread of pandemics, but it also has certain negative repercussions. According to research conducted in the United Kingdom, the COVID-19 system of social separation and segregation has had considerable negative consequences on psychological well-being and individual prosperity and well-being. Furthermore, social rejection has been linked to the possibility of mental weakening, particularly among the elderly, who may suffer from the negative impacts of loss of inspiration, the relevance of mortality, and the loss of routine and design.

IOT ARCHITECTURE FOR MANAGING COVID

The researchers advocated new methods for ensuring people's well-being, conducting checks, combating epidemics, and encouraging social isolation and self-quarantine. The cycle is encapsulated under a start-to-finish fundamental IoT-built framework that focuses on a mix of transient activities and long-haul methods. Momentary methodology includes robotized enactment of preventive cautions, playing music or strict stanzas and headings for explicit exercises like doing activity or eating the right food, long-term methodology, if necessary, with an appropriate doctor, medical caretaker, or clinician, and drawing up a characterized care and fix plan for the patient's predicament [28].

The long-term board strategy incorporates long-term flexibility in preparing for pandemic emergency situations while maintaining social removal and decreasing the risk of contamination spread and future pandemics.

These actions include the following:

- Long-range planning for dangers such as hypertension, diabetes [29], hyperthyroidism, COVID contamination, and others, posed by deviations in body and natural boundaries, as well as coming into close contact with currently affected patients. Quarantine checks of people who use robots and PDAs when they are tracked down by early analysis [30] or are found defenseless due to a fundamental medical concern or proximity to infected patients. Once the person has been identified as a patient/transporter for the infection, only then will the area be checked.
- Appropriate far-off discussion with doctor/nurse/clinician, far-off persistent checking, legitimate direction, updating care and fix plans with customary input from aggregated individual datasets, increased readiness and circumstance mindfulness through cutting-edge observing and expectation devices.
- Early detection by the acquisition of nasal samples for testing with robots, if observed powerless through contact following and deviation in critical or ecological boundaries, reducing the risk of disease for medical care workers [31].
- Brilliant metering and warnings on changing through accounts from ecological sensors installed in the checked people's homes.
- People who use robots are subjected to a quarantine check climatic conditions. As a result, current challenges with GPS and Bluetooth advance in indoor areas,

such as low assimilation power and vision blocking [32].

• Organization of robots to help people in isolation by delivering them food and clinical supplies, cleaning their existing situation, feeding them with fundamentals, and closely monitoring others who are facing the same thing, thus reducing anxiety [33] among medical care workers. The proposed paradigm for the COVID-19 tracking application is shown in Figs. (**1 - 3**) [12].

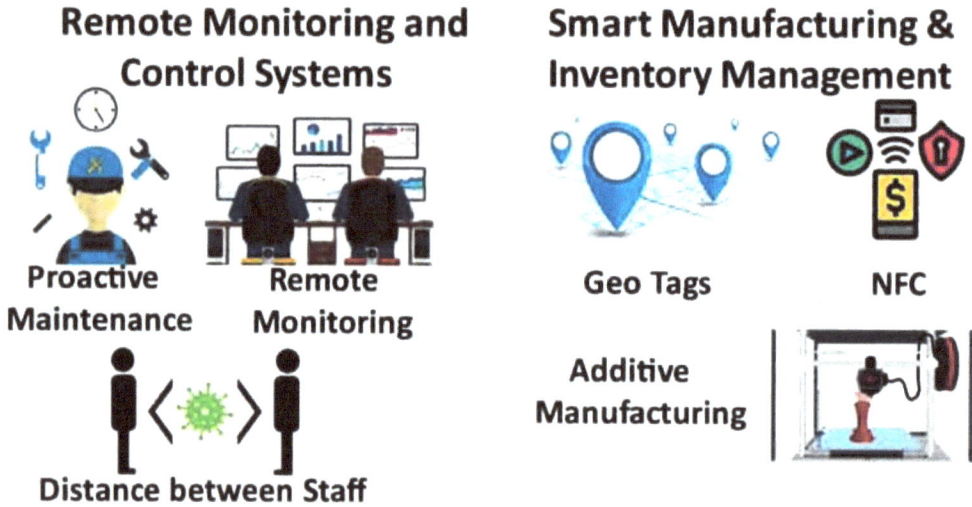

Fig. (1). Recent Increased Adoptions in Industries in the Wake of COVID-19.

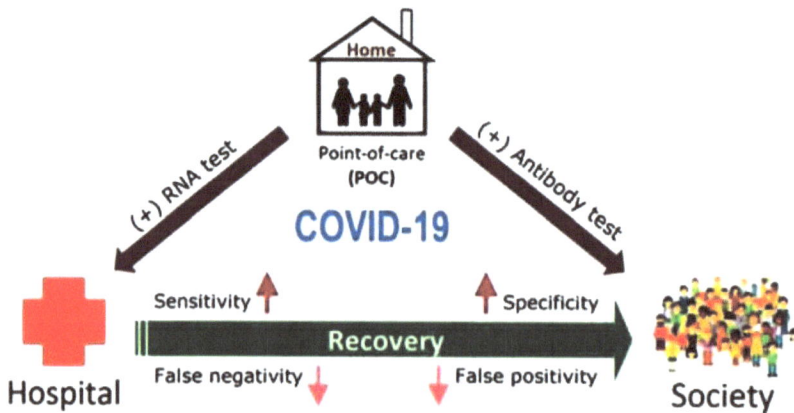

Fig. (2). Detection to recovery cycle of covid-19.

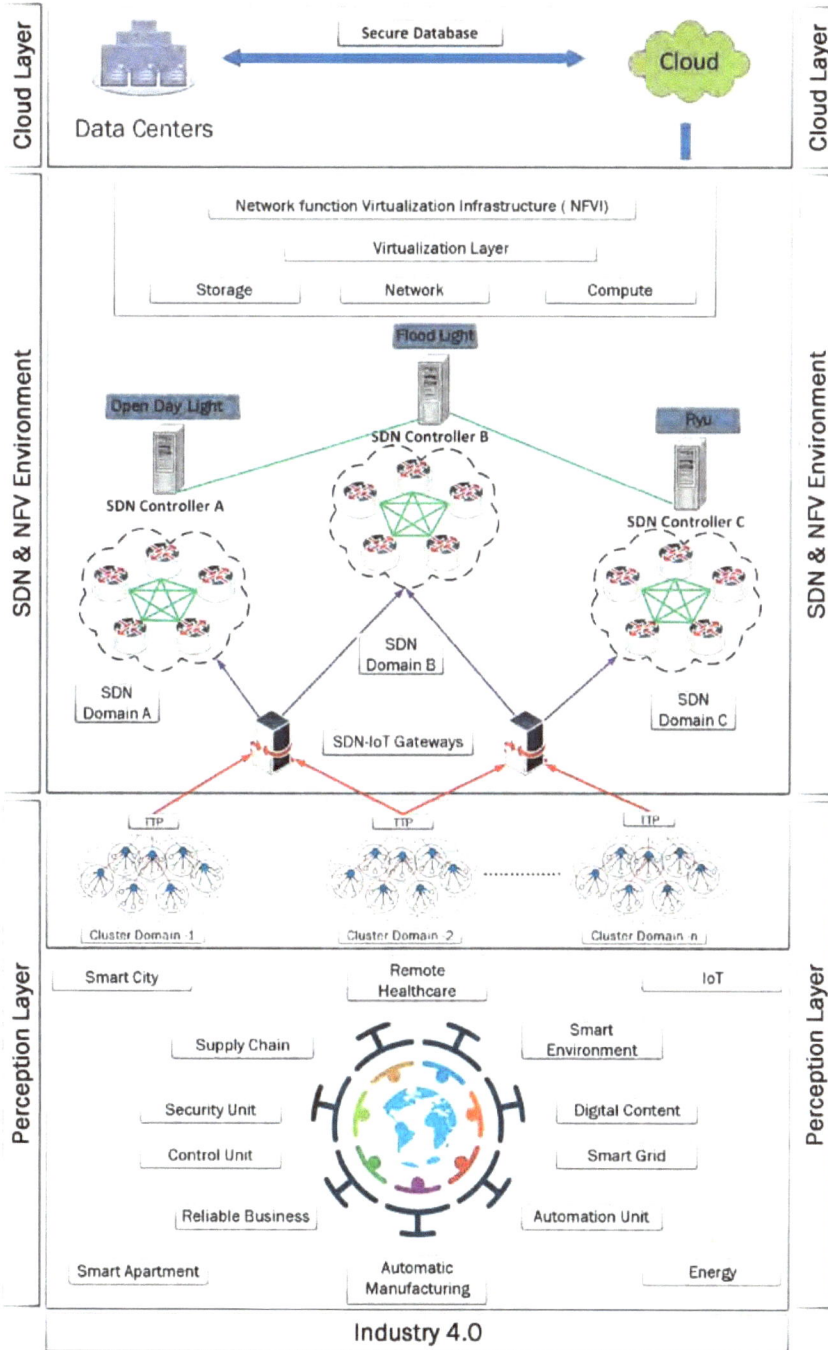

Fig. (3). IoT-based COVID-19 tracking application.

CHALLENGES AND OPPORTUNITIES

IoT execution is ordinarily tested by association, power, range, transfer speed, and expenses. In any case, the costs for the utilization of IoT in medical services are anticipated to drive more noteworthy, versatile broadband reception [34]. The expense adequacy of normalized low-energy remote advancements likewise adds to this pattern. Likewise, the huge scope utilization of innovation in the well-being area depends on the exchange of well-being information and records, which raises issues over protection and security. These worries have prompted the execution of public IoT guidelines in created markets. In any case, suitable regulations in underdeveloped countries are yet expected to help IoT reception. Finally, IoT-applied medical services are, in many cases, restricted. To reach a conclusion, a significant level of medical conditions needs an actual assessment. Furthermore, photographs and recordings conveyed utilizing IoT-fueled telemedicine may need top-notch goals and actual treatment.

The association of versatile transporters might speed up the reception of IoT in medical services. One representation in point is controller, an organization that spends significant time on checking items. The association helps Vodafone Mobile operators to screen information on controlling vaccines by continuously utilizing the Vodafone-managed IoT connectivity platform. Such portable partnerships will give new potential to IoT-empowered medical care in immature regions [35]. Over and past COVID-19, extra IoT advancement can help with future pandemics, utilizing approaches in view of insights and converging with computerized reasoning and enormous information. Sooner rather than later, IoT can accordingly be an essential facilitator for well-being change from a receptive to a proactive framework.

CONCLUSION

IoT has made significant advances during the COVID-19 pandemic to upgrade offices and the data framework in the clinical field. It upgrades the of operations in emergency clinics. Whenever gadgets/instruments are connected to the Internet, IoT empowers new clinical applications. For patients, electronic devices are acquainted in various ways by screening patients' wellbeing concerns regarding public health by monitoring climate change. This technology enables the hospital to be appropriately managed during COVID-19. Observing the medication plays a significant role in providing affirmed data. This data may likewise help the proper dissemination of reasonable hardware/gadgets for the right patient. This method is useful to diminish squandering in the emergency clinic with the right data. It diminishes the gamble of medical clinic mishaps and handles all issues with the guide of all-around archived data. This framework might assist with safeguarding expensive clinical devices from being taken. With a superior specialized arrangement, IoT gives predominant, pertinent, and dependable information. It licenses human testing scientists with the smallest risk. Practically speaking, it gives creative answers for an intense test in the clinical area during the COVID-19 pandemic. It establishes offices and manages patient recoveries, providing essential crisis assistance to minimize associated losses. The fastest acknowledgment in the clinical calling is inferable from its effectiveness. IoT is intended to oversee better ongoing diseases, clinical emergencies, work on tolerant consideration, wellness, the board of circulatory strain, well-being reviews, estimations, and audiological help, and is equipped for consistent, dependable observing of COVID-19 patients and further developed personalization of the clinical area. IoT-empowered gadgets might help advance the capacity of individual well-being data for COVID-19 patients and associate with different data sets. This innovation can help manual record-keeping to a base. It wipes out missteps and results on schedule by settling on a very informed decision.

REFERENCES

[1]   Y. Ushimaru, T. Takahashi, Y. Souma, Y. Yanagimoto, H. Nagase, K. Tanaka, Y. Miyazaki, T. Makino, Y. Kurokawa, M. Yamasaki, M. Mori, Y. Doki, and K. Nakajima, "Innovation in surgery/operating room driven by Internet of Things on medical devices", *Surg. Endosc.,* vol. 33, no. 10, pp. 3469-3477, 2019.
[http://dx.doi.org/10.1007/s00464-018-06651-4] [PMID: 30671666]

[2]   R. Basatneh, B. Najafi, and D.G. Armstrong, "Health sensors, smart home devices, and the internet of medical things: an opportunity for dramatic improvement in care for the lower extremity complications of diabetes", *J. Diabetes Sci. Technol.,* vol. 12, no. 3, pp. 577-586, 2018.
[http://dx.doi.org/10.1177/1932296818768618] [PMID: 29635931]

[3]   H. Wang, Y. Wen, D. Zhao, E.J. Ciaccio, and F. Liu, "Differential barometric-based positioning technique for indoor elevation measurement in IoT medical applications", *Technol. Health Care,* vol. 25, no. S1, pp. 295-304, 2017.
[http://dx.doi.org/10.3233/THC-171333] [PMID: 28582918]

[4]   R.P. Singh, M. Javaid, and A. Haleem, "R. Suman Internet of things (IoT) applications to fight against COVID-19 pandemic Diabetes & metabolic syndrome Clin", *Res. Rev.,* vol. 14, no. 4, pp. 521-524, 2020.

[5]   B. Farahani, F. Firouzi, V. Chang, M. Badaroglu, N. Constant, and K. Mankodiya, "Towards fog-driven IoT eHealth: Promises and challenges of IoT in medicine and healthcare", *Future Gener. Comput. Syst.,* vol. 78, pp. 659-676, 2018.
[http://dx.doi.org/10.1016/j.future.2017.04.036]

[6]   K.K. Patel, and S.M. Patel, "Internet of things-IoT: definition, characteristics, architecture, enabling technologies, application & future challenges", *Int. J. Eng. Sci. Comput.,* vol. 6, pp. 6122-6131, 2016.

[7]   L. Farhan, S.T. Shukur, A.E. Alissa, M. Alrweg, U. Raza, and R. Kharel, "A survey on the challenges and opportunities of the Internet of Things (IoT)", *Proceedings of the 2017 Eleventh International Conference on Sensing Technology (ICST),* pp. 1-5, 2017. Sydney, NSW, Australia.
[http://dx.doi.org/10.1109/ICSensT.2017.8304465]

[8]   M.S. Jalali, J.P. Kaiser, M. Siegel, and S. Madnick, "The Internet of Things Promises New Benefits and Risks: A Systematic Analysis of Adoption Dynamics of IoT Products", *IEEE Secur. Priv.,* vol. 17,

no. 2, pp. 39-48, 2019.
[http://dx.doi.org/10.1109/MSEC.2018.2888780]

[9]   T. Alam, "Internet of Things and Blockchain-based framework for Coronavirus (Covid-19) Disease", *SSRN,* 2020.
[http://dx.doi.org/10.2139/ssrn.3660503]

[10]   A.C. Chang, "Artificial intelligence and COVID-19: Present state and future vision", *Intelligence-Based Medicine,* vol. 3-4, p. 100012, 2020.
[http://dx.doi.org/10.1016/j.ibmed.2020.100012] [PMID: 33196057]

[11]   D.R. Seshadri, E.V. Davies, E.R. Harlow, J.J. Hsu, S.C. Knighton, T.A. Walker, J.E. Voos, and C.K. Drummond, "Wearable sensors for COVID-19: A call to action to harness our digital infrastructure for remote patient monitoring and virtual assessments", *Frontiers in Digital Health,* vol. 2, p. 8, 2020.
[http://dx.doi.org/10.3389/fdgth.2020.00008] [PMID: 34713021]

[12]   D. Vatansever, S. Wang, and B.J. Sahakian, "Covid-19 and promising solutions to combat symptoms of stress, anxiety and depression", *Neuropsychopharmacology,* vol. 46, no. 1, pp. 217-218, 2021.
[http://dx.doi.org/10.1038/s41386-020-00791-9] [PMID: 32792683]

[13]   G. Quer, J.M. Radin, M. Gadaleta, K. Baca-Motes, L. Ariniello, E. Ramos, V. Kheterpal, E.J. Topol, and S.R. Steinhubl, "Wearable sensor data and self-reported symptoms for COVID-19 detection", *Nat. Med.,* vol. 27, no. 1, pp. 73-77, 2021.
[http://dx.doi.org/10.1038/s41591-020-1123-x] [PMID: 33122860]

[14]   T. Mishra, M. Wang, A.A. Metwally, G.K. Bogu, A.W. Brooks, A. Bahmani, A. Alavi, A. Celli, E. Higgs, and O. Dagan-Rosenfeld, "Early detection of COVID-19 using a smartwatch", *medRxiv,* 2020.
[http://dx.doi.org/10.1101/2020.07.06.20147512]

[15]   H.L. Cao, H.A.D. Nguyen, T.H. Luu, H.T.T. Vu, D. Pham, H.H. Le, D.X.B. Nguyen, T.T. Truong, H.D. Nguyen, and C.N. Nguyen, "Localized automation solutions in response to the first wave of COVID-19: A story from Vietnam", *Int. J. Pervasive Comput. Commun.,* 2020.

[16]   N. Ahmed, R.A. Michelin, W. Xue, S. Ruj, R. Malaney, S.S. Kanhere, A. Seneviratne, W. Hu, H. Janicke, and S.K. Jha, "A survey of COVID-19 contact tracing apps", *IEEE Access,* vol. 8, pp. 134577-134601, 2020.

[17]   F. Zuo, J. Wang, J. Gao, K. Ozbay, X.J. Ban, Y. Shen, H. Yang, and S. Iyer, "An interactive data visualization and analytics tool to evaluate mobility and sociability trends during COVID-19", *arXiv,* p. 14882, 2020.

[18]   A. O'Dowd, "Covid-19: UK test and trace system still missing 80% target for reaching contacts", *BMJ,* vol. 370, p. m2875, 2020.
[http://dx.doi.org/10.1136/bmj.m2875] [PMID: 32680932]

[19]   C.M. Chen, H.W. Jyan, S.C. Chien, H.H. Jen, C.Y. Hsu, P.C. Lee, C.F. Lee, Y.T. Yang, M.Y. Chen, L.S. Chen, H.H. Chen, and C.C. Chan, "Containing COVID-19 among 627,386 persons in contact with the diamond princess cruise ship passengers who disembarked in Taiwan: Big data analytics", *J. Med. Internet Res.,* vol. 22, no. 5, p. e19540, 2020.
[http://dx.doi.org/10.2196/19540] [PMID: 32353827]

[20]   S.F. Su, and Y.Y. Han, "How Taiwan, a non-WHO member, takes actions in response to COVID-19", *J. Glob. Health,* vol. 10, no. 1, p. 010380, 2020.
[http://dx.doi.org/10.7189/jogh.10.010380] [PMID: 32582442]

[21]   C.J. Wang, C.Y. Ng, and R.H. Brook, "Response to COVID-19 in Taiwan", *JAMA,* vol. 323, no. 14, pp. 1341-1342, 2020.
[http://dx.doi.org/10.1001/jama.2020.3151] [PMID: 32125371]

[22]   N. Munsch, A. Martin, S. Gruarin, J. Nateqi, I. Abdarahmane, R. Weingartner-Ortner, and B. Knapp, "Diagnostic Accuracy of Web-Based COVID-19 Symptom Checkers: Comparison Study", *J. Med. Internet Res.,* vol. 22, no. 10, p. e21299, 2020.

[http://dx.doi.org/10.2196/21299] [PMID: 33001828]

[23]   M. Arun, E. Baraneetharan, A. Kanchana, S. Prabu, N.V. Rajeesh Kumar, and J. Stanly Jaya Prakash, "Detection and monitoring of the asymptotic COVID-19 patients using IoT devices and sensors". *Int. J. Pervasive Comput. Commun.* 2020.

[24]   O. Taiwo, and A.E. Ezugwu, "Smart healthcare support for remote patient monitoring during covid-19 quarantine", *Informatics in Medicine Unlocked,* vol. 20, p. 100428, 2020.
[http://dx.doi.org/10.1016/j.imu.2020.100428] [PMID: 32953970]

[25]   N.A. Megahed, and E.M. Ghoneim, "Antivirus-built environment: Lessons learned from Covid-19 pandemic", *Sustain Cities Soc.,* vol. 61, p. 102350, 2020.
[http://dx.doi.org/10.1016/j.scs.2020.102350] [PMID: 32834930]

[26]   L. Dietz, P.F. Horve, D.A. Coil, M. Fretz, J.A. Eisen, and K. Van Den Wymelenberg, "2019 novel coronavirus (COVID-19) pandemic: Built environment considerations to reduce transmission", *mSystems,* vol. 5, no. 2, p. e00245-20, 2020.
[http://dx.doi.org/10.1128/mSystems.00245-20] [PMID: 32265315]

[27]   M.D. Pinheiro, and N.C. Luís, "COVID-19 could leverage a sustainable built environment", *Sustainability (Basel),* vol. 12, no. 14, p. 5863, 2020.
[http://dx.doi.org/10.3390/su12145863]

[28]   A.F. Santos, P.D. Gaspar, A. Hamandosh, E.B. Aguiar, A.C. Guerra Filho, and H.J.L. Souza, "Best Practices on HVAC Design to Minimize the Risk of COVID-19 Infection within Indoor Environments", *Braz. Arch. Biol. Technol.,* vol. 63, p. e20200335, 2020.
[http://dx.doi.org/10.1590/1678-4324-2020200335]

[29]   I. Nakamoto, S. Wang, Y. Guo, and W. Zhuang, "A QR Code–Based Contact Tracing Framework for Sustainable Containment of COVID-19: Evaluation of an Approach to Assist the Return to Normal Activity", *JMIR Mhealth Uhealth,* vol. 8, no. 9, p. e22321, 2020.
[http://dx.doi.org/10.2196/22321] [PMID: 32841151]

[30]   M. Cristani, A. Del Bue, V. Murino, F. Setti, and A. Vinciarelli, "The Visual Social Distancing Problem", *arXiv,* 2020.

[31]   M. Fazio, A. Buzachis, A. Galletta, A. Celesti, and M. Villari, "A proximity-based indoor navigation system tackling the COVID-19 social distancing measures", *Proceedings of the 2020 IEEE Symposium on Computers and Communications (ISCC),* pp. 1-6, 2020.
[http://dx.doi.org/10.1109/ISCC50000.2020.9219634]

[32]   T. Fan, Z. Chen, X. Zhao, J. Liang, C. Shen, D. Manocha, J. Pan, and W. Zhang, "Autonomous social distancing in urban environments using a quadruped robot", *arXiv,* p. arXiv:2008.08889, 2020.

[33]   A.J. Sathyamoorthy, U. Patel, Y.A. Savle, M. Paul, and D. Manocha, "COVID-Robot: Monitoring social distancing constraints in crowded scenarios", *arXiv,* p. arXiv:2008.0658, 2020.

[34]   H. Jarva, M. Lappalainen, O. Luomala, P. Jokela, A.E. Jaaskelainen, A.J. Jaaskelainen, H. Kallio-Kokko, E. Kekalainen, L. Mannonen, and H. Soini, "Laboratory-based surveillance of COVID-19 in the Greater Helsinki area, Finland", *medRxiv,* 2020.

[35]   J. Sarkis, "Supply chain sustainability: Learning from the COVID-19 pandemic", *Int. J. Oper. Manag.,* 2020.

CHAPTER 9

Tackling and Predicting Pandemic through Machine Learning and IoT

Silky Goel[1,*] and **Snigdha Markanday**[1]

[1] *School of Computer Science, University of Petroleum and Energy Studies, Dehradun, India*

Abstract: "The ongoing COVID-19 situation has been challenging for the existence of humans." It has consistently surpassed the numerous physical and mental activities that humans engage in, compelling them to live within increasingly constrained boundaries. In this chapter, the use of the Internet of Things (IoT) and machine learning (ML)-based framework to tackle pandemic situations in healthcare applications has been discussed. ML and IoT-based monitoring systems track infected individuals using past information, helping with isolation. The system involves parallel computation to track and prevent pandemic diseases through predictions and analysis with artificial intelligence. The execution of ML-based IoT in the pandemic circumstance in healthcare applications has shown performance in tracking and preventing the spread of the pandemic.

Keywords: Artificial intelligence, Internet of Things, Machine learning, Pandemic.

INTRODUCTION

The recently discovered coronavirus causes a highly contagious illness known as COVID-19. It was first reported in Wuhan, China, in December 2019 and has since spread to 216 countries worldwide. There have been over 10.6 million confirmed cases, and tragically, more than 1 million people have lost their lives to this disease. These censuses are promptly expanding and the calamity is developing gradually. Healthcare services severely need innovative technology to help them in these circumstances [1]. The healthcare sector is anticipating that advancements in technology will conquer crises during emergencies. Specialists all around the world are accompanied by different procedures that can come up with a solution to these challenging circumstances. It has turned into an extremely difficult task because clinical data about the disease is not accessible yet, and the

---

* **Corresponding author Silky Goel:** School of Computer Science, University of Petroleum and Energy Studies, Dehradun, India; E-mail: silkygoel90@gmail.com

Sunil Kumar, Silky Goel, Gaytri Bakshi, Siddharth Gupta & Sayed M. El-kenawy (Eds.)

data is changing over the period of time. With this restricted information, numerous researchers accompanied different supportive innovations utilizing different ML algorithms.

In developing nations, there is a lack of clinical units for tests related to COVID-19, which might result in more contamination. ML methods can provide initial assistance in monitoring individuals for various illnesses such as heart disease, diabetes [2], coronary illness, various disorders, cancer, and COVID-19. ML is at the edge of numerous advanced technologies. Recognizing potential cases quickly can help ensure that individuals receive necessary medication and treatment as soon as possible. ML procedures are used to track COVID-19 patients at high risk.

This chapter centers around the significance and effect of ML in the battle between humans and COVID-19. It gives a complete review [3] of the technologies that came up to battle against COVID using machine learning algorithms. The chapter portrays the significant role played by machine learning in the most critical circumstances. Presently, these developments are battling against COVID-19 and will be a significant method for combatting any future pandemic.

Wearable technology that monitors a patient's physiological state is just one example of how the Internet of Things (IoT) has changed the healthcare sector [4]. Numerous advanced computational innovations like blockchain, Internet of Things (IoT), artificial intelligence (AI), machine learning (ML), and unmanned aerial vehicles (UAVs) are effectively used to handle COVID-19 issues, for example, early diagnosis, CT scan diagnosis, contact tracing, vaccine development, remote monitoring, telemedicine, drug development, and virus modeling. COVID-19's harmful effects are being mitigated by the use of artificial intelligence and data science.

HOW THE COMPUTATIONAL SOLUTIONS ARE BEING USED TO FIGHT THE BATTLE AGAINST COVID.

Detection of COVID-19

The RT-PCR test is considered the most effective method for diagnosing COVID-19 [5]. However, due to the rapid increase in the number of expected patients worldwide, there is a shortage of testing kits. As a result, many computational systems are being used to accurately diagnose people. These computer models may not be as reliable as traditional biological diagnostic methods, but in emergency situations, they have proven to be quite useful and are increasingly being used as a screening approach for detecting the virus.

Detection Based on Images

For picture recognition and classification, convolutional neural networks (CNN) [6], a well-known deep learning technique, are used. CNN has been widely used in computational healthcare services for leveraging medical imaging to diagnose a number of ailments. In a comprehensive analysis, GoogleNet was among the well-known open-source CNNs that Ardakan I *et al.* examined for the COVID-19 diagnosis. They made sure that their systems could recognize COVID and other situations related to the virus's spread. The CNN architecture was created using Xception, AlexNet, and MobileNet-v2. The most accurate model was ResNe-101, which had a precision of 99.51 percent.

Voice-based Diagnosis with Deep Learning and Machine Learning Technologies

Various technologies were utilized for diagnosis based on a person's voice. In recent months, a few COVID-19 speech deep learning and machine learning techniques have been used to develop diagnostic tools [7]. A group at Carnegie Mellon University (CMU) has developed a program that analyzes a person's voice test to determine whether they have COVID-19 or not. Despite this, they emphasize that the app should only be used as a screening tool to allow for the most accurate diagnosis. Symptomatic patients should choose the RT-PCR test due to the limited availability of PCR test kits.

The recognition of the cough caused by COVID-19, as well as other types such as non-disease related coughs, is also one of the major issues to be tackled. The structure includes both the COVID-19 diagnostic engine and a cough detector. The category for the cough is carried out using the final framework. The task of the cough detector is to determine whether the incoming sound contains a cough. The ESC-50 public dataset, which includes a wide range of natural and human sounds, trains the cough detector [8]. It used about 1800 coughing human sounds and about 3500 background sounds from this collection of data. This cough detection system computes the 120-band Mel spectrogram of the recorded cough sound. The image is then changed or transformed to an image in a grayscale that measures 320x240x1. A convolutional neural network analyzes the image created as an output or result and determines whether the sound is a cough or not.

If a cough is heard, the related image is taken into consideration as part of the COVID-19 diagnosis and analysis. This framework is made up of a cluster of different deep learning and machine learning algorithms. The system is legitimate and accurate, and the reports "Coronavirus likely" or "Coronavirus unlikely" are true if all of these algorithms reach the same conclusion. Test inconclusive is displayed, indicated, or proclaimed as the system's output if the outputs do not yield the same results. The study team made use of a dataset to train the COVID-19 diagnosis mode and used 130 pertussis cough samples, 70 COVID-19 samples, 96 bronchitis samples, and normal cough samples. The CNN-based deep transfer learning-based multi-class classifier (DTL-MC), which is similar to the system used for cough detection, is based on deep learning. This method can have an architecture even with little data because of transfer learning techniques. The following algorithm uses a machine learning-based multiclass classifier (CMLMC) [9]. In the first part of this section, the pre-processed Mel-spectrogram is substituted with the sound of a cough. Principal component analysis (PCA) is used to extract the features, and SVM is used as a classifier to categorize the data.

Models have been produced using deep learning techniques or methodologies. A model called deep transfer learning was built using the CNN architecture that was employed for data collection as shown in Fig. (**1**). The output of a binary classifier, like them [10], has a size of 2, for instance, whether COVID-19 tested positive or negative for coronavirus. A huge number of probabilities were generated based on various scenarios, including "System reports COVID-19 likely and the patient is COVID-19 positive".

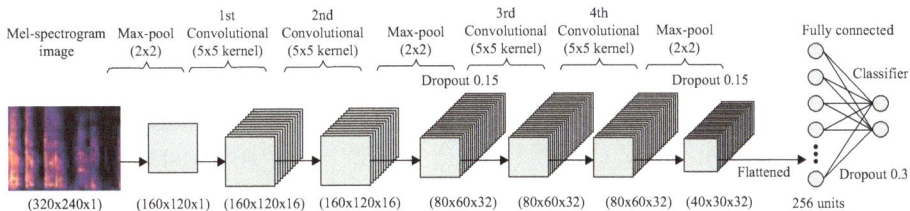

Fig. (1). Shows the CNN model for cough detection [34].

Forecast for Mortality Rate

Since the 1990s, methods of patient mortality have been predicted using machine learning. These techniques have the potential to predict COVID-19 patient fatality rates, allowing higher-risk patients to receive therapy at a higher rate. The mortality risks of several COVID-19 patients were ascertained by a study team at California State University using conventional ML algorithms [11], such as SVM, ANN, KNN, RF, DT, and LR. They were as precise as they could be, coming close to 94 percent. The individuals in the study had an average age of 56 and were COVID-19 positive, according to test confirmation. The neural network with two hidden layers offered the highest level of precision when various strategies for forecasting were utilized. A machine learning algorithm analyzed the blood samples to calculate the COVID-19 patients' mortality risks. They developed a method based on XGBoost ML that can predict COVID-19 patient mortality with accuracy up to ten days in advance. This machine learning system using decision trees identified three significant blood biomarkers that can predict death rates with up to 90% accuracy.

The Curve's Prediction

A variety of artificial intelligence and machine learning techniques have been employed to predict substantial dates in the epidemic, such as the time when the number of new cases each day is anticipated to peak. Curve forecasting is a significant and essential use of machine learning because it empowers organizations and countries to make wiser, more informed decisions [12].

A mathematical and machine learning approach was proposed by Yang *et al.* to predict the growth of the COVID-19 scenario in China. Their outcomes appeared to be largely expected. By January 23rd, 2020, China had put strict quarantine restrictions in place. Yang *et al.* made a prediction based on mathematical techniques and machine learning that COVID-19 cases in China's central area would start to increase by the middle of February and continue to rise until the end of March. Additionally, they predicted that COVID-19 cases would start to appear in mid-March and persist through late April if the quarantine in Hubei was relaxed. The significance of lockdowns and quarantines is explicated in this paper in detail. In their study, they employed two alternative prediction models. A mathematical model that mimics pandemics and epidemics was the first, called the modified SEIR. The second was a recurrent neural network known as the Long Short-Term Memory (LSTM) [13], which excels at managing data from time series. Using information from the 2003 SA RS outbreak, the LSTM was trained. The LSTM model predicted a sharp increase in China and reported additional cases on February 4th, but the peak occurred in February, pretty much exactly on the predicted date.

Research and Development on Drugs

The creation of drugs has long been aided by AI technologies [14]. Deep learning techniques have been utilized to forecast the activities of many or different biological molecules as well as the characteristics of the chemical. They have also been employed to anticipate reactions and perform retrosynthetic analyses. The activities and chemical composition of the human body have been predicted using subatomic structures and other information in a number of different ways. The development of antiviral medications to treat the SARS-CoV-2 virus is currently being accelerated and cost-effectively done using deep learning and related technologies.

Drugs that are suitable for a certain use are most typically created using generative adversarial networks (GANs) [15]. Data that is statistically equivalent to the training data supplied into the network could be gathered using GANs. The crystal structure of the 3C-like protease is known. Using a deep GAN-based generative chemical pipeline is Insilico Medicine to develop new drugs like COVID-19 inhibitors, and it has already begun manufacturing them. The research conducted by Zhavoronkov *et al.* led to the development of a variety of chemicals. They compared the structural similarities of the many chemical compounds produced by the network using the search engine of the ChEMBL database [16]. They made use of data from the ChEMBL database, a free database of biological compounds with characteristics resembling those of drugs.

IBM researchers conducted yet another trial of COVID-19 medication discovery, using deep generative models to develop and evaluate a range of therapies [17]. They advise employing molecules created through controlled creation (CogMol), a complete framework, to design novel drugs, such as microscopic atoms that specifically target viral proteins. This model combines a flexible sub-atomic VAE pre-training scheme with an extraordinarily effective multi-attribute-controlled inspection approach (Variational Autoencoder) [18]. To create useful and efficient pharmaceutical-like compounds, CogMol uses a protein-molecule binding affinity indicator trained on protein organization embeddings and a variational autoencoder. They employed three objective proteins as opposed to simply one in the former experiment. They employed non-structural proteins in their study. The spike protein is composed of 9 copies, a primary protease, and a receptor-binding domain. They discovered that 90 percent of the compounds produced are chemically genuine, and 95% of them satisfy basic requirements [19]. As a result, the model provides incredibly exciting medications for additional testing to determine their efficacy and safety against COVID-19.

Development of Vaccines

A development in vaccination science that utilizes bioinformatics is reverse vaccinology [20]. The fundamental idea behind reverse vaccination is that the best genes can be found by screening the entire genomes of pathogens using bioinformatics computational methods. A few antigens (proteins or pathogens that have been weakened) are injected into a person's body during the vaccination phase with the aim of stimulating the immune system to develop immunity to a particular infection. Artificial intelligence (AI) and machine learning can be used to anticipate which substances or proteins would be vaccines [21].

Another model is VAXIGN-ML, which is used for selecting the best mRMR and optimizing the hyperparameters that employ severe gradients [22]. The best vaccine candidate is a protein. The algorithm's accuracy and robustness are increased by optimization by minimizing or removing mistakes. The candidates for the SARS-CoV-2 vaccine were predicted using VAXIGNML as shown in Fig. (**2**) [23]. The COVID-19-causing virus', nsp8, nsp3, and S proteins, were thought to be good candidates for potent defensive antigenicity. Utilizing five supervised machine learning algorithms, the VAXIGN-ML device, with the boosting method offers the highest level of precision. The information for their review came from the protein database.

To create antibodies, understanding the particular protein designs is crucial. Even after using numerous techniques to determine a protein's constituent parts, the artificial intelligence algorithm DeepMind AlphaFold from Google chooses the direction in which a protein's structure is folded [24]. This approach is being used to determine the structure of numerous proteins associated with the virus that causes COVID-19 [25]. The structure or fold of proteins has been studied over time using a variety of technologies, including x-ray crystallography, cryo-electron microscopy, and nuclear magnetic resonance. These processes, however, are pricy and time-consuming. In contrast, the AlphaFold program is highly compact, computationally quick, and easy to use. In the AlphaFold software, a trained neural network takes the protein structure as input and generates distance and angle predictions based on that structure. It also provides a score for the quality of the predicted protein structure [26].

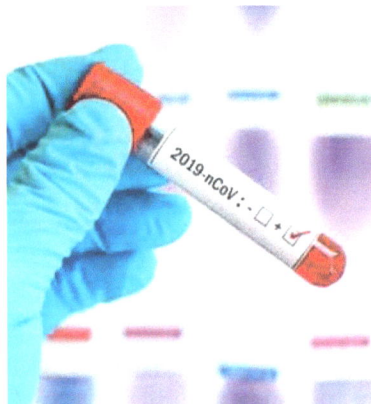

Fig. (2). Development of covid-19 vaccine [23].

Sampling Based on the Needs of the Respondents

By depending on the responsive arrangement of informants with their local networks to quickly put up a database of interactions between SARS-CoV-2 virus carriers [27].

Important components of the suggested method include:

- Developing an RDS platform for detecting dynamic, undetected instances and determining the growth of dynamic pollution on a local level [28]. We can issue prior, high-sway information as the general well-being of people with future flu-like illnesses, such as COVID-19, by evolving the capacity to send designated testing quickly to the North Carolina (NC) residents, utilizing transmission pathways to enroll local area individuals efficiently to complete electronic reviews and present for testing.
- Evaluating differential social contact designs through private organization reviews to assess the social determinants of contamination risk [29]. Recognizing new positive cases, reaching out to disadvantaged populations, and evaluating the effectiveness of RDS in identifying positive patients in underrepresented populaces. Researchers try out tests to see if the RDS works by responding swiftly with various testing modalities and arriving at more distal organization connections that are not normally reached through traditional contact following methods.
- Using RDS to illuminate and coordinate atomic disease transmission research focuses on people who are representative of the neighborhood [30]. The assessment of optional assault rates in diverse situations will be possible by combining point-by-point contact designs with transmission designs investigated by sub-atomic disease transmission research. Healthcare professionals in emergency rooms and other care settings are shielded from interaction patterns with a higher risk of transmission.

Early Warning and Alerts

COVID-19 determination and screening are being influenced by artificial intelligence. Out in the open, sensors that measure infrared temperatures have been used to detect fever. Nonetheless, this innovation relies on faculty to complete the filtering process [31]. Considering AI, cameras with multimodal technology have started to be employed to restrict the possibility of openness of cutting-edge employees at airports, emergency clinics, and medical services offices. These improved cameras can detect persons with elevated internal heat levels, compare appearances, and track a singular's progress. A few states have started using face recognition software so the COVID-19 outbreak can be contained. This invention makes it easier to monitor people who violate quarantine rules or to check the interior temperature of sick patients in a group. By combining facial recognition with other advances, facial recognition and AI provide unrivaled control in isolated scenarios. For example, the Find Face framework combined with CCTV cameras can continuously recognize people as AI surveys people's interpersonal relationships, working with brief reactions.

- **Changes in People Analysis:** It makes use of intricate recognition and historical data searches to gauge the likelihood of contaminated people.
- **Constant Inspection of Violations**: It distinguishes isolated people and tells specialists in the event that they are perceived on camera, regardless of whether they put on a veil or masks.
- **Following Compliance with Quarantine:** Programs that perceive outlines make it conceivable to screen people utilizing different cameras regardless of whether facial imaging is accessible or not.
- **Age Recognition**: AI is exceptionally valuable in evaluating time of life and is helpful in observing people over 60 who are advised to stay at home during the ongoing pandemic, given that there is a greater risk of COVID-19.

DISCUSSION AND APPLICATION

ML was used to handle the pandemic in a few major ways in the preceding segment. In any event, several measures have been proposed to mitigate COVID-19's negative consequences. Perhaps diagnosis is one of the AI applications in this COVID-19 situation. With the use of medical photos and voice, AI technology is currently being used to quickly diagnose diseases at a low cost. AI and machine learning [6, 32] are also being used for critical jobs in the discovery of drugs that can combat or fight the SARS-CoV-2 virus. Technology is also being used to generate effective vaccines, among many other important applications. COVID-19 outbreaks are also being differentiated, addressed, and forecasted using AI in many parts of the world.

In addition, IoT is crucial in tackling several COVID-19-related issues. For example, GPS-based wearable frameworks are utilized for contact tracking. Contact tracing is helpful because when one person contracts a disease, individuals who are exposed to that person are nearly certainly also unwell. By taking the necessary precautions, the illness can be managed. The Indian government developed the Arogya Setu app to connect medical care providers with Indian citizens and raise awareness of the COVID-19 crisis by making it simpler for those who are impacted by the virus to access treatment. A mobile application called Close Contact, which alerts users to nearby objects, has also been created in China. Additionally, the utilization of telemedicine services, like the trend in this setting, is toward virtual diagnosis or virtual consultation for clinical services. In the United States, just 11% of consumers used telemedicine services in 2019, but because of the COVID-19 pandemic, this number increased to roughly 46% in 2020 [33].

In the fight against COVID-19, many NLP strategies are used, particularly in the area of fake news identification. These methods are particularly beneficial for a variety of problems, such as sentiment analysis and text summarization, for analyzing the COVID-19 remarks.

Since the start of the epidemic, there has been a tremendous amount of research on this topic. Numerous research papers on this virus and its treatment have been published since February. A significant amount of information was acquired quickly. Unless deliberate attempts are taken to organize it, individual study groups might not be able to access this information. This issue can be resolved with knowledge graphs. Several different knowledge graphs have been developed by several scholars. A team of researchers built the pathophysiology, substantial causation-effect chain, and the COVID-19 knowledge graph based on academic research on the new COVID-19 that attempts to present a thorough understanding of its pathophysiology. The research on the COVID-19 diagnosis is shown in the table below.

DIGITAL TWINS AND PERSONALIZATION WELL-BEING

While epidemics thrive more in the developed world, humans have also developed means to fight diseases, such as vaccines. However, creating a vaccine takes a while, which is problematic when a virus appears out of nowhere. This was the situation with the COVID-19 pandemic, which likely originated from bats and spread to humans within a few months. The earliest possible identification of potential epidemics is necessary to halt their spread because, regrettably, technologies like vaccinations can occasionally be hard to come by. Today's technology combines information from a variety of sources and analyzes information utilizing outbreak models that account for the way and rate at which viruses grow among various demographics and geographical regions [34].

Different strategies can be applied to identify and determine the behaviors that enhance their exposure to viruses. Several organizations, like the Network Science Institute at North-Eastern University, are keeping an eye on the COVID pandemicusing large analytics of data and social sites. Social media is capable of being a detector, however it has a low sensitivity and resolution. A "digital twin" refers to a virtual copy of a recognizable object. While the concept originated in the industrial sector, some organizations have expanded it to create digital models of human organs in the fields of medicine and healthcare. PDTs synchronize all information sources, including electronic health records (EHRs), to deliver 360-degree health information (EHRs) [35], accessing healthcare information, patient entries, public documents, cell phones and gadgets, and the Internet of Things. PDTs can be utilized with machine learning algorithms to forecast a variety of client scenarios, identify early detection indicators for preventative measures, anticipate changes from baseline conditions, and make it possible to choose the best course of customized prescription.

The principal benefits of PDTs are summarized below [36]:

- **Alerts generated by themselves**: The cautions that are self-generated permit individuals to be more aware of a potential circumstance.
- **Broad Analytics:** Analyses conducted on a huge local area or nation assist with expecting a critical spread.
- **More clear focus**: A clearer center prompts less inescapable limitations, where there is less risk and stricter regulations in high-risk locations.
- **Reduced Costs:** Limitations that are more actively engaged have a lower monetary impact.
- **Greater Adaptability:** This technique is more original, allowing groups or individuals to adjust to specific conditions.
- **Greater Self-Awareness:** PDTs empower more prominent individual mindfulness and a brief way of behaving properly to the circumstance.
- **Faster Feedback**: PDTs consider constant or close continuous input with respect to activities taken utilizing the information assembled and shared.
- **Diminished Effort**: PDTs require lesser exertion and are a cheaper method for observing individuals.
- **Administration Development**: PDTs work with the improvement of administrations focused on tainted people by making virtual gatherings or networks.
- **Better Resource Use**: PDTs empower the productive utilization of assets, thinking about the accessibility of assets and contending needs.
- **Quicker Triage**: Individuals can get close enough to essential help benefits even more suitably through the internet.

CONCLUSION AND FUTURE SCOPE

AI technologies have been broadly utilized in medical services and will continue to so in the future. As AI and ML have been extremely fruitful at handling the different issues that emerge in the healthcare sector, they have likewise been effectively used for handling the issues emerging because of COVID-19. Despite having a great deal of advantages, there are yet many disadvantages of using AI in handling medical services issues, like inaccurate diagnosis. Even though AI frameworks are at present utilized for analysis, it is not quite as precise as a biological diagnosis.

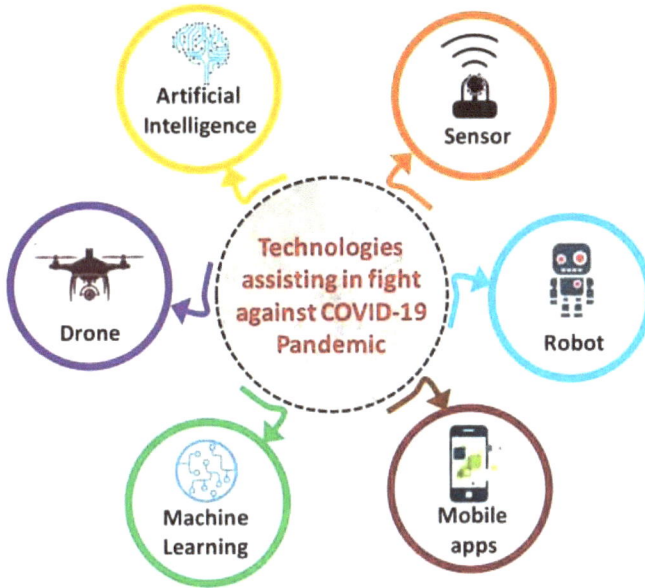

Fig. (3). Technologies assisting the fight against COVID-19 [36].

REFERENCES

[1]   A. Kumar, P.K. Gupta, and A. Srivastava, "A review of modern technologies for tackling COVID-19 pandemic", *Diabetes Metab. Syndr.,* vol. 14, no. 4, pp. 569-573, 2020.
[http://dx.doi.org/10.1016/j.dsx.2020.05.008] [PMID: 32413821]

[2]   V. Chamola, V. Hassija, V. Gupta, and M. Guizani, "A Comprehensive Review of the COVID-19 Pandemic and the Role of IoT, Drones, AI, Blockchain, and 5G in Managing its Impact", *IEEE Access,* vol. 8, pp. 90225-90265, 2020.
[http://dx.doi.org/10.1109/ACCESS.2020.2992341]

[3]   L. Wynants, "Prediction models for diagnosis and prognosis of covid-19 infection: systematic review and critical appraisal", *BMJ,* 2020.

[4]   M. Pourhomayoun, and M. Shakibi, "Predicting mortality risk in patients with COVID-19 using artificial intelligence to help medical decision-making", *medRxiv,* 2020.
[http://dx.doi.org/10.1101/2020.03.30.20047308]

[5]   S. Thapa, S. Adhikari, and S. Mishra, "Review of Text Summarization in Indian Regional Languages", *2020 International Conference on Computing Informatics & Networks (ICCIN),* 2020.

[6]   S. Tuli, S. Tuli, R. Tuli, and S.S. Gill, "Predicting the Growth and Trend of COVID-19 Pandemic using Machine Learning and Cloud Computing", *Internet of Things,* p. 100222, 2020.
[http://dx.doi.org/10.1016/j.iot.2020.100222]

[7]   N. Bansal, R. Gautam, R. Tiwari, S. Thapa, and A. Singh, "Economic Load Dispatch Using Intelligent Particle Swarm Optimization". 2021.

[8]   V. Chenthamarakshan, "Target-specific and selective drug design for covid-19 using deep generative models", *arXiv preprint arXiv,* 2020.

[9]   E. Ong, H. Wang, M.U. Wong, M. Seetharaman, N. Valdez, and Y. He, "Vaxign-ML: supervised machine learning reverse vaccinology model for improved prediction of bacterial protective antigens", *Bioinformatics,* vol. 36, no. 10, pp. 3185-3191, 2020.
[http://dx.doi.org/10.1093/bioinformatics/btaa119] [PMID: 32096826]

[10]   J. Jumper, K. Tunyasuvunakool, P. Kohli, D. Hassabis, and A. Team, "Computational predictions of protein structures associated with COVID-19", In: *DeepMind*, 2020.

[11]   R. Kumar, F. Al-Turjman, L. Anand, A. Kumar, S. Magesh, K. Vengatesan, R. Sitharthan, and M. Rajesh, "Genomic sequence analysis of lung infections using artificial intelligence technique", *Interdiscip. Sci.,* vol. 13, no. 2, pp. 192-200, 2021.
[http://dx.doi.org/10.1007/s12539-020-00414-3] [PMID: 33558984]

[12]   S.K. Nataraj, F. Al-Turjman, A.H. Adom, R. Sitharthan, M. Rajesh, and R. Kumar, "Intelligent Robotic Chair with Thought Control and Communication Aid Using Higher Order Spectra Band Features", *IEEE Sens. J.,* 2020.

[13]   S. Pradeepa, K.R. Manjula, S. Vimal, M.S. Khan, N. Chilamkurti, and A.K. Luhach, "DRFS: detecting risk factor of stroke disease from social media using machine learning techniques", *Neural Process. Lett.,* 2020.

[14]   R. Sitharthan, S. Krishnamoorthy, P. Sanjeevikumar, J.B. Holm-Nielsen, R.R. Singh, and M. Rajesh, "Torque ripple minimization of PMSM using an adaptive Elman neural networkcontrolled feedback linearization-based direct torque control strategy", *Int. Trans. Electr. Energy Syst.,* vol. 31, no. 1, p. e12685, 2021.

[15]   M. Ramamurthy, I. Krishnamurthi, S. Vimal, and Y.H. Robinson, "Deep learning based genome analysis and NGS-RNA LL identification with a novel hybrid model", *Biosystems,* vol. 197, p. 104211, 2020.
[http://dx.doi.org/10.1016/j.biosystems.2020.104211] [PMID: 32795485]

[16]   Sitharthan, R., Rajesh, M., Madurakavi, K., Raglend, J., Kumar, R., "Assessing nitrogen dioxide (NO_2) impact on health pre-and post-COVID-19 pandemic using IoT in India". *Int. J. Pervasive Comput. Commun.,* 2020.

[17]   T.K. Burki, "Coronavirus in China", *Lancet Respir. Med.,* vol. 8, no. 3, p. 238, 2020.
[http://dx.doi.org/10.1016/S2213-2600(20)30056-4] [PMID: 32027848]

[18]   W.B. Yu, G.D. Tang, L. Zhang, and R.T. Corlett, "Decoding the evolution and transmissions of the novel pneumonia coronavirus (SARS-CoV-2) using whole genomic data", *ChinaXiv,* p. 202002, 2020.
[http://dx.doi.org/10.24272/j.issn.2095-8137.2020.022]

[19]   J.F.W. Chan, S. Yuan, K.H. Kok, K.K.W. To, H. Chu, J. Yang, F. Xing, J. Liu, C.C.Y. Yip, R.W.S. Poon, H.W. Tsoi, S.K.F. Lo, K.H. Chan, V.K.M. Poon, W.M. Chan, J.D. Ip, J.P. Cai, V.C.C. Cheng, H. Chen, C.K.M. Hui, and K.Y. Yuen, "A familial cluster of pneumonia associated with the 2019 novel coronavirus indicating person-to-person transmission: a study of a family cluster", *Lancet,* vol. 395, no. 10223, pp. 514-523, 2020.
[http://dx.doi.org/10.1016/S0140-6736(20)30154-9] [PMID: 31986261]

[20]   W. Liu, Z.W. Tao, L. Wang, M.L. Yuan, K. Liu, L. Zhou, S. Wei, Y. Deng, J. Liu, H.G. Liu, M. Yang, and Y. Hu, "Analysis of factors associated with disease outcomes in hospitalized patients with 2019 novel coronavirus disease", *Chin. Med. J. (Engl.),* vol. 133, no. 9, pp. 1032-1038, 2020.
[http://dx.doi.org/10.1097/CM9.0000000000000775] [PMID: 32118640]

[21]   M. Goumenou, D. Sarigiannis, A. Tsatsakis, O. Anesti, A. Docea, D. Petrakis, D. Tsoukalas, R. Kostoff, V. Rakitskii, D. Spandidos, M. Aschner, and D. Calina, "COVID 19 in Northern Italy: An integrative overview of factors possibly influencing the sharp increase of the outbreak (Review)", *Mol. Med. Rep.,* vol. 22, no. 1, pp. 20-32, 2020.
[http://dx.doi.org/10.3892/mmr.2020.11079] [PMID: 32319647]

[22]   P. Mehta, D.F. McAuley, M. Brown, E. Sanchez, R.S. Tattersall, and J.J. Manson, "COVID-19: consider cytokine storm syndromes and immunosuppression", *Lancet,* vol. 395, no. 10229, pp. 1033-1034, 2020.
[http://dx.doi.org/10.1016/S0140-6736(20)30628-0] [PMID: 32192578]

[23]   A. Mitra, B. Deutsch, F. Ignatovich, C. Dykes, and L. Novotny, "Nano-optofluidic detection of single

viruses and nanoparticles", *ACS Nano,* vol. 4, no. 3, pp. 1305-1312, 2010.
[http://dx.doi.org/10.1021/nn901889v] [PMID: 20148575]

[24]   L. Garg, E. Chukwu, N. Nasser, C. Chakraborty, and G. Garg, "Anonymity preserving IoTbased COVID-19 and other infectious disease contact tracing model", *IEEE Access,* vol. 8, pp. 159402-159414, 2020.
[http://dx.doi.org/10.1109/ACCESS.2020.3020513] [PMID: 34786286]

[25]   R.P. Singh, M. Javaid, A. Haleem, and R. Suman, "Internet of things (IoT) applications to fight against COVID-19 pandemic", *Diabetes Metab. Syndr.,* vol. 14, no. 4, pp. 521-524, 2020.
[http://dx.doi.org/10.1016/j.dsx.2020.04.041] [PMID: 32388333]

[26]   M. Otoom, N. Otoum, M.A. Alzubaidi, Y. Etoom, and R. Banihani, "An IoT-based framework for early identification and monitoring of COVID-19 cases", *Biomed. Signal Process. Control,* vol. 62, p. 102149, 2020.
[http://dx.doi.org/10.1016/j.bspc.2020.102149] [PMID: 32834831]

[27]   A. Rahman, M.S. Hossain, N.A. Alrajeh, and F. Alsolami, "Adversarial examples–security threats to COVID-19 deep learning systems in medical IoT devices", *IEEE Internet Things J.,* vol. 8, no. 12, pp. 9603-9610, 2021.
[http://dx.doi.org/10.1109/JIOT.2020.3013710] [PMID: 36811011]

[28]   M. Ndiaye, S.S. Oyewobi, A.M. Abu-Mahfouz, G.P. Hancke, A.M. Kurien, and K. Djouani, "IoT in the wake of COVID-19: a survey on contributions challenges and evolution", *IEEE Access,* vol. 8, pp. 186821-186839, 2020.
[http://dx.doi.org/10.1109/ACCESS.2020.3030090] [PMID: 34786294]

[29]   H.N. Dai, M. Imran, and N. Haider, "Blockchain-enabled internet of medical things to combat COVID-19", *IEEE Internet of Things Magazine,* vol. 3, no. 3, pp. 52-57, 2020.
[http://dx.doi.org/10.1109/IOTM.0001.2000087]

[30]   R. Vaishya, M. Javaid, I.H. Khan, and A. Haleem, "Artificial Intelligence (AI) applications for COVID-19 pandemic", *Diabetes Metab. Syndr.,* vol. 14, no. 4, pp. 337-339, 2020.
[http://dx.doi.org/10.1016/j.dsx.2020.04.012] [PMID: 32305024]

[31]   T Devi, J.Sathya Priya, N. Deepa, "Framework for detecting the patients affected by COVID-19 at early stages using Internet of Things along with Machine Learning approaches with improved Accuracy", *Computer Communication and Informatics (ICCCI) 2022 International Conference on* pp. 1-7, 2022.

[32]   E. Mbunge, S.G. Fashoto, B. Akinnuwesi, A. Metfula, S. Simelane, and N. Ndumiso, "Ethics for integrating emerging technologies to contain COVID ☐19 in Zimbabwe", *Hum. Behav. Emerg. Technol.,* vol. 3, no. 5, pp. 876-890, 2021.
[http://dx.doi.org/10.1002/hbe2.277] [PMID: 34518816]

[33]   A. Rahman, M. Rahman, D. Kundu, M.R. Karim, S.S. Band, and M. Sookhak, "Study on IoT for SARS-CoV-2 with healthcare: present and future perspective", *Math. Biosci. Eng.,* vol. 18, no. 6, pp. 9697-9726, 2021.
[http://dx.doi.org/10.3934/mbe.2021475] [PMID: 34814364]

[34]   V. Kumar, A. Ghimire, and H.K. Hoon, "Machine Learning and IoT based solutions for detection of arrhythmia using ECG signals", *Trends in Electronics and Informatics (ICOEI) 2021 5th International Conference on,,* pp. 477-484, 2021.
[http://dx.doi.org/10.1109/ICOEI51242.2021.9452907]

[35]   N. Peiffer-Smadja, T.M. Rawson, R. Ahmad, A. Buchard, G. Pantelis, F-X. Lescure, G. Birgand, and A.H. Holmes, "Machine learning for clinical decision support in infectious diseases: a narrative review of current applications", *Clin. Microbiol. Infect.,* 2019.
[PMID: 31539636]

[36]   P. Kumar, R. Chaudhary, A. Aggarwal, P. Singh, and R. Tomar, Improving Medical Image Segmentation Techniques Using Multiphase Level Set Approach *Via* Bias Correction., *Int. J. Eng.*

Adv. Technol., 2012.

[37] S. Singh, S.K. Jangir, M. Kumar, M. Verma, S. Kumar, T.S. Walia, and S.M.M. Kamal, "Feature Importance Score☐Based Functional Link Artificial Neural Networks for Breast Cancer Classification", *BioMed Res. Int.,* vol. 2022, no. 1, p. 2696916, 2022.
[http://dx.doi.org/10.1155/2022/2696916] [PMID: 35411308]

CHAPTER 10

Deep Learning and IoT Revolutionizing Transportation Management: A Study on Smart Transportation

Inder Singh[1,*]

[1] *School of Computer Science, UPES, Uttarakhand, India*

Abstract: In our day-to-day life, we often refer to transportation as the movement of products or people from one place to another . On the other hand, management is all about controlling resources required by transportation to achieve desired objectives and goals. Transportation management plays a critical role for an individual and company. Applications for transportation management are becoming smarter as a result of the development of technologies like the Internet of Things (IoT), and connected devices are enabling their exploitation in all spheres. Hence, with the use of these technologies, the volume of data is also increasing many-fold. There are many techniques, such as machine learning (ML), deep learning (DL), and artificial intelligence (AI), that can be applied to collected data to get insights into the data and further enhance the capabilities and intelligence of the applications. Nowadays, transportation management is more efficient with the use of both deep learning and Internet of Things techniques.

Keywords: AI, DL, ML, Transportation management.

INTRODUCTION

Nowadays, deep learning and IoT play a pivotal role in improving the effectiveness and efficiency of transportation management. There are numerous research studies in these areas, which state that with the use of deep learning techniques, organizations can improve their capabilities and the intelligence of the applications. With the help of deep learning based applications, travelers can obtain appropriate and precise traffic information that allows them to acquire suitable traveling paths, traveling modes, departure times, *etc.* With the integration of IoT, we can optimize the performance of traffic. Based on the current scenario, we may assume that, by using IoT technologies and devices, we

---

[*] **Corresponding author Inder Singh:** School of Computer Science, UPES, Uttarakhand, India;
E-mail: inderddn@gmail.com

can enhance the benefits of transportation systems. The problems of the transportation systems, such as traffic congestion, route optimization problems, pollution, security, and problems with optimal use of fuel, are not only related to individual countries, but they are global problems. In this chapter, we started our discussion on the role of transportation in the growth of GDP, challenges of traditional transportation management, deep learning models and applications in smart transportation, and IoT enabled applications in smart transportation.

Role of Transportation in GDP growth

The automobile industry is a major contributor to India's GDP growth. Its contribution to GDP growth was 6.7 percent in 2016 and is predicted to rise to 12 percent by 2026. This industry will become one of the most important contributors to job creation. According to the Automotive Mission Plan, this sector was predicted to provide 10 million employments by 2022 (Source: Automotive Sector Skill Council, National Skill Development Corporation). According to World Bank data from 2014, 32 percent of the population lives in urban areas, which is predicted to rise to 40 percent by 2030, contributing up to 75 percent of GDP (Smart Transportation - transforming Indian cities, 2016).

Challenges of Traditional Transportation Management

There are so many challenges in transportation management. This may be due to not choosing the optimized route or problems in tracking the consignments.

Route Optimization Problem

Inefficiency of route management directly affects the delivery time of the order. It not only affects the delay in the delivery of the order but is also subject to vehicles stuck in traffic congestion and high maintenance costs of the vehicle.

Consignments Tracking Problem

The inability to track a consignment may be another problem due to traditional call-based tracking methods. One must organize a dedicated team to make multiple calls for consignment tracking.

Increase in Transportation Cost

Transportation cost is another key factor in transportation management. It is really a big challenge to manage or optimize the cost of transportation. There are many problems with the manual management of the transportation processes. The effect of manual transportation management increases the cost of transportation management due to the requirement of more workforce, delay in delivery, and not using the vehicle's capacity completely.

Intelligent Transportation System Framework and its Applications

Understanding the foundation of intelligent transportation system (ITS) applications allows us to identify the various data components of ITS more clearly. The ITS platform provides a framework for planning, defining, and implementing various ITS applications. The ITS architecture describes how data and information move through the system and the services it provides [1].

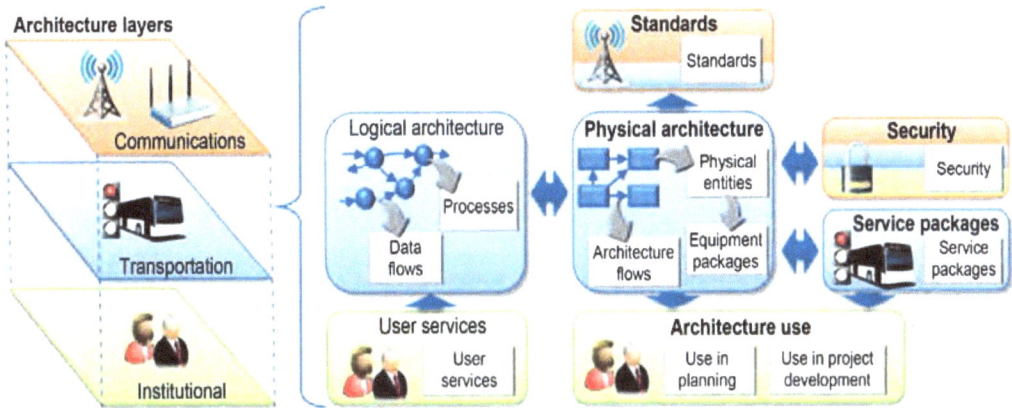

Fig. (1). Different components of ITS architecture [1].

In an ITS architecture, user services specify what the system is expected to perform. There are different components of ITS architecture.

- User services.
- User service requirements.
- Logical architecture.
- Physical architecture.
- Service packages.
- Security.
- Standards.

User services

User services are the building block that specify what the system is expected to perform. These services are portrayed from the eyes of stakeholders and users. There are several user services, and these are categorized into the following different groups:

1. Traffic and travel management.
2. Management of public transportation.
3. e-payment.
4. Operations of commercial vehicles.
5. Emergency management.
6. Modern vehicle safety systems.
7. Management of information.
8. Construction and maintenance operations.

Models of Deep Learning

There are several deep learning models.

Convolutional Neural Networks (CNN)

There are many architectures of deep learning techniques; CNN is one of the most popular architectures. There is immense use of the CNN technique in image processing applications. CNN is made up of three types of layers: convolutional, pooling, and fully connected. In each CNN, the training process is divided into two stages: feed-forward and back-propagation. There are several popular architectures of CNN; the most common are ResNet, ZFNet, VGGNet, AlexNet, and GoogLeNet. However, the primary use of CNN is in image processing applications, but there are some other application domains that also use CNN, *e.g.*, remote sensing, energy, electronics systems, computational mechanics, *etc.* Some of the application areas of CNN are condition monitoring of wind turbines, motion estimation and correction of medical imaging, prediction of aerodynamic flow, crop yield prediction, and advanced image processing [2].

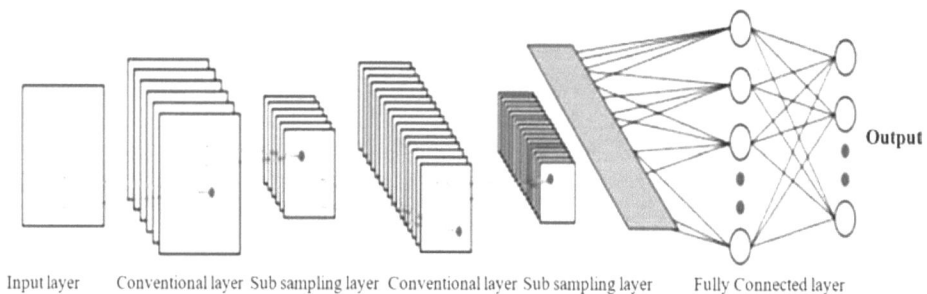

Input layer   Conventional layer Sub sampling layer Conventional layer Sub sampling layer   Fully Connected layer

Fig. (2). CNN architecture [2].

Recurrent Neural Networks (RNN)

RNN is a robust and powerful neural network. RNNs are designed in such a manner that we can utilize them in processing patterns and sequences such as speech, text, handwriting, and other such types of applications. RNNs are often used in NLP tasks because they are very efficient in text handling.

Applications of RNN are wind speed prediction, tropical cyclone intensity prediction, music genre recognition, ship trajectory restoration, and stock price trends [2].

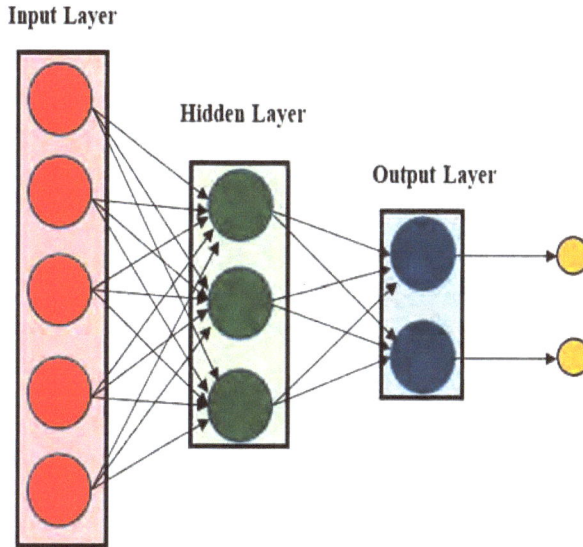

Fig. (3). Recurrent Neural Networks (RNN) architecture.

There are different types of RNN such as One to One, One to Many, Many to One, Many to Many.

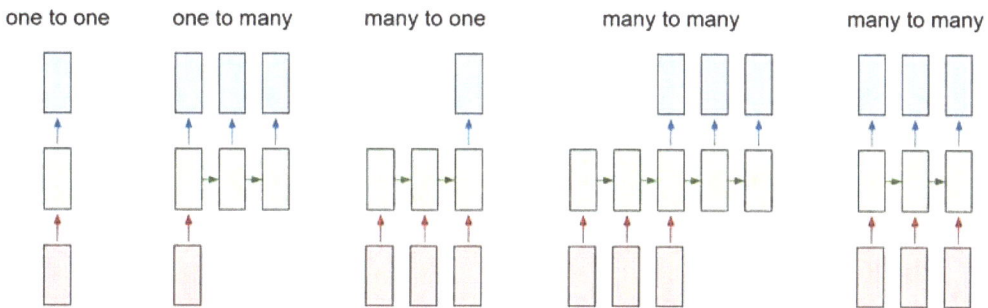

Fig. (4). Types of RNNs (Source [3]:).

Autoencoders (AE)

Autoencoders are feedforward neural networks with identical input and output values. They are made up of three parts: encoder, code, and decoder. They compresses the input values to the code with the encoder and decompresses the code with the decoder back to the input values.

Some of the applications of autoencoders are improving cyber-physical systems, electric load forecasting, laser-based scan registration, collaborative filtering, noisy image classification, and robust speaker verification [2].

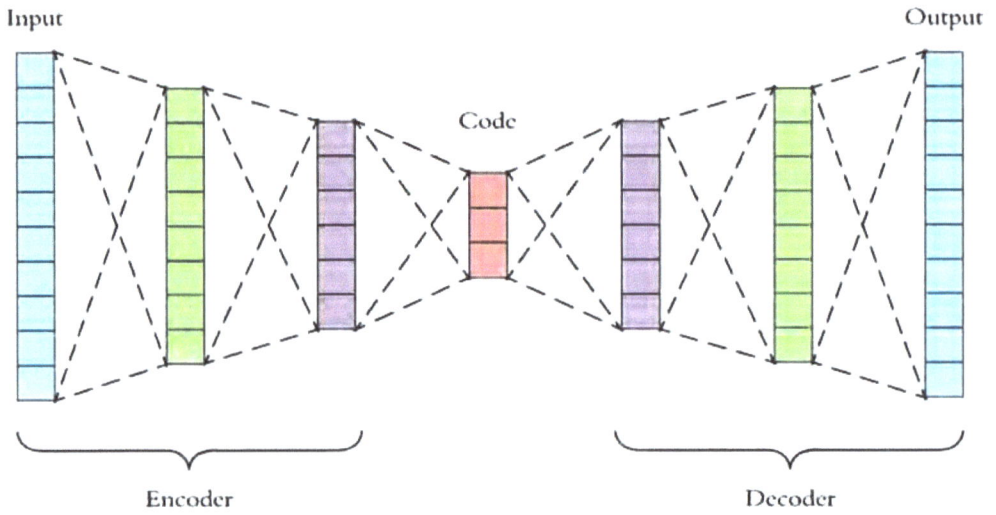

Fig. (5). Autoencoders (AE) (Arden Dertat, 2017) [10].

Long Short-Term Memory (LSTM)

For a very long time, there have been many problems in sequence prediction. It is considered one of the most difficult problems to solve. There are many problems, such as finding the patterns in the stock market's dataset, predicting sales, recognizing your way of speaking, and predicting your next word on a mobile phone's keyboard. For the given problems of sequencing, LSTMs are considered to provide the most effective solutions in the problem areas.

There are some limitations of the RNN, which can be resolved by using LSTMs. LSTM is made up of memory chunks known as cells. It moves two states to the next cell: the cell state and the hidden state. The primary function of memory blocks is to remember things. There are three mechanisms that can be used to manipulate memory, called gates (forget gate, input gate, and output gate) [4].

A few of the notable applications of LSTM are solar radiation forecasting, volatility forecasting, air quality prediction, structural seismic prediction, time series prediction, wind turbine power prediction, and earthquake trend prediction [2].

Deep Reinforcement Learning (DRL)

Deep reinforcement learning combines deep learning with reinforcement learning. DRL can solve more complex real-world decision-making problems that could not be solved by previously available machine learning algorithms. To handle unstructured data, deep learning is one of the most effective tools. It can discover patterns from a large dataset pool. It may not always be considered the best tool for the entire real time decision-making problems, but it is more efficient in many aspects [5].

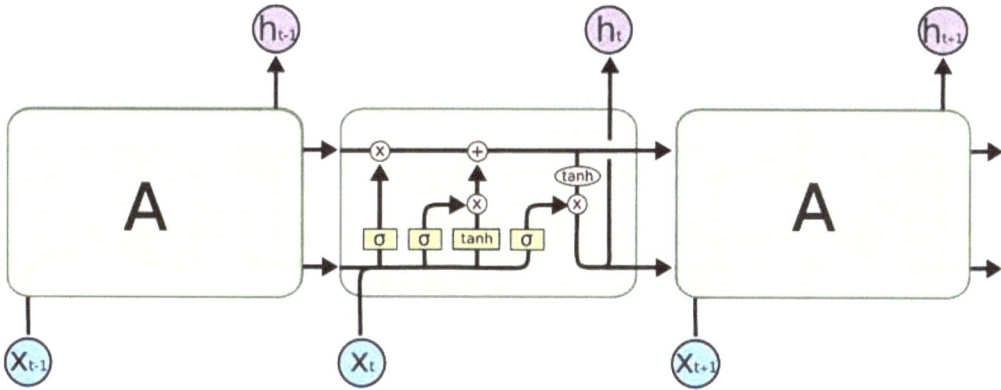

Fig. (6). Long Short-Term Memory (LSTM) (Olah, 2015) [11].

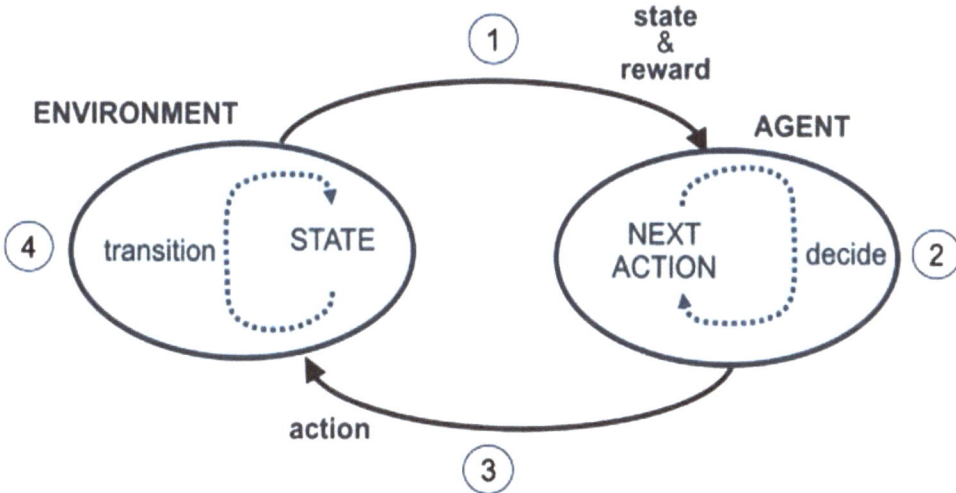

Fig. (7). Reinforcement learning cycle (TORRES.AI, 2020) [12].

Applications of Deep Learning in Smart Transportation

There are several deep learning applications in smart transportation. In this part, we addressed several deep learning applications in smart transportation. When compared to typical machine learning approaches, deep learning techniques give more efficient and optimum solutions [6, 7] (Table **1**). Several studies explained many deep learning applications for smart transportation.

Prediction of Traffic characteristics

One of the most significant deep learning applications in transportation is traffic characteristics prediction. Traffic management agencies may control traffic more efficiently by using information on traffic characteristics. Information about traffic dynamics assists drivers in making wise route choices. Among the noteworthy features that may be predicted using the traffic characteristics prediction program are traffic flow, traffic speed, and journey time.

Presumption of Traffic Incidents

Using applications for estimating traffic accidents can help traffic management authorities reduce the risk of incidents in hazardous areas and traffic congestion. The major purpose of this application, however, is not only to estimate traffic incident risk for a location/area but also to identify incidents based on traffic parameters.

Identification of Vehicle

We know that each vehicle's license plate is unique; the first step in re-identification (Re-ID) is to recognize them. The vehicle identification application can extract distinguishing features such as the color and model of the vehicle and distinguish similar plates.

Timing of Traffic signal

One of the most difficult tasks in the transportation arena is optimizing signal light time for optimal performance. To solve this optimization challenge, several analytical models employ mathematical approaches. Deep learning models may be used to get the optimal traffic signal timing.

Public Transportation and Ridesharing

Passengers utilize public transit to go around cities. To increase urban planning performance as well as passenger satisfaction, the nature of the deep neural network has equipped companies with increasingly optimal routing maps that take into account data such as passenger demand for a specific type of travel at specific locations and times. Companies that use deep learning techniques can produce more accurate forecasts than those that use standard machine learning approaches.

Visual Recognition Tasks

One of the most prominent deep learning applications in the realm of intelligent transportation systems is nonintrusive recognition and detection systems, such as camera-image-based systems.

Traffic Flow Forecasting

In data analytics and transportation modeling, traffic is a highly generic problem. The primary goal of traffic flow prediction is to predict the future number of cars on a road segment during a certain time interval. Due to shallow architecture, many methods have not been able to achieve desirable outputs.

Traffic Signal Control

In the modern transportation system, one of the biggest problems is traffic congestion. One solution to overcome traffic congestion is to extend the road infrastructure, but it is very time-consuming and expensive and not feasible for established cities. The other option is to increase the efficiency of transportation management systems (*i.e.*, Traffic Signal control (TCS)), which can optimize the flow of vehicles in order to reduce congestion.

Prediction of Travel Demand

The aim of travel demand prediction is to find out the future users who will utilize public transportation and the number of roads. Most of the studies on travel demand prediction were not related to passenger demand; instead, they used passenger demand as an input.

Autonomous Driving

There are several deep learning applications in computer vision nowadays. Autonomous driving has a strong relationship with image and video processing. The existing deep learning model is able to predict vehicle and lane detection.

IoT Technologies and Applications in Smart Transportation

IoT is a system that connects real-world objects, attaches sensors and actuators to these objects, and connects them to the Internet *via* wireless and wired network infrastructure. It uses different types of connecting devices and technologies such as ZigBee, Wi-Fi, Bluetooth, RFID, GPRS, GSM, 4G, LTE, *etc.* It allows the users to share the information between them and between things. There are many applications of the Internet of Things in the areas of smart cities, smart homes & buildings, smart healthcare, and waste management and monitoring [8].

Suitable traveling paths, traveling modes, and departure times are the crucial success factors of intelligent transportation systems, which can be obtained from precise and appropriate traffic data. The rapidly increasing rate of fuel consumption and pollution due to the growing number of vehicles is also a key factor in traffic congestion. The rapid growth of technology helps to explore and solve traffic issues (Varun Chand and Karthikeyan, 2018). Embedding the sensors and actuators to the vehicles or other mobile devices can help suggest optimized routes and easy parking reservations. It also helps in autonomous driving [9].

The economic growth of any country depends on many factors, and development in the transportation sector is one of them. Nowadays, there are a huge number of applications available to make transportation smarter. Road condition monitoring and alert application is one of the highly utilized applications [8]. Smart transportation works on the following core pillars:

- Vehicle connectivity: For the efficient utilization of the Internet of Vehicles, it is mandatory that vehicles must be connected properly.
- Transportation analytics: Companies/organizations can utilize transportation analytics for anomaly detection and demand prediction.
- Transportation control: Transportation management or transportation control is the key factor in analyzing the best route and controlling the speed of the vehicles.

There are many aspects of smart transportation. The following figure [8] demonstrates one of the aspects of smart transportation.

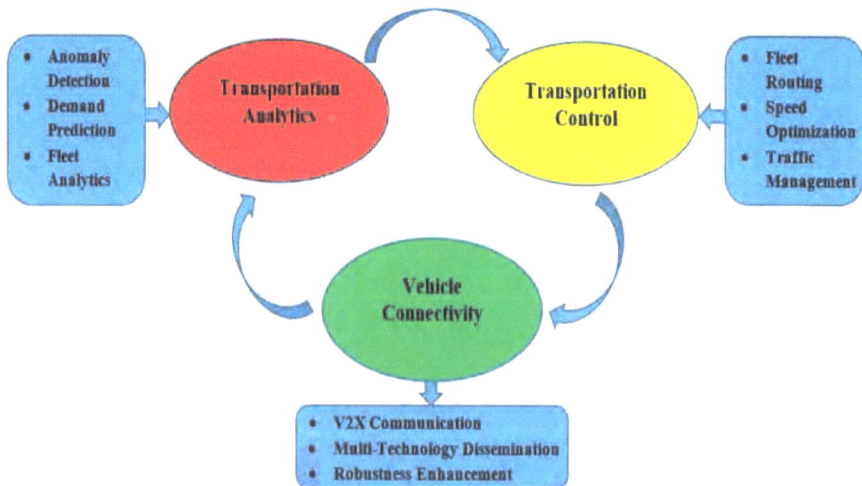

Fig. (8). Smart Transportation Aspects [8].

Use of IoT technologies in Smart Transportation

Many cutting-edge IoT-based technologies are now accessible to give a multitude of digital devices with a variety of sensing, actuating, and computing capabilities. They provide novel services in many areas *e.g.*, smart cities, smart transportation, *etc.* These services are reshaping cities by enhancing infrastructure and transportation systems, decreasing traffic congestion, managing waste, and boosting human life quality [8]. A study designed a traffic model for an IoT-based smart city, demonstrating the utilization of IoT devices and their applications in smart transportation.

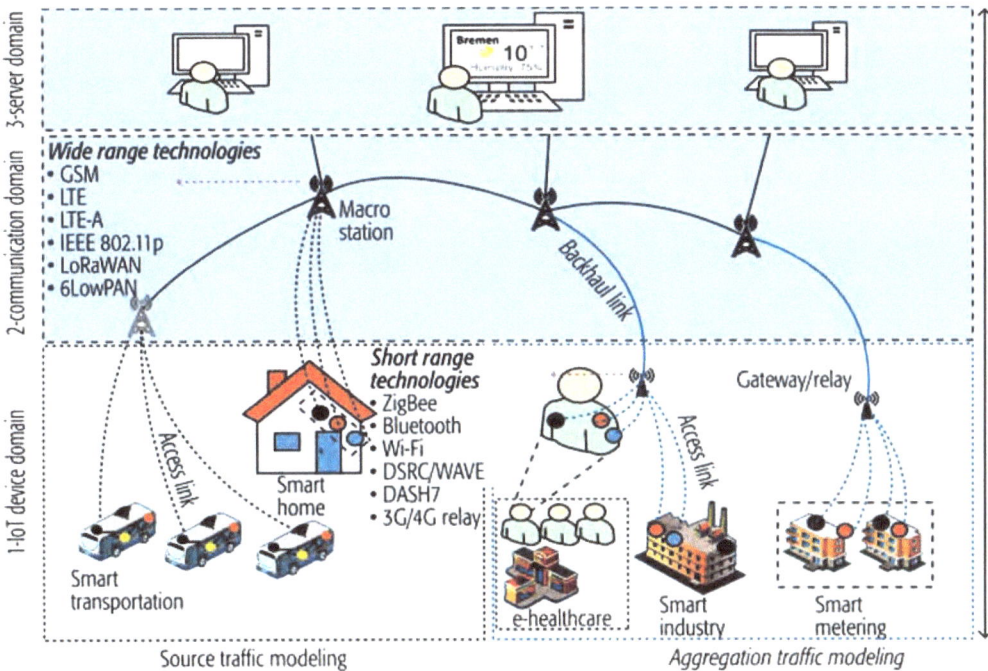

Fig. (9). Traffic model for an IoT-powered smart city [8].

Edge Computing devices used for deep learning

Intelligent decision-making can be achieved in one of two ways: cloud computing-based or edge computing-based. We can deliver cloud computing services *via* the internet; on the other hand, edge computing can be performed at the edge of the network. There are several advantages of the edge Computing approach over the cloud computing approach, such as fast and efficient decision-making and decreased data transfer costs. Edge computing is gaining popularity in the field of deep learning as well. There are many popular devices used for deep learning.

Table 1. Popular Deep Learning Edge Computing Devices Source [6]:

Specification	Jetson Xavier	Jetson TX2	Jetson Nano	Raspberry Pi 3 B+
GPU	512-core Volta GPU with 64 Tensor Cores	NVIDIA Pascal, 256 CUDA Cores	128-core Maxwell	Broadcom VideoCore IV
CPU	Octal-core NVIDIA Carmel ARMv8.2 CPU @ 2.26 GHz	HMP Dual Denver 2 + Quad ARM Cortex-A57/2 MB L2	Quad-core ARM A57 @ 1.43 GHz	Quad-core ARM Cortex-A53 @ 1.2 GHz
Memory	16 GB 256-bit LPDDR4 137 GB/s	8 GB 128-bit LPDDR4 59.7 GB/s	4 GB 64-bit LPDDR4 25.6 GB/s	1 GB LPDDR2 (900 MHz)
Display	3 × eDP 1.4, DP 1.2, HDMI 2.0	2 × DSI, 2 × DP 1.2, HDMI 2.0, eDP 1.4	HDMI 2.0, eDP 1.4	HDMI, DSI
Data Storage	32 GB eMMC 5.1	32 GB eMMC, SDIO, SATA	microSD	microSD
USB	USB-C	USB 3, USB 2	USB 3, USB 2	USB 2
Connectivity	1 Gigabit Ethernet	1 Gigabit Ethernet, 802.11ac WLAN, Bluetooth	Gigabit Ethernet	100 Base Ethernet, 2.4GHz 802.11n wireless
Mechanical	105 mm × 105 mm	50 mm × 87 mm	100 mm × 80 mm	56.5 mm × 85.60 mm
Power	10 W, 15 W, 30 W	7.5 W	5–10 W	5 W

CONCLUSION

The role of transportation management is crucial for both individuals and companies. The emergence of technologies like the Internet of Things (IoT) has led to improved applications for transportation management, and connected devices are making it possible to use these applications across industries. As a result, the amount of data being used is also growing exponentially with the adoption of these technologies. Numerous methodologies, including machine learning (ML), deep learning (DL), and artificial intelligence (AI), can be employed to analyze gathered data in order to gain valuable insights and augment the functionality and intelligence of the applications. Today's deep learning and Internet of Things approaches are making transportation management more effective.

REFERENCES

[1]   S.M. Khan, "Characteristics of Intelligent Transportation Systems and Its Relationship With Data Analytics, Data Analytics for Intelligent Transportation Systems", *Elsevier Inc.,* 2017. [http://dx.doi.org/10.1016/B978-0-12-809715-1.00001-8]

[2]   A. Mosavi, S. Ardabili, and A.R. Várkonyi-Kóczy, "List of Deep Learning Models", *Lecture Notes in*

Networks and Systems, vol. 101, pp. 202-214, 2020.
[http://dx.doi.org/10.1007/978-3-030-36841-8_20]

[3]　　A. Karpathy, *The Unreasonable Effectiveness of Recurrent Neural Networks.,* 2015.
http://karpathy.github.io/2015/05/21/rnn-effectiveness/

[4]　　P. Srivastava, *Essentials of Deep Learning : Introduction to Long Short Term Memory.,* 2017.
https://www.analyticsvidhya.com/blog/2017/12/fundamentals-of-deep-learning-introduction-to-lstm/

[5]　　https://towardsdatascience.com/drl-01-a-gentle-introduction-to-deep-reinforcement--earning-405b79866bf4

[6]　　A. K. Haghighat, *Applications of Deep Learning in Intelligent Transportation Systems, Journal of Big Data Analytics in Transportation.,* 2020.
[http://dx.doi.org/10.1007/s42421-020-00020-1]

[7]　　H. Nguyen, L-M. Kieu, T. Wen, and C. Cai, "Deep learning methods in transportation domain: a review", *IET Intell. Transp. Syst.,* vol. 12, no. 9, pp. 998-1004, 2018.
[http://dx.doi.org/10.1049/iet-its.2018.0064]

[8]　　Z.K.A. Mohammed, and E.S.A. Ahmed, "World Scientific News WSN", *World Sci. News,* vol. 67, no. 2, pp. 126-148, 2017. http://yadda.icm.edu.pl/yadda/element/bwmeta1.element. psjd-b638cb4d-d6-f-4f4c-afa5-ad309a7c4838%0Ahttps://www.infona.pl/resource/bwmeta1.element.psjd-8c8e-b68-9180-4879-85d8-a7870d5644e9

[9]　　F. Zantalis, G. Koulouras, S. Karabetsos, and D. Kandris, "A review of machine learning and IoT in smart transportation", *Future Internet,* vol. 11, no. 4, p. 94, 2019.
[http://dx.doi.org/10.3390/fi11040094]

[10]　Dertat, A, "Applied deep learning-part 3: Autoencoders", *Towards data science,* vol. 3, p. 10, 2017.

[11]　Olah, C. Understanding lstm networks. 2015.

[12]　Chaturvedi, T., Torres, A. I., Stephanopoulos, G., Thomsen, M. H., & Schmidt, J. E, "Developing process designs for biorefineries—Definitions, categories, and unit operations", *Energies,* vol. 13, no. 6, p. 1493, 2020.

Current Progression of IIoT Using Machine Learning

CHAPTER 11

Machine Learning in the Healthcare Sector

Arjun Arora[1,*] and **Swati Sharma**[1]

[1] *Cybernetics Cluster, School of Computer Science, University of Petroleum and Energy Studies, Dehradun, India*

Abstract: The healthcare sector caters to millions of people and makes a significant contribution to the local economy. The inclusion of artificial intelligence and machine learning in healthcare is not only benefiting society but also overcoming various challenges associated with it. Artificial intelligence is a branch of computer science that is used to induce human-like intelligence into machines. Machine learning is a subset of artificial intelligence that makes machines capable of learning and giving the desired conclusions without explicit programming and human support. Machine learning in the healthcare sector is making huge advancements and yielding positive results. The increasing applications of machine learning have earned it a valuable spot in the healthcare sector. From specialized robots in hospitals to automated software for disease prediction and detection, machine learning is taking over almost all areas of healthcare with the aim of reducing the workload of medical experts and also delivering services to individuals at home with cost-effective solutions. With the advancement of technology, the introduction of portable systems has led to the availability of enormous amounts of medical data, which is difficult to analyze by human experts because it takes a lot of time, effort, and analytical costs. Machines are better in speed, endurance, and pattern identification as compared to humans. With the introduction of machine learning in healthcare, the task of managing massive data has become easier as automated machine learning models not only help in data analysis but are also capable of detecting underlying data patterns that may be difficult for clinical experts to come across. Machine learning can ease the task of identifying and detecting various diseases by providing complex algorithms such as Artificial Neural Networks (ANNs). With the introduction of neural networks, the analysis can be done on various data parameters given their ability to self-learn, memorize, and provide quality treatment. Machine learning not just focuses on the physical well-being of an individual but also their mental health by coming up with artificial-intelligence-based mood trackers and self-assessing applications for stress diagnosis. One of the major applications of machine learning is to detect and identify dangerous diseases, such as diabetes and cancer, that are difficult to detect at the initial stage and are detected at subsequent stages when it is too late. The use of early detection systems can save many lives by providing timely treatment of patients. Another important application of machine learning in the healthcare field is the introduction of bionic microchips. The

* **Corresponding author Arjun Arora:** Cybernetics Cluster, School of Computer Science, University of Petroleum and Energy Studies, Dehradun, India; E-mail: a.arora@ddn.upes.ac.in

Sunil Kumar, Silky Goel, Gaytri Bakshi, Siddharth Gupta & Sayed M. El-kenawy (Eds.)

fusion of bionics and machine learning will bring a revolutionary change in the healthcare sector. One such example is implanting bionic chips in the brain to monitor brain activity for the identification of neurological disorders like epilepsy. The AI-enabled bionic hand uses a man-machine interface to interpret the patient's intent and send the commands to the artificial limb, thus helping the patient make more natural movements and controlling the prosthetics more precisely. There is a tremendous use of machine learning and artificial intelligence in providing customized solutions to patients, as one solution does not cater to many patients. Therefore, customized solutions according to their medical history are a feasible choice. Machine learning plays an enormous role in drug discovery by improving decision-making in pharmaceutical data through high-quality data. It provides immediate assistance to the patients using the healthcare chatbot systems that suggest immediate solutions to them. There is no area left in the healthcare industry of which machine learning is not a part. Machine learning in the healthcare industry can yield efficient and timely results without any human intelligence. This is just the beginning. Machine learning in healthcare has a bright future that will revolutionize the field of medicine and healthcare.

Keywords: Healthcare, IoT, ML.

INTRODUCTION

Artificial intelligence is a budding technology. There is no area left where artificial intelligence has not earned a valuable spot. One such sector is healthcare, where artificial intelligence is yielding promising results. Artificial intelligence imparts human-like thinking ability to a machine to accomplish a particular task. Machine learning is an emerging trend in the healthcare industry [1]. Machine learning is the branch of artificial intelligence that gives a machine the ability to think, identify patterns, and make decisions without any kind of explicit programming and human intervention [2]. As technology is advancing day by day, the complexity of machine learning algorithms is gradually increasing, resulting in the fast processing of complex and high dimensional data. With the introduction of machine learning algorithms such as neural networks, complex automated models can be created for detecting data patterns and also certain hidden data patterns that may not be identified by clinical experts. The inclusion of artificial intelligence in the healthcare sector is to analyze and make deductions by identifying the underlying patterns in the clinical data. With the advent of technology, the demand for portable systems to monitor a patient's health has increased, resulting in a massive collection of medical data. This huge clinical data is very difficult to be analyzed by clinical experts, and a lot of human effort and analytical costs are involved to give a clear deduction. To simplify the task of data analysis and decision-making, the role of machine learning is enormous as with its ability to learn from the data and detect the patterns, automated machine learning models can predict and diagnose several disorders, thus helping the clinical experts by reducing their workload and also giving the benefit of cost-effectiveness. The introduction of artificial intelligence in healthcare is helping to enable the human task for a better digital future. There are various applications of AI and ML in the healthcare sector for revolutionizing the services given to patients and assisting the team in performing their tasks with better precision. The whole idea of involving machine learning in different sectors is to balance the workload efficiently and have automated algorithms assign tasks that can cut off the redundant methodologies originally performed by human experts. This time can be saved by clinical experts for further research and innovation, while processing and analyzing tasks can be effectively done by automated machine learning models. This load balancing will not only help save an ample amount of time but also save a lot of computation and analytical costs. The shift of machine learning technologies over the cloud has made it more flexible to provide powerful functionality for data analysis and decision making. Artificial intelligence is not just enhancing the physical well-being of an individual but is also focusing on mental well-being [3]. The rapid increase in healthcare-based chatbots and AI-based applications for monitoring stress and helping with anxiety control has seen a drastic shift in people wanting to get services in this field. Due to the portability and flexibility of these systems, people have become more confident in seeking remedies for issues such as anxiety and stress instead of personally visiting centers for medications from clinical experts. A broad range of applications has made machine learning an integral part of the healthcare industry, and its consistent growth in medical research and analysis will not only digitize trends but also shape the future.

CHALLENGES FACED BY THE HEALTHCARE SECTOR

The health sector faces several challenges using traditional methods of analysis and clinical decision-making. Many areas do not have proper medical services for the patients or the services burn a hole in the pocket and make it difficult for the people to avail medical services at a nominal cost. Many a time, diagnosis of diseases at later stages makes it too late for treatment or medication to cure them. The challenges faced by the healthcare sector [4, 5] without the involvement of artificial intelligence and machine learning are as follows:

Massive Clinical Data

As society becomes more and more digital, the amount of data generated and collected increases and accelerates significantly. There is a huge availability of clinical data for detection, prediction, and diagnosis, such as medical images, wearable device data, electronic health records, *etc.* Analyzing this ever-expanding data becomes a challenge, and it is time-consuming for clinical experts to go through every piece of data and make deductions. There are several underlying data patterns that may not be detected by them.

Cost

Another challenge faced by the healthcare sector is the cost. Huge data processing and analysis incur large analytical costs for the medical experts and the team. It may not be feasible for many patients to avail the services and bear the expense.

Disease Diagnosis at a Later Stage

Diseases such as diabetes and cancer do not show symptoms at the initial stages. At subsequent stages, it becomes too late for any kind of treatment or medical assistance. As new diseases are emerging every now and then, they have similar symptoms that make people use home remedies instead of getting proper diagnosis and treatment. This tends to cause severe future consequences and complications [6].

In-time Assistance

Many a time, due to the unavailability of a medical expert, the patients are unable to get an in-time solution to their problem. In the worst-case scenarios, it can even be a risk to their lives.

Monitoring patient's health

In critical cases such as monitoring a patient's health in Intensive Care Units (ICU), it is very important to monitor a patient's activity at regular intervals of time. Individually keeping track of the patient's activity can be difficult for analysis by the clinical team.

Clinical Trials for Drug Discovery and Development

In order to develop a new drug or to enhance a particular drug, a lot of clinical trials are performed in order to measure the effectiveness of the drug. These clinical trials consume a lot of time and, many times, may not be successful even after spending so much time on them. Also, clinical trials require suitable people who are fit for them. Analyzing the right set of candidates for clinical trials is also a challenge.

Contagious Diseases Pose a Threat to Human Life

Contagious diseases such as COVID-19 spread rapidly from one person to another, infecting masses and, in severe cases, requiring immediate medical help and posing a threat to life. The pandemic took the lives of millions of people, including front-line workers such as the medical staff, social workers, *etc.*, making it difficult to treat people in time without catching the virus themselves. The front-line workers attending COVID cases were themselves a hub for transferring the virus to the masses due to its highly contagious nature [7].

TURNING CHALLENGES FACED BY THE HEALTHCARE SECTOR INTO OPPORTUNITIES USING MACHINE LEARNING

With the inclusion of machine learning in the healthcare sector, these challenges are opportunities for machine learning-based models for automatic decision-making. A lot of research studies are being conducted and yielding promising results for the detection and diagnosis of various disorders. Complex machine learning algorithms such as artificial neural networks are capable of processing high dimensional unsupervised data, learning from the data patterns, and making predictions. Feature extraction algorithms are helpful in identifying the important parameters for making efficient predictions, thus reducing the dimensionality of data and focusing only on the important parameters that are required for making the prediction. Machine learning will not only overcome these challenges but will also be responsible for a major breakthrough in the healthcare sector. Some of the challenges that can be overcome and be applied in the real world are as follows:

Processing massive Clinical Data

The problem of processing this huge medical data can be solved using machine learning models that have the capability to learn from the massive data of patients as well as from the recommendations given to them by the clinical experts, thus improving the efficiency of data-driven decision-making and diagnosis and obtaining insights from the deductions. With automated machine learning models, this huge data can be analyzed by them, and by learning the data patterns of the patients as well as the clinical experts, a major task will be automated instead of manual labor. This grants more time to the medical team for important cognitive activities rather than performing mundane processing tasks. These machine learning models will assist the medical team in processing complex medical data that may be associated with rare disorders. Not just analyzing clinical data but also keeping records of patients as they visit the doctor can be automated using natural language processing models that can analyze speech and record the data, thus saving the time for the doctor for manual record-keeping and focusing more on the patient's problem.

Cost-efficient Solutions

With the help of automated machine learning models, this cost can definitely be reduced to a great extent and will help the patients to avail healthcare services at a nominal cost. By analyzing the patient's medical history, the right treatment can be provided instead of observing the effect of a particular medicine to judge the recovery rate over a specific period of time. This can reduce the cost of treatment to a greater extent as it will be effective in analyzing if a patient is allergic to any medicine and reducing the chances of side effects from the medicines. The machine learning models will also help in automating the processing tasks without the need to visit the clinical experts time and again to analyze the medical records, thus saving time and visiting expenses [8].

Early Identification and Prediction of Diseases

Dangerous diseases such as diabetes and cancer have been the major causes of the death of millions of people all over the world. Various dangerous diseases may show symptoms at an early stage, but some diseases do not show any danger flags at the initial stages and get identified at the subsequent stages, where it becomes very difficult to cure and give timely treatment. A lot of research is going on to predict dangerous diseases at an early stage so that proper and timely treatment can be provided to the patients, millions of lives can be saved, and the death rate from these diseases can be controlled. With the help of machine learning models and clinical data, they can identify the suspicious segments indicating a disorder. This is also beneficial as minor changes in the clinical data may not be identified, or noise can be wrongly identified as a suspicious disorder segment. With the help of machine learning algorithms, pre-processing of clinical data can be done efficiently, and pattern detection can be achieved with higher accuracy, thus detecting the diseases at an early stage.

Timely Assistance Using Machine Learning

With the help of various applications and healthcare chatbots, timely assistance can be provided to patients in person as well as online. Healthcare applications can analyze data patterns using a questionnaire and give patients various options to connect with different clinical experts based on the domain, whether online or offline. For minor issues, the healthcare applications can give suggestions for quick remedies that can be done without the presence of an expert or that can prevent any further damage to the health until help arrives. As the technology is increasing, data in various forms, such as images and EEG data, can also be fed as input, and based on the problem, automated models can give immediate assistance.

Monitoring Patient's Health

In ICUs, continuous monitoring of patients is of high priority. With the help of machine learning, automated models can monitor a patient's activity. This will be of great help to the medical team to simultaneously monitor the health of multiple patients at a time using artificial intelligence and machine learning. Real-time health monitoring is especially beneficial in the case of long-term monitoring of the recovery rate for a patient's health using real-time data and portable medical equipment. These models will monitor the patient's health and also notify the medical team in case of an emergency by sending an urgent alarm for immediate help. Smart healthcare systems are beneficial for at-home continuous monitoring of a patient or an elderly person. Not only this, automated models are helpful for people who are unable to visit a doctor for their routine check-ups. Any irregular variation in medical data patterns, if identified by these machine learning models, will send an immediate alert to the patient's family members so that they can help him or her in time [9, 10].

Clinical Trials for Drug Discovery and Development

Clinical research is an extensive area that leads to various trials and errors for the development of drugs specific to various diseases. Clinical trials can be very time-consuming, complex, labor-intensive, and expensive, and may be subject to errors and unexpected biases that may, at times, threaten their proper implementation, acceptance, and application. All these challenges can be overcome using machine learning. With the help of artificial intelligence and machine learning, high dimensional data can be analyzed to identify all possible combinations using dynamic strategy and then filter out the ones that have a particular property specific to a disease. The pattern analysis can be done on different medicines to gain insightful inferences to perform enhancements over the existing medicines to treat different variants of a particular disease. This dynamic approach using machine learning can visually elaborate the trends over a time period for a further clinical trial. Also selecting participants for the clinical trials is also a challenge. This challenge can also be resolved by monitoring the historical medical data of the candidate for clinical trials, and suitability can be predicted. This will save time and help reduce the side effects if any. By analyzing chemical compositions and trends in drug discovery and development, important breakthroughs can happen as machine learning models are capable of identifying hidden correlations between different components [11].

Coping with Contagious Diseases Using Machine Learning

For coping with contagious diseases, machine learning has an enormous role to play. Robots in the field of medicine have been revolutionizing the healthcare sector over the past years. The advancement of technology, the enhancement of machine learning algorithms, and the introduction of additional algorithms in artificial intelligence have broadened the scope of the inclusion of robotics into healthcare. Robots have not only been used for operative tasks but also for assisting healthcare workers and medical staff in times of a disease breakout. Over the course of the COVID-19 pandemic, hospitals began deploying robots for a much broader range of tasks to reduce the risk of exposure to pathogens. With the help of robots in the COVID ward, the doctors do not come in contact with the affected patients, thus preventing the spread of the virus from the patient to the medical staff and completely providing an isolated environment for the patients to recover. These healthcare robots can also help in sanitizing the patient's room and keep it hygienic. This will give more time to the medical staff to focus on the patient and give more time to cognitive functions rather than worrying about contracting the virus. These automated healthcare robots can even provide medicines to patients by pattern matching and monitoring historical data. For immediate care, robots can prescribe medicines to patients, giving time to the medical experts to focus on more serious tasks and operations. This allows physicians, nurses, and other healthcare workers to focus on empathic patient care and provides a secure and isolated environment for both the healthcare team and patients. Robots are also useful in engaging older patients socially. These robots can also help in the distribution of essentials needed in the time of a pandemic, thus facilitating no contact delivery [12].

APPLICATIONS OF MACHINE LEARNING IN THE HEALTHCARE SECTOR

Artificial intelligence is being used in the healthcare sector to perform undertakings like treatment suggestions, analysis, and even medical procedures. The colossal guarantee of AI has prompted an increment in the review, improvement, and reception of the innovation. The increasing number of machine learning applications in healthcare permits us to look at a future where information, investigation, and advancement work inseparably to help patients without ascertaining it. In the future, it will be very normal to find machine learning-based applications installed with patient information in real-time, accessible from various medical care frameworks in different nations, expanding the adequacy of new therapy choices that were inaccessible previously. These applications of machine learning in the healthcare sector not only provide cost-effective solutions but also prepare the world for a digital future. The noteworthy contribution of artificial intelligence and machine learning in the field of medicine can unravel the challenges faced by different parts of the industry. The different areas in healthcare, such as disease detection, healthcare record monitoring, smart healthcare systems, *etc.*, prove the wide scope of the cognitive functionalities performed by automated machines [13]. The various applications of machine learning in the healthcare sector are as follows:

Monitoring Mental Health

Machine learning not only focuses on the physical well-being of an individual but also concentrates on mental health. With the help of machine learning, experts are constantly working towards helping patients with issues related to mental health. The inclusion of machine learning for monitoring mental health has given confidence to the patients to step forward for proper treatment and interaction with experts regarding their issues. There has been a considerable rise in therapy sessions over the past few years. Also, during the pandemic, the stress and anxiety issues of people have increased over time. Sudden mood changes and an increase in frustration and anger have become a cause of concern. Not just adults but children have also become victims of these mental health issues. These issues have been taken care of by machine-learning-based solutions that are showing promising results. The early detection of issues such as anxiety and stress can help in the prevention of long-term mental health-related issues such as depression. This can be done with the help of healthcare applications that can monitor a person's mood and behavior in continuous intervals. Various applications provide a questionnaire to analyze a person's mood and recommend activities to uplift in case of negative emotion. The services provided by these applications are enhanced using algorithms such as neural networks to mimic a realistic human conversation. Various applications such as meditation apps help the person in case of anxiety or a panic attack to calm down using breathing activities or suggesting engaging activities. Real-time behavior analysis helps in identifying the mental health status of a person over a period of time and predicting the condition by analyzing the change in behavioral patterns. Emotion analysis can also be done to track the daily behavior of an individual and identify negative triggers based on the day-to-day activities to prevent the negative impact of those activities on mental health. With the help of sentiment analysis, emotions can be analyzed to identify stress or anxiety. With the help of machine learning, factors affecting mental health can be identified beforehand, and quality of life can be improved to a great extent [3].

Smart Monitoring Systems

As technology is advancing day by day, it is promoting a healthier lifestyle in individuals and making them in charge of their healthy lifestyle. This way, people are becoming more and more aware of adopting a healthy lifestyle and being physically active. The pandemic has been a factor in this major drift. It has inflicted a sense of good health and physical wellness among individuals. The use of smart monitoring systems such as mobiles and wearable devices for monitoring day-to-day activities and collecting real-time data continuously is becoming more and more popular. Smartwatches and different wearables are not only for fashion and wellness. Progressively, they are helping health experts to gather and examine more extensive areas of patient information between arrangements or after the medical procedure and significant bits of knowledge that can signal treatment. Today, the demand for smartwatches is revolutionizing the healthcare sector in a completely new sense by permitting us to take responsibility for our physical and mental prosperity straight from our wrists. These days, smartwatches and fitness bands are loaded with numerous functionalities such as heart rate trackers, stress level analyzers, analyzing sleep patterns, SpO_2, and many more. These facilities are making it easier for people to keep track of their daily activity and alert them if there is an abnormal pattern detected. Not just for personal tracking, these devices help the medical team monitor the daily activities of patients. With facilities such as step count and calorie trackers, they encourage people to accomplish their targeted goals and incorporate fitness into their lives. These devices are also equipped with alarming systems and send an immediate alarm to the concerned people when abnormal data patterns such as a higher heart rate or low levels of oxygen are detected. The data collected from these devices can be viewed from different devices, making it portable and flexible to various platforms. This collected data can be monitored by healthcare professionals, and based on the inferences, the individuals can be provided with specific medical services. These smart devices also allow patients to set reminders for medication or water intake and they can take immediate action on the go. Wearables are contributing a lot to healthcare, and they mostly aim at preventive care and early detection of diseases [14, 15].

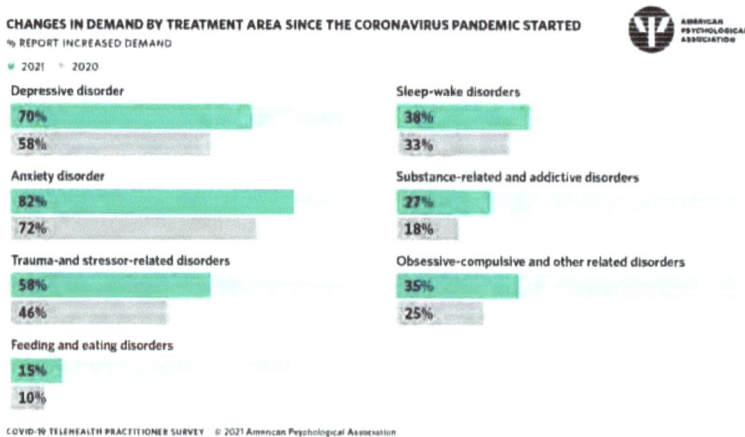

Fig. (1). Changes in demand by treatment since the start of COVID-19 [3].

Healthcare and cloud computing

Instead of using on-premise data centers for computation and analyzing huge amounts of data, the use of cloud-based functionality has increased over the past few years and is trending. Cloud computing uses virtual servers and various services for analyzing, processing, and computing massive data and saving the expenses of buying on-premise-specific infrastructure. There are huge volumes of clinical data such as medical images, EEG data, data from portable medical equipment, *etc.* This massive data requires large amounts of storage and processing capabilities for generating insights, which is not possible and is very time-consuming for normal processing systems. Investing in physical infrastructure having specific and limited functionality costs a lot and takes months of set-up. This problem is solved by using cloud platforms such as AWS, Microsoft Azure, *etc.*, to perform the same task on a budget and within minutes. Cloud platforms provide tons of facilities, including machine learning and data analytics, for processing huge amounts of data. These solutions are flexible and fault-tolerant and grant multiple access to the data simultaneously. The healthcare team can store huge volumes of data over the cloud securely for any duration and review it within minutes. The health data from wearable devices and smartphones is stored on the cloud as a backup for a quick review by the patient, doctors and health experts for unrestricted analysis. The tasks related to hardware and launching services are handled by the cloud platforms, making it easier for the patient and healthcare experts by providing abstraction without worrying about the internal working of the cloud functionalities. Also, cloud platforms provide utmost security for confidential and highly sensitive patient data without the fear of data being stolen or getting destroyed in any calamity or natural disaster. Cloud-based solutions aim to provide cost-effective solutions and charge only for the services that are being used for medical data analysis and insight generation. This is beneficial as many a time, the resources get underutilized or over-utilized. The flexible structure of the cloud allows having as many resources as required without worrying about running out of resources, unlike investing in physical data centers that are limited in functionality. Cloud platforms provide huge computation power for processing large clinical data such as medical images and deducing inferences. This data can be shared globally within minutes for further analysis by different experts all over the world. Thus, shifting to a cloud-based paradigm in the healthcare sector will benefit it with respect to different parameters such as cost, storage, and computation [17].

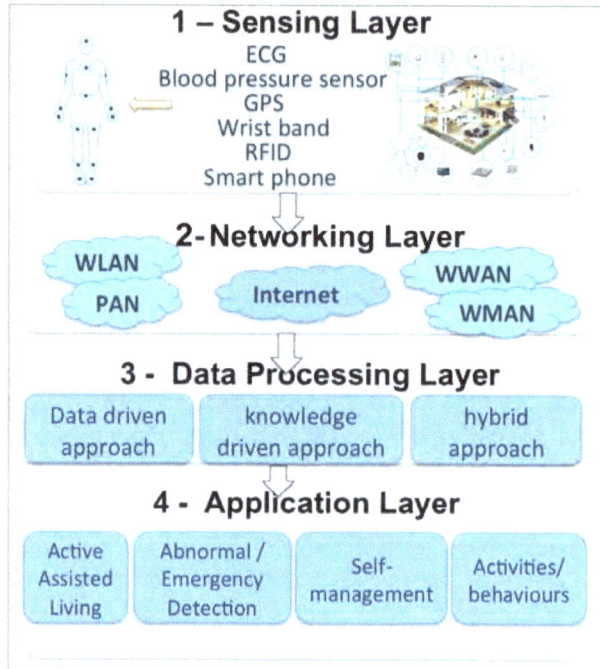

Fig. (2). Cloud-based health monitoring system [16].

Self-assessment and Tracking Applications

The use of self-assessment and tracking applications is increasing at a rapid rate, especially these days when personally paying a visit to a health expert may not be feasible. During the pandemic, initiatives such as self-assessment apps helped individuals to examine themselves on their own without much medical assistance and get treatment from home by connecting with experts online. Applications such as the Arogya setu application is one such example [19]. It provides a broad range of facilities to individuals and is being used as proof of health in many places for entry purposes. It allows the individuals to self-assess themselves and enter relevant information in case of any symptoms. With its tracking feature, the individual is able to track the location, analyze the number of COVID-19-affected cases around him, and act accordingly. It also monitors real-time data for each region daily at continuous intervals of time. It is also capable of predicting the interaction status for any individual based on the location and classifies it as safe or unsafe based on the interaction. These applications are also cost-effective and, at the same time, record real-time data and make predictions based on the activity status.

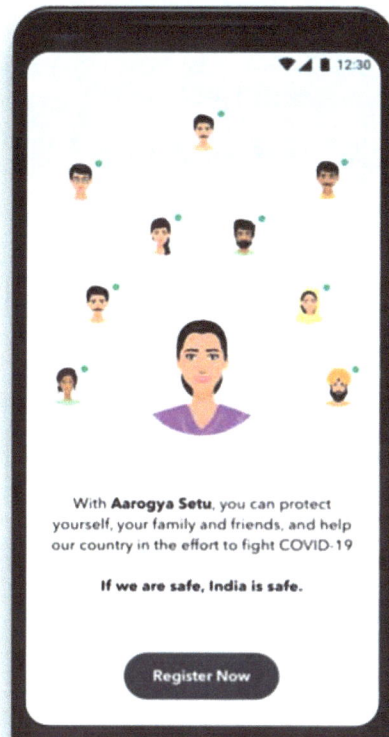

Fig. (3). A snapshot of Arogya Setu app [18].

Bionics and Machine Learning

Machine learning is making huge advancements in the area of prosthetics. The inclusion of artificial intelligence in the field of prosthetics has gradually increased and enables amputees to make the functionality of prosthetics trivial. With the predictive and analyzing capabilities of machine-learning-based automated models, the use of technology has become widespread to ease the lives of people. Incurable diseases such as epilepsy are accompanied by seizures that may pose a threat to a patient's life because of their unpredictability. These neurological disorders can be prevented with the help of small algorithmically configured bionic chips that are implanted in the brain for predicting epileptic or non-epileptic seizures by detecting irregular brain signals, giving red flags upon abnormal brain activity. Not just for neurological disorders, these bionic chips can help amputees control their limbs with the help of brain signals, thus requiring little muscle effort and easing the lives of people [21].

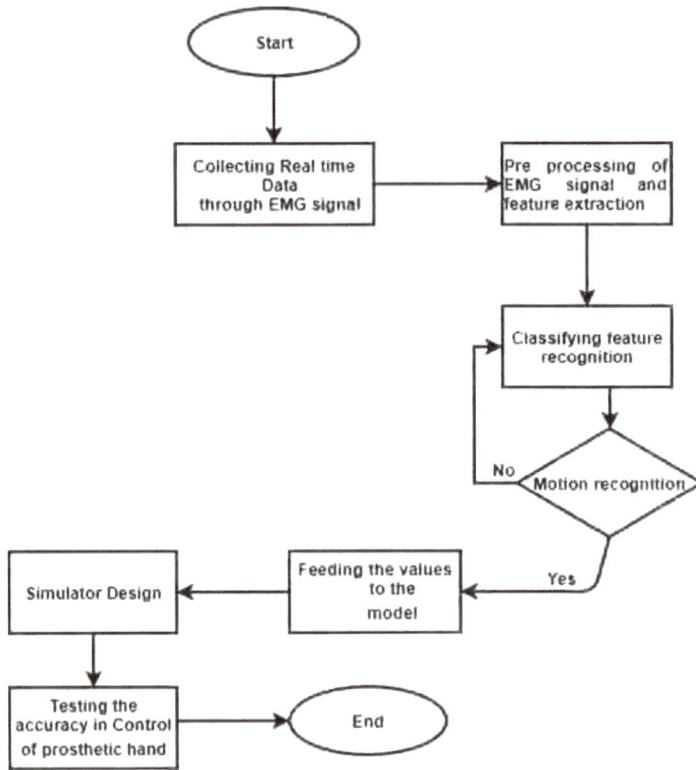

Fig. (4). Flowchart of bionic robot arm [20].

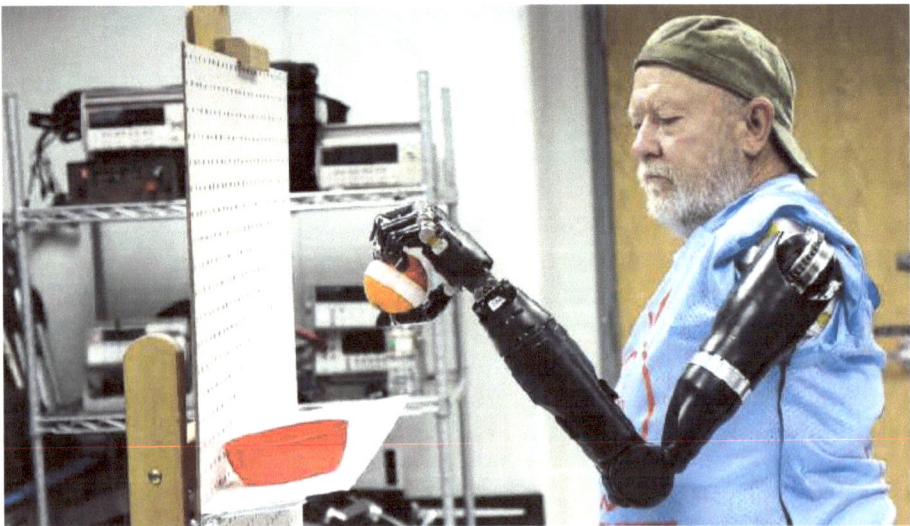

Fig. (5). Bionic Arm [22].

Early Alarming Systems

According to various research works, in various neurological diseases, brain activity becomes abnormal before the occurrence of any disorder. Diseases such as epilepsy are accompanied by seizures that have symptoms like loss of consciousness, blackout, inability to think, tightening of muscles, sudden jerks, *etc.*, and may pose a threat to the patient's life as the seizures are unpredictable, and if a seizure occurs in the middle of any activity such as driving, running, *etc.*, it is very harmful to the patient. For such scenarios, research is going on to develop early alarming systems to alert the patient beforehand so that the patient can be aware well in time and be prepared without any stress or anxiety. These alerting systems can also send immediate help signals to the family members of the patient for immediate help and thus save the patient's life from any mishap. Also, the alerting systems send the alerts well before time as soon as suspicious brain segments are detected and give ample time to the patient to seek help. These alerting systems are also helpful in identifying a disease outbreak [22].

Robots in the Healthcare Sector

Machine learning-based robots are revolutionizing the healthcare sector with continuous advancements. Robots in the healthcare industry have become an inseparable part. From major to minor tasks in the field of medicine, robotics in healthcare is becoming an integral part. Over a number of years, robots have been used to assist in surgeries. As there have been numerical upgrades and transformations in the technology, the applicability of robots in the healthcare sector has spread across a number of parts. Not just for surgeries, robots have been used by the healthcare team to provide services and assist clinical experts during the pandemic. The number of robots in hospitals and clinics increased during the COVID-19 pandemic to accomplish tasks, thereby reducing the risk of exposure to the virus. From using robots for medicine distribution to using them for hygiene purposes, the application scope for the use of robotics in the healthcare sector is huge. The deployment of robots in care centers has made the task of clinical experts and front-line workers easier by minimizing human-t--human interaction, therefore curtailing the spread of infectious diseases through human interaction. These healthcare robots can also provide medical assistance and even prescribe medicines to patients by analyzing historical medical data, thereby allowing clinical experts to focus on serious issues and perform cognitive functions effectively. The robots can even suggest similar medicines to the patients based on medical image analysis by identifying the chemical composition of the medicine that will suit the patient better and reduce the risk of severe side effects. As technology is advancing, the complexity of machine learning-based algorithms is increasing, thus providing better decision-making and pattern identification abilities and allowing the healthcare team to focus more on non-trivial tasks and empathetic patient care. Robots can help in monitoring patient data at regular intervals of time, thus reducing human intervention. Machine learning-based robots can assist clinical experts with surgical procedures by using the ability to analyze data patterns, identify the underlying hidden data patterns, and assist in better decision-making using complex computer vision models for real-time data capture and decision-making in operation theatres. The use of robots as a social convention is also helpful in improving the mental well-being of patients. The robots are used as companions to help the patients keep a healthy state of mind and keep them distracted during complex medical procedures. Robots of all kinds will keep on evolving to perform tasks in an autonomous, efficient, and accurate manner [12].

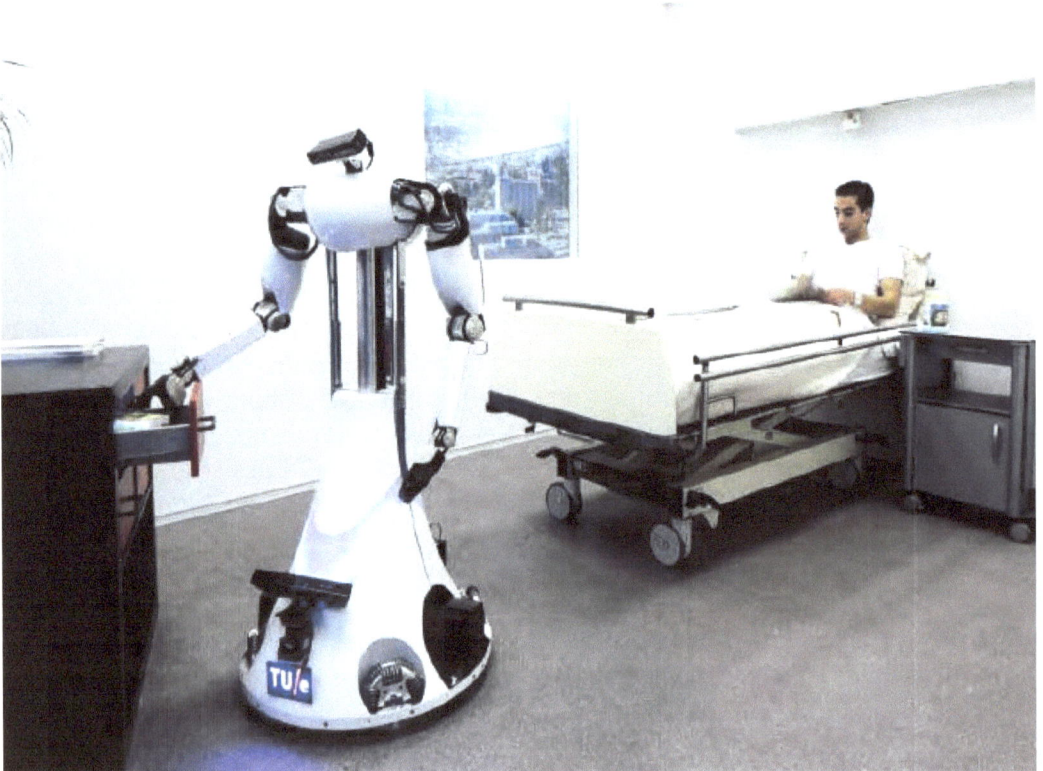

Fig. (6). Robots in healthcare [23].

Customized Healthcare Treatment and Products

Artificial intelligence and machine learning aim at providing customized solutions to the patients as one solution may not be feasible to all. With customized healthcare products, the demand for customized solutions is increasing day by day, thus facilitating the use of artificial intelligence and machine learning in the development of products. With the help of rule-based decision-making, the data of an individual is collected by means of surveys, questionnaires, or wearables or by examining historical medical data. Based on the quiz and the requirements, a customized solution is prepared by identifying the right composition to suit the needs of the people. Curated specifically for an individual, the customized solutions keep the requirements of people in mind and help them understand which product works best for them. As the availability of data is increasing day by day, the inclination towards data-driven approaches has increased the demand for customized solutions. Machine learning models use pattern identification and learning capabilities to suggest and recommend people accordingly. These personalized solutions are patient-specific, dynamic in nature, and provide a better assessment of the status. This self-analysis will help the patient go for specific choices rather than a trial-and-error approach to finding the right treatment for him or her. This also helps the clinical experts to identify the medical history of the patient based on customized solutions and helps in collective decision-making by many experts simultaneously. This will help people cut on expenses and save time, giving them more time for introspection and self-analysis [24].

Drug Discovery

Research on drug discovery is one of the latest applications of artificial intelligence in healthcare. With the help of machine learning and artificial intelligence, time and analytical costs can be reduced to a considerable extent as compared to the traditional trial–and-error approach for discovering and researching in the field of medicine. With the help of complex artificial intelligence models such as neural networks, meaningful deductions can be made regarding drug discovery. The traditional approach takes months to years to come out with the right dosage for treating a particular disease, and clinical trials further require an ample amount of time to understand the effect of medicine on the candidates and to comprehend any issues related to side effects or complications. These time-consuming practices can be simplified with the help of machine learning-based automated models that take historical data as input, identify the data trends based on the clinical decisions of the past, and suggest new techniques to tackle the problem. For drug discovery, to identify the main components to be incorporated in the medicine for giving immunity towards the toxins and reducing the rate of growth of toxins in the body, all such vital decisions can be made by machine learning and computer vision models. These models can mitigate the workload of clinical experts and also help in combating some rare disorders through meaningful deductions and analysis.

Efficient Disease Diagnosis

One of the most important applications of machine learning in healthcare is the efficient detection of diseases that may not be easily detected in the early stages or are incurable. Artificial intelligence and machine learning help clinical experts in making efficient deductions for the diagnosis of various diseases. Various researches are going on for diagnosing life-threatening diseases such as cancer and diabetes such that early detection of these diseases will help patients to get timely treatment and medication and will save millions of lives all over the world. With the help of machine learning models such as artificial neural networks, support vector machines (SVM), logistic regression, Naive Bayes classification, *etc.*, examining thousands of data volumes to detect patterns of irregularities within the data and infer whether the patient is diagnosed with a particular disease or not becomes easier for the healthcare experts. This is particularly helpful as portable systems generate massive data that is patient-specific and differs from person to person. Machine learning models provide rapid and dynamic processing that helps generate insights from the patient-specific data and suggest treatment after the diagnosis with a greater accuracy score. This also helps the clinical experts to make multiple deductions based on the machine learning decision to be extra sure and prevent any kind of false alarms as portable data can be very noisy. This noise has to be removed from the data using preprocessing techniques for efficient analysis and data-driven decisions. Also, there may be various factors in the data that may not be useful for analysis and may reduce the overall accuracy score for diagnosis. Such issues are handled by feature extraction algorithms that only select primary factors required for decision-making and classification. Feature extraction reduces the time taken by the models to process data and helps in better diagnosis with a higher accuracy score. Efficient diagnosis is very important for such diseases at an early stage because these diseases are further causes of other secondary diseases that increase the health risk for a patient.

Medical Image Analysis

Computer vision models play an enormous role in medical image analysis of various diseases. Medical image analysis is basically the in-depth analysis of 2D or 3D images of the affected organs by the machine learning models obtained from CT and MRI images. By using image datasets as input for computer vision models, deep learning networks are used to examine and learn from huge amounts of data and classify whether it is a malignant or a benign case. Many research studies are going on for different types of cancers, such as breast cancer, lung cancer, *etc.*, where the tumor is classified as a benign tumor or a malignant tumor based on the medical image analysis and deductions made by the deep learning networks. Deep learning networks are capable of learning from unsupervised data and can handle complex data very efficiently. Medical image analysis helps clinical experts to give assurance on the deductions made by machine learning models to get an extra edge for efficient decision-making. With the help of computer vision models to analyze clinical images, it can also deduce the severity of the disease by analyzing various parameters associated with it. It can also save the time and cost for the patients to go through rigorous procedures for diagnosis. In many cases, these rigorous medical procedures may not be able to diagnose the disease in time [26]. Using machine learning models can help identify these disorders that are hard to diagnose at the earlier stages. With the help of medical image processing, deeper insights can help clinical experts give the right treatment based on the severity of the disease. With the availability of various libraries by software for processing medical data, the task of image analysis becomes easier as these libraries provide functions for removing noise from the raw image and applying various filters to highlight the affected area under examination. With the help of such software and programming languages, only the area under examination is highlighted, and the irrelevant sections from the raw data are discarded for faster processing of medical images, making it faster for training automated models for efficient classification [27, 28].

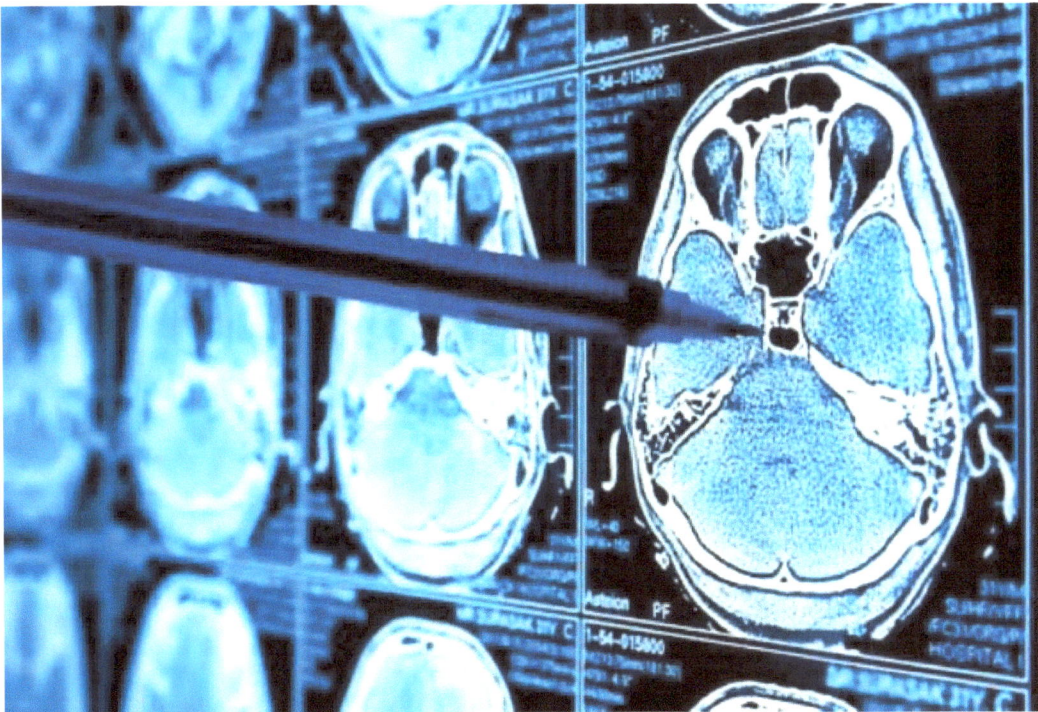

Fig. (7). Analyzing clinical images [25].

Artificial Intelligence-based Mobility Devices

With the introduction of sensor-based devices in the healthcare sector, mobility devices are getting a technological upgrade to make the lives of patients easier. Mobility devices such as wheelchairs and aids for walking are becoming artificially intelligent in detecting any obstruction and guiding the patient with the appropriate decision based on analysis. These artificially-enabled mobile devices are able to enhance the standards of living for patients and make them self-reliant and able to perform tasks themselves without assistance. These machine learning-infused devices are able to send smart alerts in case of any mishap. These devices can also detect the person's location to help his or her family and friends track the activity continuously without worrying about anything [30].

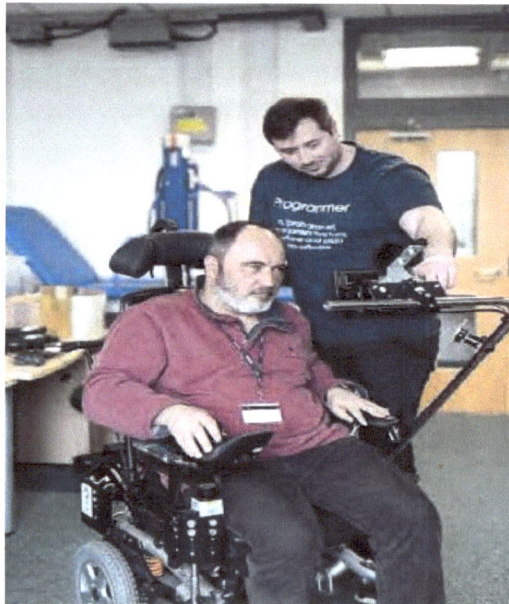

Fig. (8). AI-enabled wheelchairs [29].

CONCLUSION

The human being is the smartest and most complex structure created by God. The ability to impart human-like thinking capabilities to machines is perplexing and intriguing at the same time. Artificial intelligence and machine learning are responsible for various breakthroughs in the field of healthcare without doubt and have the capability to improve healthcare systems. As prevention is better than cure, with artificial intelligence and machine learning, we can be well prepared beforehand, and timely treatment can be provided to the patients. There are different segments of the healthcare sector, such as healthcare centers, hospitals, and clinics, the pharmaceutical sector, medical equipment manufacturers, medical care and insurance providers, the healthcare marketing sector, health records departments, *etc.*, and all these segments are benefiting enormously with the help of machine learning and artificial intelligence. Automation of time-consuming tasks may free up physician programs to enable more patient interfacing. The predictive power of AI and ML makes them more promising for predicting diseases and disorders, thus making them valuable tools for analysis. Improving access to data helps health professionals take the right steps to prevent disease. Humans should focus more on cognitive tasks and let the automation-based tasks be focused by the machine learning algorithms, thus focusing more on research and testing. Real-time data can provide better and faster diagnostic insights. Artificial intelligence is used to reduce administrative errors and conserve indispensable resources. AI is increasingly being applied to healthcare, and the boundaries and challenges continue to be faced and overcome. Machine learning is not enhancing a particular segment of the healthcare industry but is improving all the segments simultaneously. Advancements in all segments of the healthcare industry are important for the entire system to work as one army. For better decision-making, more and high-quality data is required, and for better classification, efficient decision-making has to be performed. Therefore, all segments of the industry are interlinked. The improvement in one segment will result in the improvement of other sectors in parallel. The complex machine learning and deep learning models are unleashing the hidden potential of artificial intelligence to revolutionize the healthcare sector [31, 32]. These applications are just a start for digitizing the healthcare system, and in the future, many such challenges will be overcome by machine learning. It will benefit not just the healthcare department but will make the lives of people easier all over the world.

REFERENCES

[1]   Z. Zhang, J. Lu, L. Xia, S. Wang, H. Zhang, and R. Zhao, "Digital twin system design for dual-manipulator cooperation unit", *Electronic and Automation Control Conference (ITNEC),* pp. 1431-1434, 2020.
[http://dx.doi.org/10.1109/ITNEC48623.2020.9084652]

[2]   D. An, and Y. Chen, "Digital Twin Enabled Methane Emission Abatement Using Networked Mobile Sensing and Mobile Actuation", *1st International Conference on Digital Twins and Parallel Intelligence (DTPI),* pp. 354-357, 2021.
[http://dx.doi.org/10.1109/DTPI52967.2021.9540133]

[3]   Y. Wang, Y. Cao, and F-Y. Wang, "Anomaly Detection in Digital Twin Model", *1st International Conference on Digital Twins and Parallel Intelligence (DTPI),* pp. 208-211, 2021.
[http://dx.doi.org/10.1109/DTPI52967.2021.9540116]

[4]   S. Zhang, H. Dong, U. Maschek, and H. Song, "A digital-twin-assisted fault diagnosis of railway point machine", *1st International Conference on Digital Twins and Parallel Intelligence (DTPI),* pp. 430-433, 2021.
[http://dx.doi.org/10.1109/DTPI52967.2021.9540118]

[5]   L. von Rueden, "Informed Machine Learning - A Taxonomy and Survey of Integrating Prior

Knowledge into Learning Systems", *IEEE Trans. Knowl. Data Eng.*, 2015.

[6]   M. Ross, C.A. Graves, J.W. Campbell, and J.H. Kim, "Using Support Vector Machines to Classify Student Attentiveness for the Development of Personalized Learning Systems", *2013 12th International Conference on Machine Learning and Applications, Miami, FL, USA*, pp. 352-32, 2013.
[http://dx.doi.org/10.1109/ICMLA.2013.66]

[7]   F. Ahamed, and F. Farid, "Applying Internet of Things and Machine-Learning for Personalized Healthcare: Issues and Challenges", *2018 International Conference on Machine Learning and Data Engineering (iCMLDE)*, pp. 19-21, 2018.
[http://dx.doi.org/10.1109/iCMLDE.2018.00014]

[8]   M.A. Ahmad, A. Teredesai, and C. Eckert, "Interpretable Machine Learning in Healthcare", *International Conference on Healthcare Informatics (ICHI)*, pp. 447-447, 2018.
[http://dx.doi.org/10.1109/ICHI.2018.00095]

[9]   P.K. Kushwaha, and M. Kumaresan, "Machine learning algorithm in healthcare system: A Review", *International Conference on Technological Advancements and Innovations (ICTAI)*, pp. 478-481, 2021.
[http://dx.doi.org/10.1109/ICTAI53825.2021.9673220]

[10]   K. Shailaja, B. Seetharamulu, and M.A. Jabbar, "Machine Learning in Healthcare: A Review", *Second International Conference on Electronics, Communication and Aerospace Technology (ICECA)*, 2018.
[http://dx.doi.org/10.1109/ICECA.2018.8474918]

[11]   T.I. Rohan, M.S.U. Yusuf, M. Islam, and S. Roy, "Efficient Approach to Detect Epileptic Seizure using Machine Learning Models for Modern Healthcare System", *2020 IEEE Region 10 Symposium (TENSYMP), Dhaka, Bangladesh*, pp. 1783-1786, 2020.
[http://dx.doi.org/10.1109/TENSYMP50017.2020.9230731]

[12]   S. Vyas, M. Gupta, and R. Yadav, "Converging Blockchain and Machine Learning for Healthcare", *Amity International Conference on Artificial Intelligence (AICAI)*, pp. 709-711, 2019.
[http://dx.doi.org/10.1109/AICAI.2019.8701230]

[13]   M. Dol, and A. Geetha, "A Learning Transition from Machine Learning to Deep Learning: A Survey", *International Conference on Emerging Techniques in Computational Intelligence (ICETCI)*, pp. 89-94, 2021.
[http://dx.doi.org/10.1109/ICETCI51973.2021.9574066]

[14]   D. V. K, T. K. Ramesh and S. A, "A Machine Learning based Ensemble Approach for Predictive Analysis of Healthcare Data," 2020 2nd PhD Colloquium on Ethically Driven Innovation and Technology for Society (PhD EDITS), 2020, pp. 1-2,

[15]   J. Wojtusiak, "Semantic Data Types in Machine Learning from Healthcare Data", *2012 11th International Conference on Machine Learning and Applications, Boca Raton, FL, USA*, pp. 197-202, 2012.
[http://dx.doi.org/10.1109/ICMLA.2012.41]

[16]   J.C. Alcaraz, S. Moghaddamnia, N. Poschadel, and J. Peissig, "Machine Learning as Digital Therapy Assessment for Mobile Gait Rehabilitation", *2018 IEEE 28th International Workshop on Machine Learning for Signal Processing (MLSP), Aalborg, Denmark*, pp. 89-94, 2018.
[http://dx.doi.org/10.1109/MLSP.2018.8517005]

[17]   A. Arora, N. Rakesh, and K.K. Mishra, "Reliable Packet Delivery in Vehicular Networks Using WAVE for Communication Among High Speed Vehicles", In: *Networking Communication and Data Knowledge Engineering.*, G.M. Perez, K.K. Mishra, S. Tiwari, M.C. Trivedi, Eds., vol. Vol. 3. Springer Singapore: Singapore, 2018, pp. 65-77.
[http://dx.doi.org/10.1007/978-981-10-4585-1_6]

[18]   G.D. Singh, S. Kumar, H. Alshazly, S.A. Idris, M. Verma, and S.M. Mostafa, "A novel routing protocol for realistic traffic network scenarios in VANET", *Wirel. Commun. Mob. Comput.*, vol. 2021, no. 1, p. 7817249, 2021.

[http://dx.doi.org/10.1155/2021/7817249]

[19]   B. Kaur, and A. Arora, "Emotional Intelligence: Rendering Association amongst the Technology Approach and Non-Fiscal Efficiency Aspects", *2020 IEEE 1st International Conference for Convergence in Engineering (ICCE), Kolkata, India,* pp. 11-15, 2020.
[http://dx.doi.org/10.1109/ICCE50343.2020.9290678]

[20]   G.D. Singh, M. Prateek, S. Kumar, M. Verma, D. Singh, and H.N. Lee, "Hybrid genetic firefly algorithm-based routing protocol for VANETs", *IEEE Access,* vol. 10, pp. 9142-9151, 2022.
[http://dx.doi.org/10.1109/ACCESS.2022.3142811]

[21]   A. Aggarwal, P. Dimri, and A. Agarwal, "Statistical Performance Evaluation of Various Metaheuristic Scheduling Techniques for Cloud Environment", *J. Comput. Theor. Nanosci.,* vol. 17, no. 9, pp. 4593-4597, 2020.
[http://dx.doi.org/10.1166/jctn.2020.9285]

[22]   V. Sapra, L. Sapra, J.K. Sandhu, and G. Chhabra, "Biomedical Diagnostics through Nanocomputing", In: *Nanotechnology.* Jenny Stanford Publishing, 2021, pp. 443-460.
[http://dx.doi.org/10.1201/9781003120261-13]

[23]   H-C. Soong, N.B.A. Jalil, R. Kumar Ayyasamy, and R. Akbar, "The Essential of Sentiment Analysis and Opinion Mining in Social Media : Introduction and Survey of the Recent Approaches and Techniques", *2019 IEEE 9th Symposium on Computer Applications & Industrial Electronics (ISCAIE), Malaysia,* pp. 272-277, 2019.
[http://dx.doi.org/10.1109/ISCAIE.2019.8743799]

[24]   G. Chhabra, "An Approach for the Transformation of Human Emotion and Energy-Field using Sound Therapy", *Turkish Journal of Computer and Mathematics Education,* vol. 12, no. 6, pp. 3172-3183, 2021. [TURCOMAT].

[25]   Saad, 'Opinion Mining on US Airline Twitter Data Using Machine Learning Techniques', in 2020 16th International Computer Engineering Conference (ICENCO), Dec. 2020, pp. 59–63,
[http://dx.doi.org/10.1109/ICENCO49778.2020.9357390]

[26]   P. Kumar, R. Chaudhary, A. Aggarwal, P. Singh, and R. Tomar, Improving Medical Image Segmentation Techniques Using Multiphase Level Set Approach *Via* Bias Correction., *Int. J. Eng. Adv. Technol.,* 2012. [IJEAT].

[27]   Y.M. Tun, and P. Hninn Myint, "A Two-Phase Approach for Stance Classification in Twitter Using Name Entity Recognition and Term Frequency Feature", *2019 IEEE/ACIS 18th International Conference on Computer and Information Science (ICIS), Beijing, China,* pp. 77-81, 2019.
[http://dx.doi.org/10.1109/ICIS46139.2019.8940282]

[28]   M. Wongkar, and A. Angdresey, "Sentiment Analysis Using Naive Bayes Algorithm Of The Data Crawler: Twitter", *2019 Fourth International Conference on Informatics and Computing (ICIC),* pp. 1-5, 2019.
[http://dx.doi.org/10.1109/ICIC47613.2019.8985884]

[29]   Md. Mahiuddin, "Real Time Sentiment Analysis and Opinion Mining on Refugee Crisis", *2019 5th International Conference on Advances in Electrical Engineering (ICAEE), Dhaka, Bangladesh,* pp. 699-705, 2019.
[http://dx.doi.org/10.1109/ICAEE48663.2019.8975462]

[30]   R. Mouty, and A. Gazdar, "The Effect of the Similarity Between the Two Names of Twitter Users on the Credibility of Their Publications", *2019 Joint 8th International Conference on Informatics, Electronics & Vision (ICIEV) and 2019 3rd International Conference on Imaging, Vision & Pattern Recognition (icIVPR), Spokane, WA, USA,* pp. 196-201, 2019.
[http://dx.doi.org/10.1109/ICIEV.2019.8858561]

[31]   P. Nagarkar, A. Khan, S. Raikar, and A. Zantye, "Twitter Data Mining for Targeted Marketing", *2020 Second International Conference on Inventive Research in Computing Applications (ICIRCA),* pp. 44-50, 2020.

[http://dx.doi.org/10.1109/ICIRCA48905.2020.9183005]

[32]   F. Riquelme, P. Gonzalez-Cantergiani, D. Hans, R. Villarroel, and R. Munoz, "Identifying Opinion Leaders on Social Networks Through Milestones Definition", *IEEE Access,* vol. 7, pp. 75670-75677, 2019.
[http://dx.doi.org/10.1109/ACCESS.2019.2922155]

CHAPTER 12

IoT-Based Intelligent Transportation System through IoTV

Gagan Deep Singh[1,*]

1 Cybernetics Cluster, School of Computer Science, University of Petroleum \& Energy Studies (UPES), Bidholi, Dehradun-248007, India

Abstract: Since India gained independence, the number of vehicles in the country has increased by 170 times, while the road infrastructure has only expanded nine times in proportion. The rate of vehicle population growth is approximately two and a half million per year. Road fatalities far exceed those from rail, air, and terrorism, and it is predicted that by 2030, road accidents will be the fifth largest cause of human deaths. Technology, specifically IoT-based intelligent transportation systems (ITS), can address the challenges posed by inadequate road infrastructure and development. International consortia can collaborate to develop solutions tailored to such conditions. This chapter presents facts related to Indian transport and road accidents and proposes an IoT-based intelligent transportation system, termed IoTV, to improve transportation and reduce accident rates. The authors recommend an IoTV solution for ITS in their paper.

Keywords: Automobile, Intelligent transportation system, IoT, IoTV, Road infrastructure, Road accidents.

INTRODUCTION

The emergence of radio communication and its recent technology has given a new platform to scientists and researchers in network communication. The wireless technology do not need any centralized control and can manage, rearrange, organize, and even repair the nodes/links by itself. The present development in ad-hoc network technologies and dedicated short-range communication has given rise to vehicular ad-hoc networks (VANET). In VANET technology, there will be communication through wireless means for vehicle-to-vehicle (V2V), infrastructure-to-vehicle communication (I2V), and even road-to-vehicle (R2V) communication. The basis of this communication has evolved from existing mobile ad-hoc networks (MANET). The future transport network architecture will

---

* **Corresponding author Gagan Deep Singh:** Cybernetics Cluster, School of Computer Science, University of Petroleum \& Energy Studies (UPES), Bidholi, Dehradun-248007, India; E-mail: gagan@ddn.upes.ac.in

rely on the intelligent transportation system (ITS). Critical tasks such as the safety and security of vehicles/passengers, network congestions, smoother traffic monitoring and controlling, *etc.*, will be managed by ITS [1].

The "Crash Avoidance Matrices Partnership (CAMP), Advance Driver Assistance System (ADASE), FLEETNET, and CARTALK" are some of the famous applications that were developed by various automobile manufacturers and governments through public-private partnerships [2]. This network of vehicles makes a communication system for drivers as well as vehicles that avoids acute situations such as road obstacles and accidents, driver assistance systems, sudden emergency brakes on highways, traffic jams, and sudden increases in vehicle speed, along with the clear pathways for ambulance, police, VIPs, fire brigade, *etc.* VANET is also able to provide luxury applications like an infotainment system at an on-board display of vehicles, weather reports, vehicle health monitoring and status, *etc.* Fig. (**1**) shows the overall working of the VANET structure.

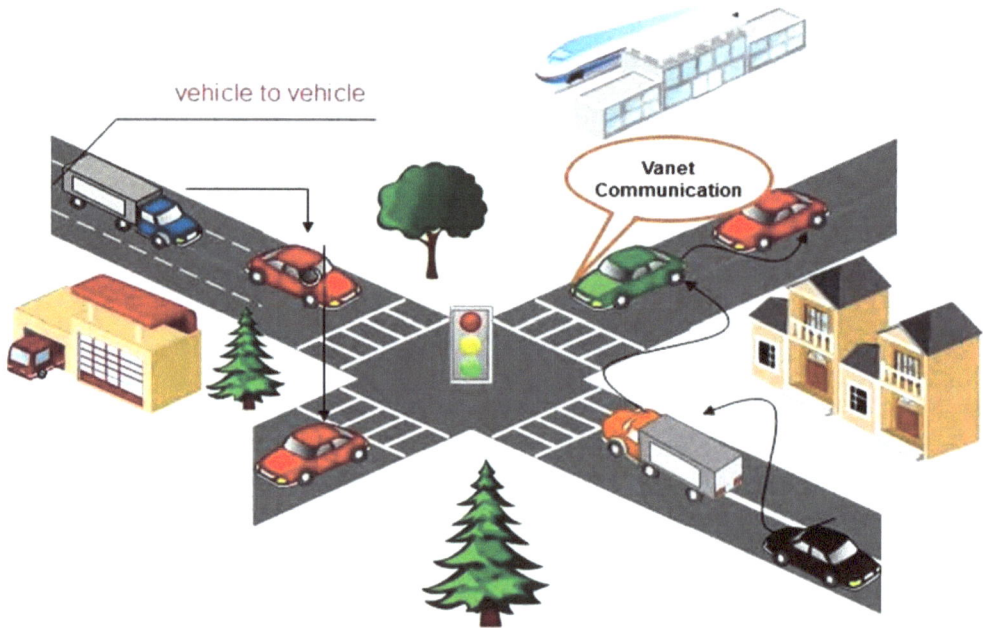

Fig. (1). VANET structure.

The Internet of Things (IoT) has also emerged as one of the most important technologies that will be used in all areas in the coming days. This will act as a nervous system for any of the communication technology. IoT can provide communication among any of the available devices, equipment, or components. This compromises the connection of intelligent systems on the internet with seamless connectivity at any time and anywhere to anyone in the system. It has been estimated that by 2025, the traffic data flow will grow 1000 times more than before, and over 50 billion IoT devices will establish an intelligent network [3].

IoT is a combination of network devices that communicate with each other and gather data from various sensors and data processing and web-based applications. The sensors are used to detect the data and gather the relevant information. This data is transmitted through the network equipment on the cloud for further processing. Various web technologies are used for data mining, leading to the extraction of relevant information. This derived information can be made useful by some dedicated applications that may be installed on some workstations [4]. These online IoT-based devices are made available through a combination of hardware and software that can fulfill the users' demands at 24/7 availability. This makes the availability of the services for all desirable users at several locations but at the same [5].

ITS will also consist of interconnected vehicles and their related infrastructure. This compromises VANET, the combination of devices that work on IoT, vehicles, and all the IoT-based routing equipment that works for VANET. IoT will soon introduce new characteristics in VANET, such as vehicle-to-sensors (V2S), vehicle-to-person (V2), vehicle-to-roadside setups (V2R), and vehicle-t--intelligent transportation infrastructure (V2I), and this is known as vehicle-t--everything (V2E) [6]. In this chapter, the author proposes the Internet of Things for vehicles *i.e.*, IoTV.

The IoTV architecture and its framework can be applied to connect V2V, V2I, and ITS for managing and processing autonomous vehicles within VANET [7]. IoTV is best suited for situations where humans may not be able to work at their full potential, like natural disasters such as earthquakes and landslides. Autonomous vehicles can then diagnose the affected region and find vacant routes to inform the ambulance, and in this way, free passage can be provided. The same can also be applied to efficient routings in intelligent transportation systems where VANET deploys Swarm Intelligence techniques like ACO [8], PSO, firefly, *etc* [9].

The Authors propose the IoTV paradigm through a framework capable of providing efficient communication for autonomous automobiles. The paper focuses basically on the following major points.

- IoTV framework with layered architecture is proposed that focuses on the functionalities, operations, and representations of the different layers.
- A communication framework is proposed that encompasses four fundamental aspects of IoTV: automobiles, users, network communication, and cloud technology.

NETWORK MODEL OF IOTV ENVIRONMENT

The IoTV network model represents the complete system for communication in the IoTV network architecture. Fig. (**2**) represents the proposed network model environment. This model shows the interaction among different components using IoT-based communication. This system consists of V2R, V2V, V2I, and V2S that work for ITS and create an IoTV environment [10]. Further, the IoTV network model presents four major important elements. The first element in this is the user who will avail all the desired services provided through IoTV in ITS. The second element is the network of connected vehicles that makes VANET. The third is the network connection, which consists of various network and routing equipment along with topology. The fourth element is cloud computing, which is responsible for various ITS-related applications running on the cloud for IoTV.

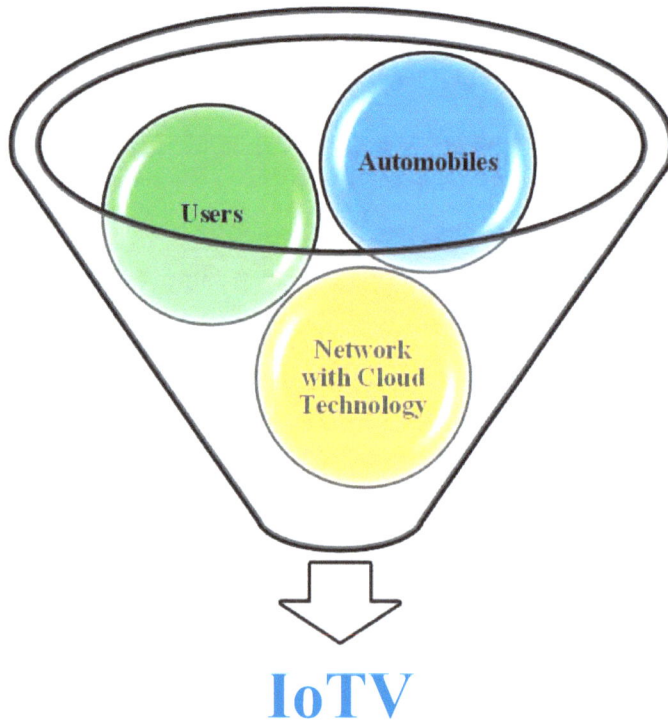

Fig. (2). Fundamental elements of IoTV.

Users

In this model, users are represented as the beneficiaries of the IoTV services. These users can be car drivers, commuters, passengers, and any other person who is somehow responsible for establishing communication in VANET. Thus, IoTV helps in broadcasting different services that facilitate the drivers to get updates on destination routes, such as congestion and traffic jam information, statistics on carbon emissions, and emergencies like calling an ambulance, police, and fire services in case of accidents [11]. The proposed IoTV is beneficial for emergencies when drivers need time-to-time information on road clearance or during natural disasters like landslides in hilly regions such as Uttarakhand.

Automobiles

In this model, automobiles are referred to as connected vehicles with preinstalled sensors. The sensors are responsible for fetching the information while driving. This information that is gathered is related to driving habits, condition of bad roads, weather, visibility, and several other driving information [12]. The on-board system these days already has sufficient features that provide the entire information of the vehicle. IoTV proposes an integrated 5G connectivity within the vehicle that makes IoT-based sensors get seamless connectivity of the internet. This helps the vehicle to fetch information from the cloud, and even the captured data can be uploadedto cloud-based applications. Now, this processed data can be broadcast on VANET, and all the automobiles connected through the proposed IoTV system can retrieve the relevant information. For this, a mobile SIM can be installed somewhere near the dashboard of the vehicle, and the same can be used for V2I to get connectivity anytime and anywhere through the GSM network. This will also save infrastructural costs, and roadside infrastructure can be utilized to set up the IoTV environment in the future [13].

Network

In the proposed model, the most important element is the third component, namely network connections in IoTV. This component is responsible for how all other elements of this model will be connected to each other. As already proposed in the second element, a GSM SIM will fulfill all the requirements of internet connectivity for IoTV, but some other network architectures like wireless access in vehicular environment (WAVE) and short-range like Bluetooth can also be used for V2V and V2S communication [14]. The emergence of 5G will change the entire way of network communication in ITS and make it possible to deploy ITS that works on the proposed IoTV network environment model [15]. VANET has the capability that it can sustain itself within its established network as each vehicle can act as a node and create its own topology to broadcast data packets. In this case, each vehicle can act as an access point and work as a router for other nodes. This makes it a self-managed communication that does not need any central control system. This network is also able to update itself with some other input feeds that may be provided by the IoT sensors in a V2I-based communication [16].

Cloud Technology

The proposed IoTV is not complete if it does not include cloud technology. The last element proposed is the cloud technology, which may act as a central nervous system. As proposed in the second and third elements, the data captured by the sensors may be uploaded to the cloud and is further processed by various applications for analysis, decision support systems, *etc.* The other vehicles or drivers can fetch that information while driving on its display boards. For this, the vehicle must be connected to the IoTV environment. The sensors on the vehicle can capture the vehicle data, such as damage in any of the spare parts, and this data can be sent to the cloud through IoTV. This information can be processed and sent to the nearby garages for instant repair with an acknowledgment to the driver [17]. This makes the journey even safer, and accidents caused by vehicle breakdowns can be avoided.

PROPOSED ARCHITECTURE OF IOTV

To avail the ITS services in the proposed IoTV environment, IoTV needs to perform the following functionalities: First, the IoT-based sensors need to collect the status of the vehicle, whether it is fit for touring or not. Some other relevant information related to nearby vehicles, route information, weather information, *etc.*, is gathered and then sent to the next element to process. Here, VANET plays a role inestablishing communication among other vehicles. V2I provides connectivity for the cloud. When information reaches the cloud application, then appropriate information will be broadcast to the vehicles that are connected to the IoTV environment. This information is finalized using available decision support systems and algorithms based on artificial intelligence. This presented integration of VANET, V2I, and IoT will create a complete IoTV system that supports intelligent transportation systems. The work proposes an architecture, as shown in Fig. (**3**), which will resolve all the issues to help develop IoT-based solutions for vehicles, termed Internet of Things for Vehicles (IoTV). The proposed architecture has four major components that provide a platform for all the supported communication models in IoTV. These components are IoTV services, network communication, cloud technology, and clients/users.

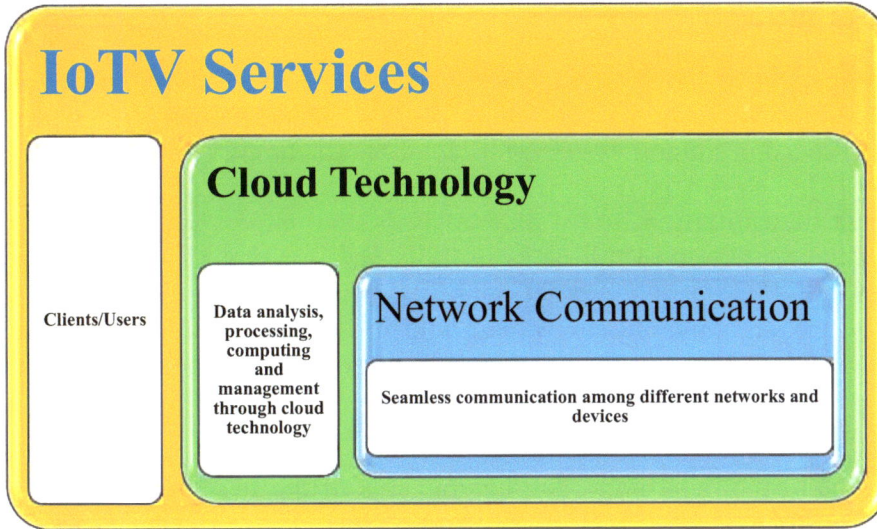

Fig. (3). Proposed IoTV.

The proposed IoTV is able to synchronize with all previous technologies as per TCP and OSI models to avail the services in the present IoT-enabled VANET environment. Though security is also a major concern, presently, it is not in the scope of the chapter. So, security may be taken care of and will work among all layers as individual protocols in each layer. The proposed IoTV model makes connectivity more accurate, scalable, and robust with present network communication architectures. Through this, the available infrastructure, such as GSM mobile towers, installed optical fiber connectivity, and all other radio communication models, can be utilized under V2I. This will provide seamless communication among different network devices in the proposed IoTV system. The discussion on each component is presented further.

IoTV Services

This component of IoTV architecture will be a services-oriented layer that facilitates users and automobiles with smart applications, which provide information, infotainment, vehicle safety, route information, weather updates, nearby garages, fuel stations, and many other relevant services. It will fetch accurate and rational analysis of information through cloud technology through network communication. Hence, cloud technology deployed for IoTV must rely on the best internet services. Soon, there will be satellite-based internet connectivity *e.g.*, Starlink. As soon as Starlink starts providing internet connectivity, it will be easier to implement IoTV.

Cloud Technology

This component of IoTV architecture incorporates smart cloud infrastructure. It performs the gathering of data, saving of data, analysis, and further processing works on decision support systems for cloud-based computations. As illustrated in a study [18], the primary responsibilities of this layer are IoTV cloud computing, intelligent transportation, IoTV data analysis, and expert systems. This will be used for the deduction of toll taxes in India on all major national highways and expressways. The Starlink internet can be used for providing cloud-based services at all toll tax stations, and IoTV can help in automatic payment as soon as it crosses the toll station. This may be like the present smart tag system.

Clients and Users

This is one of the most important components of the IoTV architecture, as it is responsible for various actuators and sensors installed at roadside units (RSUs), vehicles, and other available VANET infrastructure. The main function here is to capture detailed information on vehicles in VANET and its related services. It collects data from other devices of the IoTV ecosystem and broadcasts it to the cloud setup through the available network. The data may have information related to speed, location, status of the vehicles and route-related information, traffic conditions, weather conditions, infotainment, security, and other relevant information of drivers and commuters. The main responsibility of this layer is that the collected information is passed on to the other layer using the most secure and accurate method. This also supports all the user-based services that may relate to on board display of all the automobiles.

Network Communication

This component of IoTV architecture is mainly responsible for the seamless communication among heterogeneous and different networks in an IoTV environment. This facilitates network communication for IoT-based sensors, Bluetooth, WAVE, mobile GSM networks, 4G/5G, and satellite networks like Elon Musk's Starlink to provide secure, reliable, and fast communication between different VANET equipment. Then, the collected information is further transmitted over to the cloud for the next level of data analysis and processing.

In the proposed IoTV architecture, the presented network depends on the types of connection in VANET. This can be inter-vehicular communication and/or intra-vehicular communication. Inter-vehicular communication mainly focuses on the network that is outside the vehicle and responsible for long-range communication. Hence, WAVE communication technology is proposed in this as it is best suited for the environment where high mobility of the nodes is observed, such as in road transportation. Through this high data rate, services will be achieved for IoTV [19].

Intra-vehicular communication is proposed for short-range communications, which can be achieved through ZigBee/Bluetooth. So, for this, a high-frequency range is not required; hence, the high and random mobility of the vehicles will not get disturbed. This has been proved in previous studies, where the receiver selects the network from available networks through its signal strength [20, 21]. The challenge here is which network may be selected for which service. However, this may also be resolved by deploying the proposed IoTV architecture that works on robust and seamless internet connectivity, such as Starlink.

IOTV SCENARIO-BASED STUDY

This section is focused on IoTV-based scenario that will illustrate the working of the proposed IoTV framework. Let's assume a scenario where an emergency vehicle like an ambulance needs the fastest communication in intelligent transportation during emergency situations. Then, IoT sensors installed in ambulances will gather data and broadcast it to the available IoTV network environment. This broadcasting is used to disseminate information to all the nearby vehicles for passage [22, 23].

The proposed IoTV environment is best suited for where the platooning of vehicles is required, like in the convoys of VIPs. The routing algorithms in VANET also need to be re-evaluated to synchronize with the IoTV. In the near future, it will be observed that intelligent transportation will be implemented and deployed in real-time scenarios, and the proposed IoTV architecture may be adopted by the industry and various consortiums that fulfill the need for smart traffic management and transportation [24].

CONCLUSION

The integration of various communication architectures and IoT in VANET is the basis of the principle of intelligent transportation through interconnected vehicles and other infrastructure. This chapter proposes an IoTV structure that is IoT-enabled in the management of traffic and future transportation systems. Due to the emergence of VANET, IoT, and satellite internet connectivity *e.g.*, Starlink, the world will observe a revolutionary change in the transportation system.

The chapter presents the proposed IoTV architecture, consisting of four major components: clients/users, Network communication, cloud technology, and IoTV services. The integration of these covers four main functions of an intelligent transportation system that enables the integration of components and network modules for interoperability. The real-time scenario-based working of the proposed IoTV is also discussed, through which it can be concluded that the IoTV will be very beneficial for the implementation of intelligent transportation, with the hope that this may reduce the day-to-day problems of road commuters. These technologies are very helpful for developing countries like India as the huge development of transportation infrastructure is in progress. The sudden rise of vehicles in the coming years may raise the problem of traffic management, and VANET, with the integration of IoTV, may provide a complete solution for it.

REFERENCES

[1]   G.D. Singh, R. Tomar, H.G. Sastry, and M. Prateek, "A review on VANET routing protocols and wireless standards", In: *Smart Innovation.* vol. 78. Systems and Technologies, 2018, pp. 329-340.
[http://dx.doi.org/10.1007/978-981-10-5547-8_34]

[2]   G.D. Singh, D.M. Prateek, and D.H. Sastry G, "Swarm Intelligence Based Algorithm for Efficient Routing in VANET", *Int. J. Innov. Technol. Explor. Eng.,* vol. 9, no. 5, pp. 1124-1136, 2020.
[http://dx.doi.org/10.35940/ijitee.E2857.039520]

[3]   S. Kumar, P. Tiwari, and M. Zymbler, "Internet of Things is a revolutionary approach for future technology enhancement: a review", *J. Big Data,* vol. 6, no. 1, p. 111, 2019.
[http://dx.doi.org/10.1186/s40537-019-0268-2]

[4]   "Data Mining for Internet of Things - IEEE Access." Available from: https://ieeeaccess.ieee.org/closed-special-sections/data-mining-for-internet-of-things/ (accessed Apr. 13, 2022).

[5]   Peter, M. N., & Rani, M. P. (2021). V2V communication and authentication: the internet of things vehicles (IoTV). Wireless personal communications, 120(1), 231-247. https://link.springer.com/article/10.1007/s11277-021-08449-5

[6]   G. D. Singh, M. Prateek and G. H. Sastry, "Methodology to perform simulation experiments for realistic VANET scenarios using open source software tools," vol. 24, no. 06, pp. 10170–10175, 2020. Available from: https://www.psychosocial.com/article/PR261013/23173/

[7]   G.D. Singh, M. Prateek, and G.H. Sastry, "A Novel Algorithm for efficient routing in Vehicular Ad hoc Network using Swarm Intelligence optimization techniques", , vol. 29, no. 7, pp. 1132-1143, 2020.

[8]   G.D. Singh, S. Kumar, H. Alshazly, S.A. Idris, M. Verma, and S.M. Mostafa, "A Novel Routing Protocol for Realistic Traffic Network Scenarios in VANET", *Wirel. Commun. Mob. Comput.,* vol. 2021, no. 1, p. 7817249, 2021.
[http://dx.doi.org/10.1155/2021/7817249]

[9]   G.D. Singh, M. Prateek, S. Kumar, M. Verma, D. Singh, and H.N. Lee, "Hybrid Genetic Firefly Algorithm-Based Routing Protocol for VANETs", *IEEE Access,* vol. 10, pp. 9142-9151, 2022.
[http://dx.doi.org/10.1109/ACCESS.2022.3142811]

[10] C.M. Silva, B.M. Masini, G. Ferrari, and I. Thibault, "A Survey on Infrastructure-Based Vehicular Networks", *Mob. Inf. Syst.,* vol. 2017, pp. 1-28, 2017.
[http://dx.doi.org/10.1155/2017/6123868]

[11] B. Lidestam, B. Thorslund, H. Selander, D. Näsman, and J. Dahlman, "In-Car Warnings of Emergency Vehicles Approaching: Effects on Car Drivers' Propensity to Give Way", *Frontiers in Sustainable Cities,* vol. 2, p. 19, 2020.
[http://dx.doi.org/10.3389/frsc.2020.00019]

[12] M. Kaur, J. Malhotra, and P.D. Kaur, "A VANET-IoT based Accident Detection and Management System for the Emergency Rescue Services in a Smart City", *ICRITO 2020 - IEEE 8th Int. Conf. Reliab. Infocom Technol. Optim. (Trends Futur. Dir.,* vol. 964, p. 968, 2020.

[http://dx.doi.org/10.1109/ICRITO48877.2020.9198010]

[13] R. Hussain and S. Zeadally, "Autonomous Cars: Research Results, Issues, and Future Challenges," *IEEE Communications Surveys and Tutorials*, vol. 21, no. 2. Institute of Electrical and Electronics Engineers Inc., pp. 1275–1313, 01, 2019.
[http://dx.doi.org/10.1109/COMST.2018.2869360]

[14] M. Shahzad, and J. Antoniou, "Quality of user experience in 5G-VANET", *IEEE Int. Work. Comput. Aided Model. Des. Commun. Links Networks, CAMAD,* 2019.
[http://dx.doi.org/10.1109/CAMAD.2019.8858442]

[15] R. Hussain, F. Hussain, and S. Zeadally, "Integration of VANET and 5G Security: A review of design and implementation issues", *Future Gener. Comput. Syst.,* vol. 101, pp. 843-864, 2019.
[http://dx.doi.org/10.1016/j.future.2019.07.006]

[16] G.D. Singh, D.M. Prateek, and D.H. Sastry G, "Swarm Intelligence based efficient routing algorithm for platooning in VANET through Ant Colony Optimization", *Int. J. Innov. Technol. Explor. Eng.,* vol. 8, no. 9, pp. 1238-1244, 2019.
[http://dx.doi.org/10.35940/ijitee.I7888.078919]

[17] S. Sharma, and A. Kaul, "VANETs Cloud: Architecture, Applications, Challenges, and Issues", *Arch. Comput. Methods Eng. 2020 284,* vol. 28, no. 4, pp. 2081-2102, 2020.
[http://dx.doi.org/10.1007/s11831-020-09447-9]

[18] O. Kaiwartya, A.H. Abdullah, Y. Cao, A. Altameem, M. Prasad, C.T. Lin, and X. Liu, "Internet of Vehicles: Motivation, Layered Architecture, Network Model, Challenges, and Future Aspects", *IEEE Access,* vol. 4, pp. 5356-5373, 2016.
[http://dx.doi.org/10.1109/ACCESS.2016.2603219]

[19] S.A. Elsagheer Mohamed, and K.A. AlShalfan, "Intelligent Traffic Management System Based on the Internet of Vehicles (IoV)", *J. Adv. Transp.,* vol. 2021, pp. 1-23, 2021.
[http://dx.doi.org/10.1155/2021/4037533]

[20] Z. Tang, Y. Zhao, L. Yang, S. Qi, D. Fang, X. Chen, X. Gong, and Z. Wang, "Exploiting Wireless Received Signal Strength Indicators to Detect Evil-Twin Attacks in Smart Homes", *Mob. Inf. Syst.,* vol. 2017, pp. 1-14, 2017.
[http://dx.doi.org/10.1155/2017/1248578]

[21] A. Choudhury, A. Aggarwal, K. Rangra, and A. Bhatt, "The Components of Big Data and Knowledge Management Will Change Radically How People Collaborate and Develop Complex Research", In: *Big Data Governance and Perspectives in Knowledge Management.* IGI Global, 2019, pp. 241-257.
[http://dx.doi.org/10.4018/978-1-5225-7077-6.ch011]

[22] R. Chaudhary, P. Singh, and A. Agarwal, "A security solution for the transmission of confidential data and efficient file authentication based on DES, AES, DSS and RSA", *Int. J. Innov. Technol. Explor. Eng.,* vol. 1, no. 3, pp. 5-11, 2012.

[23] G. Bathla, P. Singh, S. Kumar, M. Verma, D. Garg, and K. Kotecha, "Recop: Fine-grained Opinions and Collaborative Filtering based Recommender System for Industry 5.0", 2021.

[24] Chithaluru, P., Tanwar, R. and Kumar, S., "Cyber-Attacks and Their Impact on Real Life: What Are Real-Life Cyber-Attacks, How Do They Affect Real Life and What Should We Do About Them?". In *Information Security and Optimization*, Chapman and Hall/CRC. 2020. pp. 61-77.

Implication of Waste in Boosting Economy

CHAPTER 13

Role of Industrial IoT for Energy Production Using Byproducts

Hitesh Kumar Sharma[1,*] and **Shlok Mohanty**[2]

[1] *Cybernetics Cluster, School of Computer Science and Engineering, University of Petroleum and Energy studies, Dehradun, India*

[2] *School of Computer Science and Engineering, University of Petroleum and Energy studies, Dehradun, India*

Abstract: Energy production from fossil fuels is limited as fossil fuel resources are limited on Earth. We have to find alternate resources for energy production. Energy production from waste material or by-products can help us in two major ways: by reducing waste on Earth and by producing energy without affecting conserved resources. Industrial IoT (IIoT) is an advanced IT-based technology that can help us detect the most useful waste and determine its availability in different places. It will also help us automate the complete lifecycle of energy production from by-products and distribute it to the required places.

In this chapter, we will discuss the role of Industrial IoT in the production of consumables from waste products/by-products. We will explain the various applications of IIoT in this whole process and the challenges faced in integrating this technology into it.

Keywords: Energy production, Industrial internet of things (IIoT), Waste management.

INTRODUCTION

Gases are mostly considered harmful to all living beings and have become one of the major concerns of the world. Mostly, the gases that are generated from factories and other working environments are fatal and hazardous to health. There are many gases as well that can be very useful for us, mostly noble gases and natural gases, such as helium, neon, *etc.* Most of the population is careless regarding their health and hygiene. Due to poor eating habits, many health issues have been reported. This often leads to the need for medication or hospitalization

[*] **Corresponding author 1Hitesh Kumar Sharma:** Cybernetics Cluster, School of Computer Science and Engineering, University of Petroleum and Energy studies, Dehradun, India; E-mail: hksharma@ddn.upes.ac.in

Sunil Kumar, Silky Goel, Gaytri Bakshi, Siddharth Gupta & Sayed M. El-kenawy (Eds.)

if the conditions worsen. In severe cases, individuals may require oxygen for breathing, which can be administered using helium, especially for those with asthma. Helium can also be useful for welding purposes and magnet production and can be considered a great example of mono and diatomic gases for the protection of welding companies. Electricity is the most important for us for performing tasks such as working on our computers, watching television, and reading and writing purposes, which can be done using electronics and electrical appliances [1, 2]. We need electricity and power to carry out various activities and tasks using energy resources, which help produce electrical energy. One of the energy resources is geothermal. Sometimes, cooling of the machines is needed for their proper working so that they do not get overheated as they stop working or get damaged. Modernized energy systems are now generally being used for the improvement of security and efficient functioning using smart city theories and conceptions. Effective management of building systems such as lighting, heating, and air conditioning can reduce energy costs and promote increased comfort during a person's prolonged stay in a room. The links between the work of intelligent tools and the amount of energy costs are necessary for alternative implementations for their improvement [3].

INTERNET OF INDUSTRIAL THINGS (IIOT): AN EXTENSION OF IOT

IoT is an IT and electronics-based advanced technology that uses digital devices like sensors for collecting data, cloud-computing platforms for storing captured data, and AMIL (Artificial Intelligence and Machine Learning)-based algorithms for analyzing the stored data [4, 5]. The physical and digital components present in the system, which can be both centralized or distributed, provide networking and computational functioning. CPSs, in general, are used as devices that have the capacity to determine the possibility of changing the actuator's state or to draw the attention of the human operator according to the environment being sensed. ICS has some similarities to the current traditional information technology systems where the systems are isolated, running various control protocols with the help of the hardware and software that are specialized where components are not physically connected to the IT networks and systems [6, 7]. The propriety solutions have been replaced by low-cost internet protocols. In a central location, adjustments are made to open or close switches, monitor alarms, and collect data. SCADA applications are formed of the following elements: the machine to be controlled and monitored, which can take up the power plant, a water system, a network and system of traffic lights, and the other is the platform system. The industrial machinery sensors and actuators are connected to the local processing and the internet. Industrial IoT provides and helps companies use devices, such as sensors, software, and machine-to-machine learning, to gather and analyze operation management and add value services. IoT can also be defined as interconnected objects and devices that manage, mine, and access the data they generate. The objects that are connected with each other are sensors and actuators, which can have some special functionalities and are able to communicate with the other equipment for generating, exchanging, and consuming data. In the virtual network, each object is represented as a node, which is continuously involved in the transmission of a huge volume of data about itself and its surroundings. Devices such as locks in smart bikes and smart kettles cannot be considered for industrial purposes. Connecting the network with the cloud aims to connect industrial assets [8].

The Industrial IoT (IIoT) is an extension of IoT, which includes sensors, communication networks, storage platforms, analytical platforms, and robotic components for the automation of industrial processes. IIoT comprises embedded systems, cloud computing, edge computing, generic technologies in smart factories, and other related software. IIoT is usually built for smartphones and wireless devices, basically for connecting the engines and sensors to the cloud network. There are certain taxonomies for the industrial IoT, such as device-centric, stack-centric, IoT sensors, IoT-based smart environment, and IoT architecture. In order to meet the 4G mobile telecommunication standards by the International Telecommunication Union-Radio Communications sector (ITU-R), which usually focuses not only on the throughput and latency rates but also on the ultralow cost, which enables adoption at a large scale that is economically feasible, the deployment of the device is enabled by coverage extension on the basis of versatility and reliability. Mostly, the challenges faced by the IIoT are due to data security [9]. Data security is how we manage and keep the data safe and protected from attackers and other criminal activities who can easily grab the information from the data that has been leaked or extracted by some unfair means. For the upcoming development of the 5G technology, ultra-reliable low-latency communications have been used for the development of 5G. Three-level integration in industrial IoT can be achieved by using different suppliers to integrate cross-technologies of smart devices. Different enterprises make use of integrations related to cross-domain businesses from various industries and sectors. IoT in healthcare is where different technologies of various fields, such as communication and interconnected apps, allow the functioning of devices, sensors, and people as a whole smart system for monitoring, tracking, and storing patients' information related to their healthcare for ongoing care [10].

IIOT FOR WASTE MANAGEMENT

IoT devices, along with machine learning, have made great improvements in various fields, and one of these fields is the waste management system.

IoT helps in the collection and management of data, and machine learning and artificial intelligence algorithms can be used for the processing of the collected data (Fig. **1**). Algorithms that are used are as follows: K Nearest Neighbor, Logistic Regression, and Long Short-term Memory for predicting the gas concentrations present in the air. IoT is used with cloud computing, where cloud services are provided so that the data collected by the IoT devices can be transferred to the cloud. Cloud computing is used for storing data securely and safely without any threats, and it can be retrieved easily from anywhere [11].

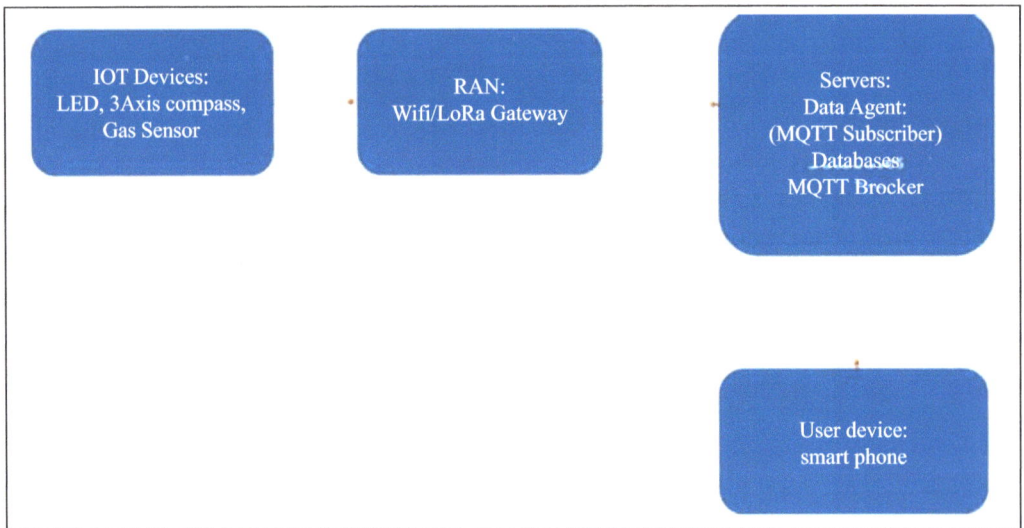

IOT Devices: LED, 3Axis compass, Gas Sensor	RAN: Wifi/LoRa Gateway	Servers: Data Agent: (MQTT Subscriber) Databases MQTT Brocker
		User device: smart phone

Fig. (1). IIoT Hardware/ software components.

E-waste management solutions come in a variety of forms and are broken down into several categories, including reduction and employment, animal feeding, recycling, composting, fermentation, landfilling, burning, and land application. Right after the reception, exploitation can be carried out using a number of tactics, including employment and reduction, which will strive to reduce the number of throwaway items consumed. IoT has contributed to the development of solutions for facilitating the use of diverse approaches at each step of waste management.

In terms of the garbage levels present in the waste bins, a smart waste collecting system was proposed [ref:http://ijrit.net/papers/December2017/V1I204.pdf]. As shown in Fig. (**2**), with the aid of the sensors, data is gathered and then sent for processing by the mechanisms. It is used or observed for the selection of the trash cans, and depending on that, several trash cans are picked up from various locations. The revised, optimized routes are delivered each day to the workers' navigational devices. This system's crucial and beneficial aspect is that it was created using lessons learned from the past, making decisions about the waste's status every day, as well as forecasting its future state [12, 13].

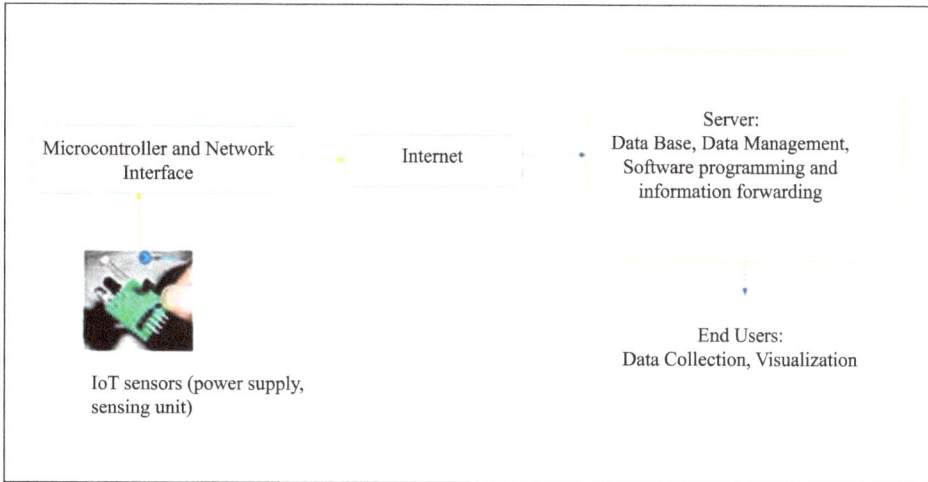

Fig. (2). IIoT basic flow of information.

METHODS FOR WASTE TO ENERGY PRODUCTION

The waste can be used for the production of energy in various ways. In Fig. (**3**), we have shown various ways to produce energy from societal/ industrial waste.

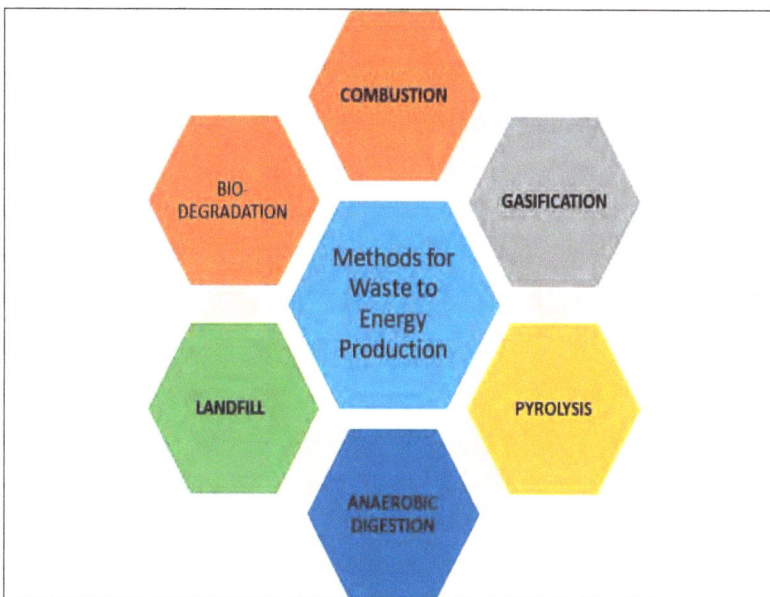

Fig. (3). Methods for energy production from waste.

These are:

- **Combustion:** The waste material is burned to produce heat, which can be used to produce energy.
- **Gasification:** The waste material is converted into gas so that the produced gas can be used for energy generation.
- **Pyrolysis:** In this method, the waste is heated to generate energy in the absence of air.
- **Anaerobic** Digestion: In this process, the waste is converted into bio-mass without the presence of oxygen.
- **Landfill:** In this process, the waste is put in a large pit and left for some days for gas production in natural ways.
- **Bio-Degradation:** In this process, the waste is converted into a fuel substance to be combusted for producing energy.

METHOD FOR DETERMINING WASTE MANAGEMENT LEVELS

The measurement of the distance from the top of the trash can to the bottom of the waste can is used to determine the level of rubbish. The sonar that is used to build the prototype should be able to measure with an accuracy of 3 mm for particular garbage bins, such as the Ultrasonic Module (HC-SR04), for range computation. In order to extend the time before the gadgets expire, it is helpful to use the battery as efficiently as possible. The tempo of data Energy usage is significantly impacted by technologies that are mostly wireless for sensing and transmitting rates [14, 15]. Data collection and transmission can occur once or twice each day. The systems are being made to learn using various algorithms and models, which are mostly related to the statistics for analyzing the sample data. Characteristics that are measurable can be used for characterizing the sample data. ML algorithms are implemented in order to find out the correlations among features and output values (known as the labels). The information we get through the training process of the model is then used to identify the patterns and make decisions based on the new data [16].

CONCLUSION

Energy production from by-products or waste is useful for waste reduction and energy production. IIoT can play an important role in converting waste into energy. The identification of waste production, location, type identification, data collection, data storage, data processing, and efficient decision-making for efficient generation can be managed by IIoT. Even energy production plan controlling can be done by industrial robots, which are part of IIoT.

REFERENCES

[1] H.K. Sharma, "E-COCOMO: the extended cost constructive model for cleanroom software engineering", *Database Systems Journal,* vol. 4, no. 4, pp. 3-11, 2013.

[2] J.C. Patni, and H.K. Sharma, "Air Quality Prediction using Artificial Neural Networks", *2019 International Conference on Automation, Computational and Technology Management, ICACTM 2019,* pp. 568-572, 2019.
[http://dx.doi.org/10.1109/ICACTM.2019.8776774]

[3] A. Aggarwal, P. Dimri, and A. Agarwal, "Statistical Performance Evaluation of Various Metaheuristic Scheduling Techniques for Cloud Environment", *J. Comput. Theor. Nanosci.,* vol. 17, no. 9, pp. 4593-4597, 2020.
[http://dx.doi.org/10.1166/jctn.2020.9285]

[4] A. Aggarwal, P. Dimri, and A. Agarwal, "Survey on scheduling algorithms for multiple workflows in cloud computing environment", *Int. J. Comput. Sci. Eng.,* vol. 7, no. 6, pp. 565-570, 2019.

[5] A. Aggarwal, P. Dimri, A. Agarwal, M. Verma, H.A. Alhumyani, and M. Masud, "IFFO: An Improved Fruit Fly Optimization Algorithm for Multiple Workflow Scheduling Minimizing Cost and Makespan in Cloud Computing Environments", *Math. Probl. Eng.,* vol. 2021, pp. 1-9, 2021.
[http://dx.doi.org/10.1155/2021/5205530]

[6] S. Singh, S.K. Jangir, M. Kumar, M. Verma, S. Kumar, T.S. Walia, and S.M.M. Kamal, "[Retracted] Feature Importance Score-Based Functional Link Artificial Neural Networks for Breast Cancer Classification", *BioMed Res. Int.,* vol. 2022, no. 1, p. 2696916, 2022.
[http://dx.doi.org/10.1155/2022/2696916] [PMID: 35411308]

[7] A. Aggarwal, P. Dimri, A. Agarwal, and A. Bhatt, "Self adaptive fruit fly algorithm for multiple workflow scheduling in cloud computing environment", *Kybernetes,* 2020.

[8] M. Arya, H.G. Sastry, A. Motwani, S. Kumar, and A. Zaguia, "A Novel Extra Tree Ensemble Optimized DL Framework (ETEODL) for Early Detection of Diabetes", *Frontiers in Public Health,* vol. 9, 2021.

[9] G. Bathla, P. Singh, S. Kumar, M. Verma, D. Garg, and K. Kotecha, "Recop: Fine-grained Opinions and Collaborative Filtering based Recommender System for Industry 5.0", *Sot Computing,* 2021.

[10] A. Bhatt, P. Dimri, and A. Aggarwal, "Self-adaptive brainstorming for jobshop scheduling in multicloud environment", *Softw. Pract. Exper.,* vol. 50, no. 8, pp. 1381-1398, 2020.
[http://dx.doi.org/10.1002/spe.2819]

[11] R. Tomar, H. Kumar, A. Dumka, and A. Anand, "Traffic management in MPLS network using GNS simulator using class for different services", *2nd International Conference on Computing for Sustainable Global Development (INDIACom),* 2015.

[12] S. Goel, S. Gupta, A. Panwar, S. Kumar, M. Verma, S. Bourouis, and M.A. Ullah, "Deep Learning Approach for Stages of Severity Classification in Diabetic Retinopathy Using Color Fundus Retinal Images", *Math. Probl. Eng.,* vol. 2021, pp. 1-8, 2021.
[http://dx.doi.org/10.1155/2021/7627566]

[13] S. Kumar, G.H. Sastry, V. Marriboyina, H. Alshazly, S.A. Idris, M. Verma, and M. Kaur, "Semantic Information Extraction from Multi-Corpora Using Deep Learning", *Comput. Mater. Continua,* pp. 1-17, 2021.

[14] S. Kumar, V. Marriboyina, and V. Marriboyina, "Information Extraction From the Agricultural and Weather Domains Using Deep Learning Approaches", *Int. J. Soft. Innov.,* vol. 10, no. 1, pp. 1-12, 2022.
[http://dx.doi.org/10.4018/IJSI.293266]

[15] G.D. Singh, M. Prateek, S. Kumar, M. Verma, D. Singh, and H.N. Lee, "Hybrid genetic firefly algorithm-based routing protocol for VANETs", *IEEE Access,* vol. 10, pp. 9142-9151, 2022.
[http://dx.doi.org/10.1109/ACCESS.2022.3142811]

[16]   G.D. Singh, S. Kumar, H. Alshazly, S.A. Idris, M. Verma, and S.M. Mostafa, "A Novel Routing Protocol for Realistic Traffic Network Scenarios in VANET", *Wirel. Commun. Mob. Comput.,* vol. 2021, no. 1, p. 7817249, 2021.
[http://dx.doi.org/10.1155/2021/7817249]

List of Acronyms

AAL	Ambient Assisted Living
ADASE	Advance Driver Assistance System
AI	Artificial Intelligence
AMED	Agency Medical Research and Development
ANN	Artificial Neural Networks
AoA	Angle of Arrival
ARTS	Advanced Rural Transport System
ATIS	Advanced Traveler Information System
ATMS	Advanced Traffic Management System
AVCS	Advanced Vehicle Control System
BAN	Body Area Networks
BC	Block Chain
BDA	Big Data Analysis
BS	Base Station
CAMP	Crash Avoidance Matrices Partnership
CDSS	Clinical Decision Support System
CMU	Carnegie Mellon University
CNN	Convolutional Neural Network
CVO	Commercial Vehicle Operations
DDoS	Distributed Denial of Services
DL	Deep Learning
DNN	Deep Neural network
DoS	Denial of Service
DSM	Digital Soil Mapping
EDA	Electro Dermal Activity
EEPROM	Electronic Enable Read Only Memory
GAN	Generative Adversarial Networks
I2I	Infrastructure to Infrastructure
I2V	Infrastructure to Vehicle
ICU	Intensive Care Units
IIoT	Industrial Internet of thing
IMU	Inertial Measurement Unit

IoHT	Internet from Healthcare Thing
IoT	Internet of Things
IoTV	Internet of Things for Vehicle
ISS	Intelligent Smart System
ITS	Intelligent Transportation System
JST	Japan Science and Technology
KNN	K-nearest neighbor
M2M	Machine To Machine
MANET	Mobile Ad hoc Networks
MC	Micro Calcification
ML	Machine Learning
NCB	National Bio-economy Council
NFC	Near Field Communication
NHS	National Health Services
NITE	National Institute of Technology and Evaluation
OT	Operational Technology
PCA	Principal Component Analysis
PLC	Programmable Logic Controller
RAMS	Road Asset Management System
RSU	Roadside Unit
RVC	Road Vehicle Communications
SCAP	Security Content Automation Protocol
UAV	Unmanned Aerial Vehicle
USB	Universal Serial Bus
V2I	Vehicle To Infrastructure
V2I	Vehicle To Transportation Infrastructure
V2R	Vehicle To Roadside
V2S	Vehicle To Sensor
V2V	Vehicle to Vehicle
VANET	Vehicular Ad hoc Network
VCC	Vehicular Cloud Computing

SUBJECT INDEX

A

Advance driver assistance system (ADASE) 169
Advanced technologies 28, 180
  electronics-based 180
AI-based 19, 72, 79
  algorithms 72
  devices 79
  software 19
AI-enabled wheelchairs 163
Air conditioning 180
Algorithms 9, 146, 158
  automated 146
  genetic 9
  learning-based 158
AlphaFold 122
  program 122
  software 122
Applications 131, 137
  for transportation management 131
  of deep learning in smart transportation 137
Architecture 2, 40, 42, 85, 119, 133, 134, 135, 168, 173
  service-oriented 2
  transport network 168
Artificial intelligence 14, 15, 16, 72, 74, 80, 84, 116, 117, 144, 145, 146, 150, 151, 159, 160, 163, 164, 180, 182
  algorithms 182
  and machine learning 159, 163, 180
  -based Mobility Devices 163
  techniques 84
Artificial neural networks (ANN) 9, 10, 15, 55, 56, 57, 59, 65, 66, 67, 68, 144, 148
Automated irrigation system (AIS) 28, 34, 35
Automation, cognitive 83
Automobiles, autonomous 170

B

Bayes' theorem 8, 91

Bluetooth signals 106
Brain 56, 65, 66, 68, 156
  activity, abnormal 156
  tumor segmentation 56, 65, 66
  tumors 56, 65, 68
Breast cancer 55, 56, 57, 67, 161
Business 29, 31, 33, 34, 75, 76, 79, 98
  sustainable 75
  system-based 34

C

Cameras 28, 51, 76, 123, 124
  drone-based 28
Cancer 56, 57, 66, 67, 68, 117, 144, 147, 149, 161
  detection, breast 57, 67
  lung 56, 66, 68, 161
CCTV cameras 123
ChEMBL database 121
Chemical 46, 95, 120, 150, 158
  composition 95, 120, 150, 158
  etching 46
Chip 35, 43, 44, 45, 46, 47
  internal 44
Clinical decision support system (CDSS) 21
Cloud 31, 84, 87, 94, 99, 100, 141, 146, 154, 170, 171, 172, 173, 174, 175, 176
  secure 31
  technology 171, 173, 174, 175, 176
Cloud-based 155, 175
  computations 175
  health monitoring system 155
Cloud computing 18, 19, 141, 154, 171, 181, 182
  approach 141
  services 141
  technology 18, 25
CNN 11, 118, 119, 134
  architecture 11, 118, 119, 134
  -based deep transfer 119
  model for cough detection 119

www.ingramcontent.com/pod-product-compliance
Lightning Source LLC
Chambersburg PA
CBHW050845220326
41598CB00006B/437